P9-DVO-846

The 2011 PRAIRIE GARDEN

WESTERN CANADA'S ONLY GARDENING ANNUAL

WRITTEN BY & FOR WESTERN GARDENERS

A non-profit publication dedicated to the advancement of horticulture in the Prairie Provinces

72nd Annual Edition

2011 Theme
Healthy Gardening

16 page Colour Section
Special 200 page edition CALGARY PUBLIC LIBRARY

General Gardening Information   JAN - - 2011

Copyright © October, 2010 The Prairie Garden Committee, Winnipeg, MB

All rights reserved.
The material in this publication is for informational purposes only. The
views expressed by contributors are not necessarily those of The Prairie Garden
Committee. Reference to commercial products or tradenames is made with the
understanding that no discrimination is intended and no endorsement by The
Prairie Garden Committee is implied.
The contents in this publication may not be reproduced or used in any fashion
without the written consent of The Prairie Garden Committee, other than short
excerpts as may appear in book reviews and literature citations.

ISBN 978-0-9736849-6-4

Published by:
The Prairie Garden Committee
P.O. Box 517
WINNIPEG, MB R3C 2J3

Co-Chairs . . . . Ed Czarnecki & Colleen Zacharias
Editor . . . . .Richard Denesiuk
Treasurer. . . . . Jean Pomo
Secretary. . . . . .Linda Pearn
Associate Editors . . . . Roger Brown, Reg Curle, Ed Czarnecki ,
Valerie Denesiuk, Susanne Olver, Linda Pearn,
Jean Pomo, Andy Tekauz, Bonnie Tulloch,
Kevin Twomey, Sandy Venton,
Frances Wershler & Colleen Zacharias

Price: $12.00 per copy
Special quantity prices available to horticultural societies,
garden clubs, commercial outlets, etc.
For inquiries and order form, see page xxx.

Printed in Canada by:
Kromar Printing Ltd.

Acknowledgements

The Prairie Garden is a non-profit publication. We appreciate support from a number of companies who share our interest in prairie horticulture. The following companies provided financial assistance toward this edition of *The Prairie Garden*. Their help is crucial in bringing this book to you at minimum cost as production and distribution costs rise annually. We welcome and thank the companies who provided sponsorship this year. Readers may contact them at the addresses below and can recognize their products by their logos, found on the back cover and on our Web site: **www.theprairiegarden.ca**

Barkman Concrete Ltd. - 909 Gateway Rd., Winnipeg, MB R2K 3L1
    Ph: 204-667-3310 website: barkmanconcrete.com,
    e-mail: wpgsales@barkmanconcrete.com

Friends of the Assiniboine Park Conservatory - 15 Conservatory
    Drive, Winnipeg, MB R3P 2N5 Ph: 204-837-4324 website:
    friendsconservatory.com, e-mail: friendsconservatory@mts.net

Jeffries Nurseries Ltd. - P.O. Box 402, Portage la Prairie, MB R1N 3B7
    Ph: 204-857-5288 website: jeffriesnurseries.com, e-mail: jeffnurs@mts.net

Kackenhoff Nurseries Ltd. - P.O. Box 2000, St. Norbert, MB R3V 1L4
    Ph: 204-269-1377

The Lily Nook - P.O. Box 846, Neepawa, MB R0J 1H0 Ph. 204-476-3225
    website: lilynook.mb.ca, e-mail: info@lilynook.mb.ca

Lindenberg Seeds Limited - 803 Princess Ave., Brandon, MB R7A 0P5
    Ph: 204-727-0575 website: lindenbergseeds.mb.ca, e-mail:
    lindenbergr@lindenbergseeds.mb.ca

Prairie Horticulture Certificate Program The University of Manitoba,
    Winnipeg, MB R3T 2N2 Ph: 1-888-216-7011, ext. 6037,
    website: umanitoba.ca/coned/mpcp/phc, e-mail: w_otto@umanitoba.ca

Schriemer's Home & Garden Showplace - 1505 Molson St., Winnipeg,
    MB R2G 3S6 Ph: 204-668-8357 website: schriemers.ca, e-mail: info@
    schriemers.ca

Shelmerdine Garden Center Ltd. - 7800 Roblin Boulevard, Winnipeg, MB
    R4H 1B6   Ph: 204-895-7203, website: shelmerdine.com, email: info@
    shelmerdine.com

St. Mary's Nursery & Garden Centre Ltd. - 2901 St. Mary's
    Rd., Winnipeg, MB R2N 4A6 Ph: 204-255-7353 website:
    stmarysnurseryandgardencentre.ca, e-mail: stmgardn@mts.net

T&T Seeds - P.O. Box 1710, Winnipeg, MB R3C 3P6 Ph: 204-895-9962
    website: ttseeds.com, e-mail: garden@ttseeds.com

The 2011 Prairie Garden
Table of Contents

Front cover photo: Bee on New England Aster by Sarah Coulber
Photo credits are in parentheses on or near all photos

An Editorial Note
by Richard Denesiuk, The Prairie Garden editor

"Gardens, scholars say, are the first sign of commitment to a community. When people plant corn they are saying, let's stay here. And by their connection to the land, they are connected to one another." - Anne Raver

Why do we garden? There are so many reasons, but one that strikes a common chord among gardeners is that it makes us feel healthy, connected to nature and a vibrant part of our environment. Not only is gardening good for our physical health, but also for our mental health. How vital our garden becomes, and how impacted it is by *our* efforts – is based on the knowledge of gardening practices we have acquired.

My first memories of gardening are as a child, 'grazing' on some delicious vegetable, and being fascinated with the symphony of bugs, birds and plants. That alliance of flora and fauna has forever imprinted on me the fascination I have for all gardens – both natural and constructed.

This year's theme *Healthy Gardening* was chosen by The Prairie Garden committee in an effort to focus our attention on the basics of gardening – tried and true practises and their healthful implications. Throughout this edition you will find short articles by committee members who share their personal views on what constitutes a healthy garden and the basic elements that might go into creating one. The first two, by co-chairs Colleen Zacharias and Ed Czarnecki, appear on this page.

This is a special 200 page edition with a wealth of articles – we just had to go for more pages than normal to get them all in! Thanks to all our contributors who have given us the great articles you are about to read. They are diverse, thought provoking and some may be controversial. I know you will enjoy this edition! 🎗

Best-Laid Plans
by Colleen Zacharias, co-chair of The Prairie Garden committee

Many new homeowners will decide at some point that they would like to add a 'garden' or a landscaped area to enhance their property. Depending on their level of experience, they will either tackle the project themselves, enlist the assistance of a more experienced friend or family member, or hire a professional.

Once the plan for the new bed goes from drawing paper to reality, there is always an initial sense of satisfaction and pride. But that should only represent the beginning of the project, not the end result. The best laid plans will never reach their full potential without the commitment to maintain and nurture – otherwise, the garden will only fall into neglect over time and bear little resemblance to the bright promise it once offered. Understanding the efforts, from spring through fall, that go into maintaining a garden, is the first step to creating a healthy garden.

Gardening is a bit like parenting – the right amount of care and nutrition is required in order to give a living thing the essentials it needs to thrive and survive in a harsh world.

A 'healthy' garden is easily identi-fied: the observer is able to readily see that the plants are well tended by looking at their upright, sturdy stems, unblemished foliage or attractive, open blooms. Regardless of the size of the garden plot, plants will have been given room to breathe. The soil will be largely weed-free with the moisture levels matched to the needs of the plants. Other factors such as the proper amount of sunlight or shade will be taken into consideration. There is genuine joy, too, in helping to overcome the challenges that our plants face from time to time.

A sensible, consistent approach to maintaining a garden is far more rewarding than the ultimate embarrassment that a neglected plot becomes. It takes a bit of labour and practical know-how, but the 'end' results are always rewarding. 🦎

Location, Location, Location
by Ed Czarnecki, co-chair of The Prairie Garden committee

A fundamental criterion in any type of gardening is the location, which would reflect the amount of sunlight, the soil type (pH, organic matter and texture) and the type of drainage available.

As an example, a shady area would be more suitable for plant types such as impatiens, begonia or hosta, while a flat-surfaced heavy clay soil would require adequate drainage and soil preparation before attempting to grow flowers or vegetables.

Gardeners in the outer treed areas of Winnipeg and other urban places also need to somehow protect their plots from deer, rabbits, ground hogs and other 'critters' who seem to have a more varied palate. Gardening can be as challenging or as relaxing as you would like and each year brings on the anticipation of something new to discover and enjoy. 🦎

A Gardener's Prayer

Author Unknown

May the bunnies never nibble on
your young and tender shoots.

May your transplants settle in
and put down hardy roots.

May your weeds come out real easy
and your lawn be fungus free.

May you never put your back out
or inhale a bumblebee.

May your roses never stab you
or your hoses spring a leak.

And may everyone come 'a calling'
when your garden's at its peak.

May you never grow too weary
as you toil for hours and hours.

And may you never be too busy
to stop and smell the flowers!

Creating a Beautiful and Beneficial Garden
by Sarah Coulber

Sarah works for the Canadian Wildlife Federation in its Backyard Habitat Program.

Echinacea and purple prairie clover (Sarah Coulber)

It seems that no matter who you are or what you do, we all have an inherent affinity with nature, even if we're not conscious of it. Whether it's enjoying the bright blooms in the grocery store or getting away to the cottage, science has proven that just noticing elements of nature can do wonders for our body, mind and emotions. Recovery rates after surgery are quicker when patients can look out a window to the trees beyond, and pain tolerance is improved at the dentist's office with a simple poster of nature to look at. Emotionally abused and mentally challenged individuals have also shown remarkable improvement, even healing, when working with animals and plants in a variety of therapy programs.

Nature also provides us with the basics such as clean air, water, food, construction materials – even our health and hygiene products ulti-mately come from nature! It makes sense that we would want to support that which supports us. But how?

Giving Back in the Garden

Many Canadians are accomplishing big things in a way they love: gardening! Whether you have a small urban patch or large rolling estate, you too can shape your greenspace to do more than just look good. You can leave existing natural areas intact, or garden in a way to support the wildlife that we rely on, including bees, butterflies and other insects for their pollinating services. Thanks to them we enjoy chocolate, fruit, cotton pajamas and much more! Greenspace will also support the bright birds and butterflies that delight our senses with their colours and sounds, and countless other species that are important in ways we are not always aware.

Canadians and Americans are discovering satisfaction in giving back to nature and are thrilled to see migrating songbirds, quiet turtles and mosquito-hungry bats visit their garden.

Lorena Baker in rural Saskatchewan found that as her garden evolved, so too did her awareness of the local wildlife and the pleasure she got from enjoying their visits. "It brightens my day to see the birds in the middle of a cold snowy day", comments Lorena, "and I get excited at seeing the first hummingbird in May."

For Robert and Hendrika Hamilton in Alberta, their efforts to naturalize their subdivision property with 1,500 trees and shrubs, native plants and water features is described as "a project we truly enjoy. Visits from wildlife are satisfying and rewarding and every day we enjoy it more and more!"

Vincent Fudge in Manitoba has noticed that both his animal and human neighbours enjoy his garden transformation from a weedy lawn to lush oasis. "There is an endless show of people stopping, admiring, asking questions", recounts Vincent. "I have had neighbours tell me they have relatives who time their visits according to what is blooming in my yard. That is truly flattering. I even have beautiful garden ornaments and sculptures that people have placed in my yard as a thank you for making the neighbourhood beautiful." In choosing to work with the soil and native species, he's even had

some special surprises along the way including native orchids popping up. "I now love the soil conditions, and invite the wildlife. Native plants fit the bill perfectly. I think they had a plan when they started showing me their wonderful bag of tricks."

While these gardeners live in different provinces and have different size properties and design preferences, they all applied the same wildlife-friendly gardening principles. You too can reap the rewards with your greenspace.

The Four Needs of Wildlife: Food, Water, Shelter and Space

Food

Grow a variety of trees, shrubs, vines and perennials to provide nectar, pollen, seeds and fruit. Consider the four seasons as you plan your garden, with early spring flowers for returning and awakening animals right through to seeds and berries that remain during the winter months. Supplementing with feeders is fine, but keep in mind that food from a natural habitat is imperative if the species you wish to attract are to survive.

Water

If you don't have a natural source of water and your budget is tight, don't worry, even a simple dish of water will work. Clean the dish when it begins to look dirty and change the water at least twice a week. This helps eliminate both germs and mosquitoes.

Shelter

By growing a variety of plants, you give animals places to rest, nest and escape both predators and inclement weather. Evergreen trees (plants that retain their needles) are helpful to stave off cold winter winds, while deciduous trees (plants that shed their leaves) provide cooling in the summer months. The trunks of both are useful for cavity nesting birds, as are snags (dead standing trees). To keep your snag safe for humans, trim any branches that cause concern. Make or leave existing rock and brush piles, put up a bat house and let some logs remain on the ground. Even a simple flower can give shelter to beneficial insects and spiders.

Space

Including diverse layers of vegetation with varying heights and textures increases the 'space' of your habitat. For example, allowing a vine to add dimension to a bare fence is like adding rooms and furniture to a bare four-walled house.

Earth-Friendly Gardening

Avoid pesticides, both insecticides and herbicides, as they can harm beneficial organisms such as butterflies, bees and even hummingbirds. While hummingbirds do rely on nectar for carbohydrates, they need protein which they get from insects and spiders. If this food source is contaminated or eliminated by pesticides, the hummingbird's health can be at risk. Pesticides can also be harmful to human health and enter our waterways, affecting environments far beyond our gardens.

By returning the land to a natural state, you will invite allies such as bug-eating birds, bats, toads and insects who will help keep 'pest' insect species in check.

Lessen weeds by using mulch in garden beds and cut your grass at 7–8 cm (3 in) high for healthier roots as well as to make it harder for weed seeds to germinate.

Other ways to be a green gardener are to use natural fertilizers, such as compost or well-aged manure; recycle by leaving your grass clippings where they fall to return nutrients to your soil; mulch your garden; and conserve water by watering only when necessary.

Incorporate Native Plants

Plants that have grown wild in your area for many centuries generally require less maintenance as they are more pest and weather resistant. This means that if they are planted in a suitable location, they shouldn't require regular watering once their roots are established.

They also tend to be better able to meet the needs of local wildlife than many exotic plants. Some cultivated plants have blooms that make it harder for pollinators to find their food while others have lost their pollen producing capacity entirely.

CWF's Guide to Creating a Wildlife-Friendly Garden

You've just read where the Canadian Wildlife Federation (CWF) comes in – a national charitable organization working to connect Canadians with the natural world around them and preserve our wild spaces. With the rapid loss of wildlife habitat for many reasons, including development, many are pointing to gardens as a means of maintaining a life-line to countless wildlife species. CWF has a Backyard Habitat program that supports Canadians wishing to return their outdoor space to a more natural state - be it sprucing up a tiny downtown patio or restoring large tracts of land in the country.

Food, Water, Shelter and Space are the basic ideas CWF encourages Canadians to incorporate in their garden design and practice; these can work regardless of your gardening style – formal, cottage or all natural look.

No matter how many of these ideas you are able to apply to your property, something is better than nothing and may simply be the first step to bringing greater balance to your area and our planet as a whole. To support you in making your space more wildlife-friendly, check out some of CWF's Backyard Habitat resources below.

CANADIAN FÉDÉRATION
WILDLIFE CANADIENNE
FEDERATION DE LA FAUNE

CWF Resources

CWF has a Certification program that recognizes Canadians who have taken the time and energy to create wildlife habitat, large or small. If you think your property meets the needs of wildlife, we'd love to hear from you! We have numerous posters and handouts showcasing Canadian species that include tips on how to support them in your garden.

Other CWF initiatives include National Wildlife Week, Rivers to Oceans Week, Hinterland Who's Who (in partnership with Environment Canada's Canadian Wildlife Service), Wild Education and the Canadian Conservation Achievement Awards Program.

Our <WildAboutGardening. org> website is another great resource for information on wildlife-friendly gardening, including a Native Plant Encyclopedia and Native Plant Supplier List to help you choose and purchase plants native to your area. Our Seasonal Gardening Guide section is updated each season with regular features on plants, animals, certified gardens, native plant nurseries, a guest column and free desktop wallpaper. Surrounding CWF's headquarters in Ottawa is a native plant demonstration garden. You can view maps and photos online or, if you are in the area, stop by and visit! To find out more, please visit <www.CanadianWildlifeFederation.ca>. 🐾

Compost – Great for Your Plants and the Environment!

by Kate Bergen

Kate is the Backyard Composting Coordinator for Resource Conservation Manitoba's Compost Action Project.

Most gardeners know that compost is an amazing natural fertilizer for your plants. In addition to adding nutrients to the soil, compost has immense benefits that are only now being discovered – or *rediscovered*, as compost has been used in agriculture for thousands of years. Composting at home allows you to create your own free compost, while at the same time it reduces your environmental impact. There is compost research that shows compost controls plant pathogens, giving us a better understanding of the many ways compost benefits your garden.

Composting is one of the most important things that individuals can do to help protect the environment. In an age where so many environmental problems seem overwhelming for the average person to tackle, composting allows the home gardener to easily make a significant difference in the community. Compostable materials make up an astonishing 40-75% of household waste in Canada. By composting, you will really *see* the difference you are making

once these organic materials are out of your garbage. In a landfill, organic materials like food waste, yard trimmings, grass and paper break down in the absence of oxygen (anaerobically), thereby producing methane, a powerful greenhouse gas that contributes to climate change and is more potent than carbon dioxide. As well as producing methane, organics also mix with other materials in the landfill to produce toxic liquids that contaminate soil and pollute our ground water. By composting you not only prevent pollution, but you also keep this resource out of the landfill and produce a valuable product – compost!

Well balanced compost

Compost benefits soil in remarkable ways. If you have problem soil, amending it with compost is one of the best ways to improve its fertility and structure. Depending upon the soil, its condition and whether it needs amending and with what – a soil test would best indicate what a sample of soil needs or does not need. Compost is often called a natural fertilizer, even though it works very differently than a synthetic fertilizer. Synthetic fertilizers can actually harm soils by reducing the abundance and diversity of microorganisms. Even slow release fertilizers that attempt to mimic the way that compost releases nutrients cannot compare with the complex ways that compost improves soil. Unlike synthetic fertilizers that supply a limited number of specific nutrients designed for direct uptake by plants, compost actually benefits plants indirectly by *feeding your soil*.

Anyone who has used compost to amend clay or sandy soils has likely seen the benefit of improved soil structure. This structural improvement is due to the organic matter that compost adds to the soil. One of the major benefits of additional organic matter to clay type soils is improved porosity to air and water. In sandy soils, compost helps to create larger soil particles that are able to retain more water. The organic material in compost is also responsible for the fertility benefits that result from compost application.

Adding organic material to your soil feeds the numerous organisms that make up a healthy soil. Once these microorganisms such as bacteria and fungi are fed, you can put them to work for your plants! Keeping them happy and well fed means they will work hard to make important nutrients like nitrogen, potassium and phosphorus available to plants.

Compost also binds to other important minerals in the soil and prevents them from leaching away with rain. When plant roots come into contact with these tied up minerals they are able to extract them from the organic material in the soil as needed. Other than peat type soils, the higher the levels of organic matter in your soil, the greater the ability for the soil to maintain proper mineral levels.

If you are concerned about contaminated soils, compost application is an excellent way to help with remediation. Compost also has an amazing ability to neutralize the effects of heavy metals and other toxins that may be present in the soil. Compost can form stable complexes with heavy metals and prevent them from being taken up by your plants. Unlike most beneficial soil minerals, most heavy metals are not water soluble, so it is extremely advantageous to have them held in a stable form through complexes with compost. *(Note: Although compost can aid in remediation, if you are working with highly contaminated soils, or are unsure of the history of your land, you may want to have it tested prior to use.)*

Compost plays an important role in plant disease control, as healthy soil is the first step in warding off problems. Healthy soils help maintain healthy plants that can more easily fight off disease. Compost is not only feeding microorganisms that in turn feed your plants, it also maintains an abundance of diversity in your soils. As with all ecosystems on Earth, biodiversity is one of the most important factors (if not the most important factor) in maintaining a healthy environment. Enhancing the diversity of microorganisms in your soil can prevent disease causing organisms from building up large populations and will help keep diseases in check.

New research is now revealing surprising ways that soil microorganisms can benefit plants through complex interactions that activate and enhance natural defence mechanisms in plants. Plants defend themselves against herbivore and pathogen attack in a variety of ways, including the activation of defensive mechanisms in response to damage and stress.

Recently, it has been discovered that plant resistance can also be activated or enhanced without these stressors through the use of different elicitors, including interactions with naturally occurring soil microorganisms. For example, some soil microorganisms release chemical signals that stimulate plants to produce antimicrobial compounds in the plant tissue that can prevent pathogens from spreading throughout the plant. Other signals can lead to the production of compounds that increase leaf toughness, making plants more resistant to disease-causing organisms that penetrate plant tissue. Plants may also respond to different soil microorganisms by producing compounds that are toxic to insects feeding on the plants, yet are beneficial to us humans – like antioxidants!

Interaction between soil microorganisms and plants may also produce volatile organic compounds (VOCs) that can help defend plants against pathogen and insect attack. Some VOCs have been shown to be antimicrobial and can directly control pathogens on the surface of plants, while other VOCs can indirectly control pathogens by activating defences throughout the plant. VOC production can also lead to beneficial, but complicated, responses from insects. Some insect herbivores detect VOCs and are deterred from feeding on plant tissue, while some VOCs will actually attract parasitic insects that feed on undesirable insect herbivores! Many of these intricate interactions between the soil, plants, pathogens and insects are only now starting to be revealed. Although the complex nature of these interactions may not be fully understood, the most important aspect of this research is that there are immense benefits to maintaining healthy soils and diverse populations of microorganisms.

The benefits of composting are numerous and remarkable, and although there is almost no risk to using compost, there are a few things you may want to consider. If you plan to use pure compost for germinating seeds or as a medium for growing highly sensitive plants, it is important to understand whether your compost is 'finished' or not. If your compost is not fully broken down there can be high levels of organic acids that could negatively affect some plants. However, this is not a real concern for the average gardener incorporating compost into their garden.

Another potential problem is the composting of plant material when a disease problem is present in the garden. If you are composting large amounts of diseased plants, ensure that your compost is reaching adequate temperatures to kill disease causing organisms. Most pathogens, as well as weed seeds, will be destroyed after 3 days at 55^0 Celsius (131^0 F) or hotter. Get a compost thermometer and familiarize yourself with the proper temperatures for control. A final consideration is the use of chemically treated plant material in your compost. Generally speaking, most chemical fertilizers and pesticides wash away quite quickly after application – which should be reason enough to stop using them! There are some really nasty, persistent chemicals out there, such as certain compounds used to control some ants, that have been shown to survive the composting process. The best way to avoid potential problems is to avoid the use of chemicals altogether.

As we rediscover all the amazing benefits of compost that have been known for thousands of years, we realize that we cannot continuously take material out of the soil without giving back. If you have not yet embraced composting, now is a great time to start. If you are already an active composter, there is always more to learn about the benefits and uses of this remarkable substance. Check out the tips for getting started and call the Compost Info Line if you have any questions or concerns.

Information and resources
Books on composting:
    The Rodale Book of Composting
    The Humanure Handbook
Resource Conservation Manitoba's Compost
    Info Line: 925-3777 or email compost@
    resourceconservation.mb.ca
Visit www.resourceconservation.mb.ca
The Manitoba Eco Network's Organic Lawn
    Care: <www.mbeconetwork.org>

Recommended Book

The Truth about Organic Gardening; Benefits, Drawbacks and The Bottom Line by Jeff Gillman, Timber Press. Gillman is currently an associate Professor in the department of horticultural science at the University of Minnesota.

Now that you know why to compost, here's how to get started!

Bin

Although you do not need a bin, many people choose to have a bin to keep the material contained, and to maximize yard space. If space is limited, there are many ready-made commercial bins that can be purchased at a hardware store or garden centre.

If you have the space, building your own bin out of old pallets or other wood will allow you to compost even more materials faster. Contact Resource Conservation Manitoba for bin building plans and other tips.

Materials

The most important thing about composting is balancing what we call the 'Green and Brown' materials that you add to the bin. Greens are nitrogen rich materials such as kitchen waste, fresh plant materials and fresh grass clippings. Browns are carbon rich materials like dead dry leaves, wood chips, and paper products. For successful composting keep these in balance by adding 50% greens and 50% browns by weight not volume. This can be tricky in our climate when most green materials are available in spring and summer, while brown materials like dead leaves are available in the fall.

The best tip is to store your leaves in the fall. If you don't have a supply of stored leaves, you can use shredded paper, saw dust or wood chips. Just make sure that the wood was not chemically treated. By keeping greens and browns balanced, your compost should have the right level of moisture, but during dry times of the year you may need to add water to the pile to keep it moist.

Turn the contents of the bin when it gets hot to help accelerate the compost process. If you do not want to turn the bin, just be sure to keep the greens and browns balanced. If you find you are filling your bin up before the compost is finished, you may want to consider a second bin.

Resource Conservation Manitoba

A non-profit centre for applied sustainability

Healing Aspects of our Gardens
by Lynn M. Collicutt

Lynn is retired from Agriculture Canada's Morden Research Station in Manitoba where she developed hardy ornamental plants for prairie gardeners. She is a former member of The Prairie Garden committee.

Beyond the health benefits of growing and eating vegetables from our gardens, there are many healing aspects that our gardens, landscapes and natural spaces give us.

Our eyes attune and resonate with colours and textures. Just the green foliage of plants is restful to many. As shown in studies of advertising, decorating and health issues, we react to different colours. We can use this knowledge as we plan our garden spaces: vibrant yellows, oranges and reds are energizing and uplifting; blues and violets more soothing; whites and silvers refreshing.

As we garden over the years, our awareness grows and we begin to notice subtleties such as plant textures. Broad leaves of bergenia and hostas accentuate the more delicate fronds of ferns or meadow rue. Grasses waving in the wind encourage us to appreciate movement and flexibility.

Visual beauty in our gardens and in nature helps us to transcend our everyday existence. A single rose bloom, a container overflowing with vibrant coloured annuals, a full perennial border – all bring us visual appreciation.

Engaging our senses anchors us in the present time and pulls us back from past and future thoughts, worries, or guilt. Touch is a sense we sometimes don't think of when planting our gardens. Fuzzy leaves of *Stachys lanata* (Lamb's ear), soft mosses, and smooth stones all encourage us to reach out and touch.

Include scented plants to touch and smell as you walk by or sit on your patios and decks. The area of aromatherapy is well documented so we can plant citrus scents of lemon verbena, heavy perfumes of hyacinth and roses, or invigorating rosemary. Scents are personal, so engage your nose and brain to venture out and choose what you like. Plant the tall white nicotine by your kitchen window, so the scent wafts through late in the day, or place containers of heliotrope and white nemesia by your favourite outdoor seat.

Sounds of birds, leaves rustling and water evoke relaxation in our outdoor spaces, so include bird friendly habitats, fountains, waterfalls or even a simple spout in a barrel.

Working with our hands as we plant, repot, prune or deadhead becomes almost like an outdoor meditative activity. Gardeners can be lost in their landscapes for hours, happily putting aside worries and concerns. Being in the present moment is a known stress reliever.

Our sense of nurturing is encouraged by planting seeds, watching 'old friend' perennials return year after year, or establishing long term trees and shrubs.

Creativity engages the soul. We can approach garden bed design much as an artist paints, but with the added complexities of time, space and height. Creation of container planters can be like painting a mini picture canvas.

Studies are beginning to emerge that show an enhancement in the health of those who involve themselves with growing and interacting with natural areas. By connecting with gardening and nature, we reconnect with a part of ourselves. 🦌

Two Healing Plants
by Susanne Olver

Susanne Olver is a retired greenhouse supervisor from the Dept of Botany, University of Manitoba.

Aloe vera

One plant I would not want to be without is 'the Burn Plant', *Aloe vera sinensis*. It is the best first aid for minor burns, scrapes, cuts and razor burns. It has even been found to be helpful for medical radiation burns.

The *Aloe vera*, although it is a succulent, prefers a semi-sunny to semi-shady position in the house. In summertime it does well with a once a week watering – in winter once a month or less.

There are two types of *Aloe vera*: a large one (*A. vera barbadensis*), most commonly sold in plant stores, and a smaller one, the *A. vera sinensis*. The larger one usually has only one stem, about a foot high when sold; the smaller one, which is not as available in the market, can be found in many households. The smaller *Aloe vera sinensis* grows in clusters, about 15 cm (6 in) high and seems to be more effective as a pain reliever than its larger cousin. I cannot vouch for this, as I have only the smaller one, standing on my kitchen window sill. Whenever I cut or burn myself I take one of the lower leaves, slit it open and apply the gel-like sap to the affected area. Use the inside of the leaf to spread the gel – it will be germ free. Warning: do not treat large open or deep wounds or anything that requires medical help by using any home treatment!

The Cooking Onion

The second plant that I rely on and highly recommend is the common onion. The fact that onions are a healthy part of our diet goes without saying. No need to give more recipes for their use. It is not as well known, however, that the fresh juice of a cooking onion can serve as an excellent first aid treatment for wasp and bee stings.

The 'hotter' the onion, the better. Sweet or green onions, although they might help a little, are not as effective. The quicker that the sap of the fresh cut onion is applied to the sting, the better, because once the venom is absorbed by the body, the onion juice is not able to neutralize it – although it will still have some cooling effect.

It is a good idea to carry a small onion and a pocket knife when going camping or blueberry picking. I learned this old remedy from a retired nurse who grew up in the country in northern Germany. As children they roamed around the Heath country, which was alive with wasps. Her father insisted that they always took an onion along. I tried this remedy, one time, on two little boys who came running into the house howling. The little one had stepped into a wasps nest and had 7 stings to his face! The older boy also had a few stings. They were in agony. I quickly got an onion, cut it and rubbed it onto the stings. By the time I finished treating the little one he had already stopped crying—it worked that quickly. His face hardly swelled up; the same with the older one. The site of the sting might still be a bit sensitive later on – repeated treatments will help here, too.

Again, caution: persons with bee sting allergies should not depend on this treatment and should seek medical help immediately. However, the onion still might help to neutralize the venom and reduce the pain. 🐝

The Basic Garden
by Susanne Olver

The basic garden, for me, is one that provides me with joy, relaxation, some fresh food – and health.

Even the smallest garden, from balcony, inner city backyard, to any larger sized lot can provide this – a place to sit, relax and enjoy nature. Eating your own freshly picked pesticide-free fruit and vegetables, provides culinary pleasure. A balcony can provide room for some fresh herbs and a pot or two of tomatoes. Almost all gardens can give us fresh fruit and vegetables, even flowers, on which to feast the eye. All this, if possible, unadulterated by toxic chemicals – is healthy for us and the creatures that might come and visit our 'Basic Garden'.

It's OK to be a Lazy Gardener
by Carla Zelmer

Dr Carla Zelmer is a Research Associate in the Department of Plant Science, University of Manitoba.

Psssst! Over here! Yeah, come closer because I don't want those gardening experts to hear me. What I'm about to say might be considered heresy, and I may need to share a table at a conference with them sometime. I just wanted you to know – it's ok to be a lazy gardener. In fact, it's ok to start small, to not clean up your gardens in the fall, to not be totally devoted, to not consider seed catalogues as a cozy winter read. It's ok – really. I know, you've been told to do so many things. To double dig your gardens, to plant in straight rows, to hill your squash, to eradicate all weeds, to fertilize, prune and rototill. I think it is time to consider the benefits of just doing a little, and enjoying it.

You might be feeling a little uneasy about this. After all, if gardening didn't require all that work, why would anyone do more work than was necessary? Well, there are a couple of answers to that, one of them being that high maintenance gardening is a relaxing hobby for some. I personally know gardeners who love deadheading, lopping off their troubles as the spent flowers fall. The perfection of their gardens brings peace, control and order to their lives.

Another reason is that gardeners come from all over the world, and in some places particular techniques are used to solve local problems. Put all those people together, and gather together all their gardening advice, and you'll end up with reams of recommendations, many of which may not be needed in the area where you live.

This became clear in a community garden where I had a plot many years ago. It was a community garden for a University, and so many of the gardeners were in Canada for the first time in their lives. When we planted, there was a huge diversity of styles. Some built mounds ('burial mounds' a neighbour complained) to raise up their seedlings, so they would not drown in the rains. Some carved deep trenches throughout their plots, to aid in irrigation during the dry season. There were wide even paths separating straight-rowed crops in some gardens, and in others, seed was flung onto the ground and raked in, resulting in a wonderful randomness.

It was this little garden that also taught me that a lot of the conventional wisdom could be laid aside without an unacceptable loss of productivity. I had always been a backyard/apartment gardener and so, when I arrived in Edmonton to start my Master of Science degree on June 1, I quickly secured a plot in the community garden. Four days later, I was in hospital with appendicitis, and wasn't discharged until 10 days after my surgery. June 15th, I wandered out to the garden plots and envied the gardens with their emerging seedlings and vigorous transplants. I had only a few packages of seeds, no idea where to get transplants and no energy to do any digging. I did have tomato seeds, but they should have been planted weeks ago. I despaired of getting anything from my garden, the one I hoped we could live off of during the summer. My husband was in the field on research, having been hustled there before my release by an advisory committee member who thought I'd be 'just fine'.

After a few hours of self pity (I won't admit to any more than that!), I decided that I would do just what I could. To lose a whole summer of gardening was just too painful. I didn't abandon my garden—how could I? I left the weeds where they were, sat down on the warming soil, seed packages in one hand, a teaspoon in the other, and dropped the seeds one by one in shallow holes I made with the spoon. I didn't know how long my energy would hold

out, so I planted several types of seeds around me as I sat. Even the tomato seeds went in. Over the next while, I didn't water (not allowed to lift), scrubbed out weeds with the toe of my shoe, if they got too high, and didn't bother to fertilize. It was an unusual garden, not neatly planted or organized, but it produced! The tightly-spaced plants defeated most of the weeds, the vigour of the plants seemed about the same as our more garden-devoted neighbours, and amazingly, my early season tomatoes (Siberian?) were only a week behind those of the other gardens for harvestable fruit. It was a successful experiment into how little one could do and still eat from a garden plot.

The intermingling of different types of vegetables turned out to be a benefit. This way of planting different crops together (sometimes called polyculture) was a great way to optimize the production from a small space, and defeat some insect pests at the same time. The method itself is quite old and is well used in small scale agriculture all over the world. It works because each plant species has a different structure, a different requirement for nutrients and a different tolerance for shading. Tall plants can support climbers, and the base of taller plants can provide a shadier, cooler environment for plants that ramble along the ground. Since all of the available bare ground is used by plants, there is less room for weeds and they often get crowded out. Insect pests can also be reduced, because most female insects locate their specific host plants by smell, and the fragrances in a mixed plot intermingle, making it harder for them to find the right plant to lay their eggs on.

What about the soil that I didn't turn, the weeds I failed to pull and the fertilizing I didn't do? I have since learned that my garden may have done well because of those perennial weeds.

Have you heard about mycorrhizas? These are relationships formed between plants and certain types of soil fungi. It is a mutualism: the fungi seek out nutrients in the soil in places too small for root hairs to penetrate and deliver the nutrients right to the plant roots. In return, the plants give the fungi sugars from photosynthesis. Many of these fungi can't survive without the plants. It is an old relationship, and it is natural to almost all of the world's plant families. Tilling the soil tends to break up the networks of fungal filaments, so it takes longer for the seedlings and the fungi to find each other. If the plot of land has been free of plants for a long time, mycorrhizal fungi may be greatly reduced, and may survive in the soil only as spores. This means that my pesky perennial weeds may have served as an oasis for the beneficial fungi until my garden seedlings began to grow and produce some sugars for bartering. With the help of this intact fungal network, my plants had less need for fertilizer. In fact, it is known that heavy applications of fertilizers can damage the intimate relationship between the plants and their fungal 'friends'. My unruly garden had tapped into the benefits of working with nature.

Am I suggesting, because of this experience, that you ignore all conventional wisdom about gardening? No, not exactly. What I am suggesting is that we can leave the gardening advice behind when we need to; that we can think about working with nature rather than against it in our gardening practices; that we admit to ourselves that we really don't need all the control we try to have over the plants and process in our gardens.

So go ahead and try it. Maybe you'll get stubby carrots because the ground was too hard. Can you eat stubby carrots? Of course you can! Go ahead and do what ever you can manage – just plant! 🌱

Gardening Humour

A couple of gardeners were discussing various new hybrids that they might grow in their gardens and one gardener said to the other, "Did you hear about the new potato that was a cross between a potato and a sponge?" After a negative response from his listener the gardener reported, **"It doesn't have much flavour, but it sure holds a lot of gravy."**

Autumn—Endings and Beginnings
by Jeannette Adams

Jeannette is a Master Gardener and involved with the Millennium Gardens and the West Kildonan Horticultural Society in Winnipeg, MB.

In the spring of 2010, during my rounds of garden centres, I heard a common lament from my fellow gardeners that so many of their plants had been lost over the Manitoban winter. Everyone had their own theory about why this had happened, but the most frequent one was 'a lack of snow cover.' As true as that may be, there were other contributing factors. The wet summer of 2009 discouraged plants, especially newly planted ones, from establishing strong root systems. The dry autumn weather may have caused spaces to form around the roots, allowing an early, harsh frost to penetrate deeper into the soil. Warm temperatures extended well into the fall, delaying dormancy. Once the cold weather arrived, there was little snow cover to offer protection and many plants were dead before the end of December.

In the spring of 2010, we were challenged with very wet conditions, and when fall arrived, our preparations for the coming winter became especially important. Conditions will always vary from year to year. Here are some suggestions on what to consider when preparing to over-winter your garden.

Unless you have wonderful drainage in your garden, your soil has probably become quite hard or soggy from the continuous moisture. As you start your clean-up, take time to work up the soil and carefully loosen the lumps. Fall is a good time to add some organic material. If some of your hardy bulbs did not perform very well, it may be that they need to be divided or replaced. Hopefully, you know where they are and can dig down to check on their condition. Tulips, especially, hate too much moisture and rot easily.

People often ask as to how much should they clean-up in the fall. There is a balance to be struck between knowing what to remove and what to leave standing. I suggest all annuals should be pulled out to avoid having a mushy mess to deal with in the spring. Also, remove the foliage on any perennials that freeze completely down, such as hostas. Secondly, anything that shows any signs of disease or insect problems should be cut back and the material discarded or destroyed. Do not add this material to your compost as the disease microorganisms may overwinter and infect your compost. Late blooming perennials are usually nice to leave standing as most have strong stems and interesting seed heads that will add interest to your winter garden. Ornamental grasses, perennial and annual, also add interest in winter and can be easily cut down (or annuals pulled out) in spring. Roses, especially tender ones, need special care and need to be properly covered. Hardy roses do not need as much protection, but they need to be allowed to go into a proper dormancy. Do not fertilize, therefore, after the end of July. As fall approaches, cut back on watering roses and other plants (except evergreens) in your garden. Allow some rosehips to form once the blooms slow down, as this will signal the plant it is time to prepare for winter. Once we're into late autumn, be sure to clean up the foliage and discard any leaves that may be on the ground around the rose plant. You can cut off all the rosehips to limit the chances of having overwintering insects and disease.

If the fall is dry, give your flower beds and shrubs a good watering as close to freeze-up as possible so that there aren't spaces in the soil for frost to seep down.

Those gardeners who are growing vegetables should harvest all their produce and pull out all the stalks and weeds. If healthy, these can be added to your compost. It is a good idea to work up your soil in fall as this will expose any insects or larva that may want to overwinter.

In years with wet conditions, you may find that large lumps will get broken down with frost action, allowing for less work in the spring.

Fall is also the time to gather seeds and divide some of your perennials. Daylilies, lilies, peonies and your early blooming perennials can be divided in the fall. Iris should be divided and replanted in late July or early August. Summer and late summer blooming perennials should be left to be divided in the spring.

Once the leaves have dropped off your shrubs, you should check them for any insect or disease damage. It is possible to prune in late fall, but if you can access these plants in late winter, it is best to leave pruning until then. However, it's best to prune your early spring bloomers in early summer.

Now, the question of whether to mulch or not to mulch? I have done both and have experienced varying results. Since we can never predict what type of winter we will have, it is wise to take some precautions. If you have tender plants, then you should apply some type of mulch. Perennials that have evergreen foliage, such as thyme or creeping phlox, need protection, as the winds in late fall and early spring can do a lot of damage to them. Perennials with strong growths of foliage can be left standing to trap snow.

There are many different types of mulch. The most important

consideration is that it be dry, loose and free of disease. Straw should be pulled apart before applying and weed stalks or portions exhibiting signs of mould removed. Consider that you may be introducing some new weeds and insects into your yard with straw, so if you have your own leaves or clippings, it may be your better option. I find oak leaves make a great mulch if you can get them to stay in place. Wait to apply your mulch until there is a degree of frost in the ground. This is always tricky because we can get a big dump of snow and then mulching is not possible. However, you would then have the snow cover that hopefully will stay until spring. When spring arrives, do not be too anxious to remove the mulch. I have lost more plants due to windy cold snaps in spring than to winter cold.

As we enjoy the colours and scents of fall with a degree of sadness, let's look forward to a season of rest and planning for the excitement of spring. 🦐

Healthy Trees, Gardens and People
by Michael Allen

Michael is a Consulting Urban and Environmental Forester and Certified Arborist (Viburnum Tree Experts) who regularly diagnoses tree and woody shrub problems for property owners who aspire to have healthy gardens.

As an observer of all that I see around me, I am constantly amazed by the close relationship between healthy trees and gardens, and the people who own them.

Who among us is truly totally healthy? 'Healthy' is both a real and a relative concept. Most people cope with health issues. Some do it better than others. It depends on the health issue itself. If we can wake up each day and exclaim "Wow, am I fortunate to be alive!" it is likely that we are in good health. What about the health of trees? You can not simply walk into your back yard toward your big maple tree and ask "Well, how are you doing today, tree?" How can you tell if your tree is healthy, somewhat healthy, or not at all healthy? This assumes that you are even thinking about the tree's health in the first place. If you have mystical leanings you might seek out an animated connection between the tree and yourself as one author did through meditation:

"You experience your individuality as a healthy leaf. You feel sap flowing from the vine of your innermost self. You feel your life force coming from the central core of your own eternal love. You are the leaves and branches in time and space but you are the vine in spirit and in essence." [1]

In such circumstances you obviously feel at peace with the tree and sense that its health likely mirrors your own. Be that as it may, the tree may have one or more serious problems. Doctors warn us not to self diagnose possible ailments. We are asked instead to get an informed professional opinion through an annual medical check-up.

Your big tree opens its buds as usual in May, and out come the little green leaves. The tree looks great and you decide to do spring chores believing your tree looks healthy. You assume that nature looks after its own. Two weeks later you are at the barbeque and something different catches your eye. The maple leaves are turning somewhat yellow in colour. You think to yourself "I remember that happening last year at this time as well, but the tree survived." You think, "Perhaps turning yellow in spring is normal for leaves on an old maple tree." It is amazing that if our own skin turned yellow we would get to a doctor fairly quickly. It might mean we have jaundice. However, it is easy to rationalize that green leaves that turn yellow are nothing to be too concerned about.

It's mid-June and as you cut the grass you notice that your maple tree has curling leaves that have turned yellowish-white with brown edges and tips. You also notice that the leaves have sprouted thousands of green spherical bumps. "This is new and it can't be good", you think to yourself. What do you do? You decide to fertilize the tree as you conclude fertilizer is simply plant medicine. You head off to your favourite hardware store to get the fertilizer as you can easily do the job yourself.

As the summer wears on, your maple is starting to drop its dry, crinkled leaves and there is not a green leaf to be found on the entire tree. Panic sets in as you realize the maple tree may be dying.

Some people will go to their computer and see if they can find a solution 'online'. You might find a local site that you can contact for advice or you might discover several computer sites from many areas around North America. It is very easy to get extremely confused at this point. You may decide that the tree is not worth all this worry and have it removed.

At this stage you need a professional, such as a tree expert, to diagnose your tree situation as none of your intervention attempts have worked. There are a number of resources that can be found on the

Prairies. You could call a university horticulture department; a municipal government agency that deals with trees; a well known plant nursery or two; look for tree experts in the local yellow pages, or find a tree help book in a local library or book store. Eventually you will stumble upon one or more contacts that can help you.

We are all looking for instant results in whatever we undertake. Gardening and tree care in particular are no exceptions. If we take care of our own bodies by following appropriate medical advice, staying fit through exercise and eating sensibly, we tend to feel good about ourselves. If we tend to self diagnose our ailments and buy a variety of relief remedies in the pharmacy over a long period of time, we may find ourselves constantly feeling stressed. I find that too often gardeners or would be gardeners expose their plants to a variety of 'quick fix' products without really knowing what they are doing. The result is that generally, trees and other plants will become even more stressed. For example, tree nutrition problems maybe 'diagnosed' as a pest issue and people will spray insecticides on the plant. Pest issues can be mistakenly 'diagnosed' as a

disease problem and people will use a fungicide to deal with it. Unfortunately, I see this misuse of chemical garden products all the time.

Trees and other plants are living entities. Although they are different in the way they function compared to people and animals, they do require the same basic life essentials as people: air, water and nutrition. If your tree is not getting any or all of these essentials basics, or is only getting them in a limited way, it will show signs of weakness and stress. Stressed trees and other plants then become targets for pests and diseases, or they may be so structurally weakened that they break apart in strong winds or by heavy snow loadings.

There is at least one real cause for a tree or plant problem. Be sure that you can get the best advice for that problem if you are uncertain how to treat it properly. ❧

See colour photo on page 95.

References:
(1) Ken Carey, Return of the Bird Tribes 1988 Harper Collins paperback edition, 1991, Grand Coulee, WA, pg 175

Tips for Planting Pots

Scale is important when planting containers. Remember that plants should be at least twice the height of a container. When planting a large pot with one big central shrub or plant restrict the other plants in the pot to one or two varieties.

More Than Just Another Pretty Garden
by Darlene McPherson

Darlene is an avid gardener in St. James, Winnipeg, MB. Darlene gives butterfly garden talks to schools, is a volunteer Arthritis Self Management Leader, and uses art and gardening as activities to assist in healing.

No two gardens or gardeners are alike, but we all share a love of being 'out in the garden'! We all want to create a healthy garden – one that can survive disease and brave the elements. Creating our healthy garden gives us time to meditate, and enjoy. Making gardening friends and sharing cuttings, plants and tips is something we all do! So, to be diagnosed with a medical condition that could prevent a person from ever gardening again can be devastating.

In 1953, as a wee baby, I was diagnosed with polio, although having a partially paralysed right arm never posed a real problem. As I became older I gardened using my left arm, always finding ways to compensate and adapt.

My health began to change after being diagnosed with Post Polio Syndrome in 1987. Fatigue, sore muscles and joints made gardening painful. Fortunately, a specialist referred me to occupational therapy and to physiotherapy where I received helpful aids that relieved many symptoms and exercises designed to help strengthen my muscles. Occupational therapy and physiotherapy helped me get back into successful gardening!

By 1989, because of recurrent pain and swelling in my fingers, wrists, hips, knees and feet, my family doctor referred me to a Rheumatologist who diagnosed me with rheumatoid arthritis. Hearing that diagnosis at the age of thirty-six was overwhelming! I didn't know much about the disease but what I had heard was frightening. I was devastated. Would I ever garden again?

My rheumatologist referred me to a physiotherapist who developed a series of daily 'range-of-motion' exercises. The exercises focused on strengthening my ligaments and tendons around the joints from my toes to my neck. These sessions helped me understand that exercise was very important in maintaining my flexibility and

(Darlene McPherson)

strength. As well, an occupational therapist gave me wrist splints to wear that helped to stabilize my wrists and give them the support they needed. I found that both therapists listened carefully to me. The therapists knew the value of gardening as a great activity for maintaining joint flexibility, bone density and quality of life. Their input encouraged me to continue gardening. I realized early on that the amount of time and effort I put into following their suggestions, exercise routine and aids, would determine how successful I would be in gardening and in managing my daily activities as a young mother and wife.

For the next ten years my gardening was enthusiastic and productive. I planted flowers near the foundation of the house, a small kitchen garden and a water feature. The garden looked beautiful. Installing the water feature was exciting because it involved my two sons aged seven and nine at the time. The boys had so much fun digging the hole for the little pond. My husband helped out in placing all the rocks around the pond. 'My' gardening became 'our' gardening adventure! Each year the May long weekend found my family and me, like my fellow gardeners, planting the garden. I loved spending time working in the garden and I especially loved sharing this activity with 'my guys'. There is nothing like the delight of seeing the first bud and sharing this with your family!

My life changed completely in 1998. I could no longer walk up and down stairs and perform simple tasks. Gardening was once again painful and fatiguing. I had to leave my part time job. My rheumatologist adjusted my medications and prescribed a drug called prednisone.

By March 1999, I was hospitalized for nearly two weeks as medical professionals tried to stabilize my condition. When I was discharged, I spent a great deal of time staring out the living room window. Looking at a plain green lawn did nothing to raise my spirits. However, this passive activity planted the seed of an idea — I would create a butterfly garden! The idea really grew and blossomed after my rheumatologist referred me to the Day Patient Program at the Rehabilitation Hospital, Winnipeg. During this week long program I learned much from the team of professionals consisting of physiotherapists, occupational therapists, a nurse, dietitian and social worker. I also learned so much from my fellow group members about the disease and various strategies. We were shown many adaptive aids and tools.

"So many people spend a great deal of time trying to make sense out of the senseless. Don't stop doing the things you love, just change the way you do them!" said my occupational therapist, May Chan. Her words of encouragement gave me hope and the motivation to carry on — I would continue to garden, but on my terms!

Important information centred on following the **Four P's**. You must: First **plan**, then **prioritize**, next, **pace** yourself and finally monitor your **position** – in other words make sure you are using good body mechanics. I now had a strategy for creating a butterfly garden! The Four P's put me in control of my actions and gave me a purpose.

My planning involved my husband and sons. As a family we decided that it would be a butterfly garden composed of 12 small, manageable beds connected by a grass path, wide enough for a wheelchair to pass through. Designed so I could take care of it on my own, I had the option of reducing beds if my condition worsened. I could eliminate beds and it would still look visually appealing. We created the garden over a two-year period.

I read a great deal of information on how to create a butterfly garden. I selected perennial plants suited to the butterflies' needs and the prairie environment. These plants require less water so that was a plus as well. I added some annual, biennial and various 'butterfly attracting' flower seeds. Using family teamwork our butterfly garden was created in our front yard by the year 2000.

I enrolled in the six week Arthritis Self Management Program offered by the Arthritis Society, Winnipeg. The title intrigued me as it emphasized self-management. To me that spoke of empowerment! I learned so much from the program and my fellow group members. The program is very comprehensive and several of the topics really spoke to me: breaking the pain cycle, goal setting, exercise and positive self-talk. What I especially liked was the section in the textbook on adaptive aids that showed photographs of people using the products. These particular topics helped me become a better gardener and I realized how easy it was to purchase these adaptive aids. One of the most encouraging things about this program was that I could take the information and adapt it to my own particular situation and needs. The Arthritis Society has so many informative pamphlets to choose from, including how to garden when you have arthritis! I went from 'suffering', to 'coping', to 'managing' rheumatoid arthritis.

As an arthritis manager I started each gardening day with my range-of-motion exercises. I followed the Four P's and:
• Made a mental list of garden jobs
• Decided which jobs I would do first in the garden that day
• Worked only for thirty minutes at a task – the timer I carried with me would always let me know when time was up. I made sure that for every thirty minutes worked, I would take a break for fifteen minutes. I made sure that I had a rest period every day.
• Constantly checked my body mechanics – was I standing, lifting or carrying using good

body mechanics? When I weeded, I first loosened the soil with a garden fork, then pulled the weeds out with my fingers. This placed less stress on those joints. Wearing wrist splints with the bar removed allowed me more flexibility of wrist movement while still providing excellent support.

Other disease management strategies I employed:
• Icing joints before I worked and after.
• Taking warm showers to ease and relax muscles.
• Using a sprinkler for watering the beds and long necked garden wands for plant baskets and hard to reach flowers.
• Using my son's old wagon for carrying 'large handle' easy-to-use gardening tools and soil bags. This made it easy on my joints and kept fatigue and pain at bay.
• Sitting on a small work stool with side pockets while I gardened. I could store my garden gloves, seed packets, scissors and timer in the pockets.

Fifty years after contracting polio, I had surgery on my right arm in 2003. For the first time in my life, I could bend my arm at the elbow! My physiotherapist gave me many exercises to do, which taught me how to use, bend and strengthen my right arm. My rheumatologist adjusted my medication again and gardening was easier. Perfect timing — the following year, 2004, our garden was in the

Nature Manitoba Garden Tour! The surgery, exercises and new medication really made getting ready for the tour manageable.

By 2007, my beautiful, healthy garden was transformed into a healing garden. I had spent so many years putting things *into* the garden that I never really sat back and let my healthy garden *give back* to me! How many times did I sit there and have butterflies land on me, watch the hummingbird flit from flower to flower or hear the peeping of newly hatched chickadees? It was truly a healing experience! I hadn't noticed before, but over the years our garden had been transformed from something 'pretty to look at' to a garden that was in harmony with its environment. It supported many different birds, butterflies and most importantly, it supported me. But, it went even beyond that: over the years people in the neighbourhood dropped by, bringing with them gifts of plants to add to the garden. Our garden had long ago become a 'friends and neighbours' garden that brightens everyone's day and lifts their spirits. I was just so busy creating a healthy garden, I never noticed!

There are so many possibilities open to us when we garden. A healthy garden is a survivor – much like a gardener with a medical condition. On your own terms, take time to create, to dream and heal. &

See page 94 and 101 for colour photos.

The Abilities Garden
by K.A. Beattie

*Ken is the Assiniboine Park Horticulturist in Winnipeg, MB,
the author of an informative gardening book series,
and has hosted many radio and television gardening programs.*

Assiniboine Park initiated the design of a quite unique gardening space adjacent to the Conservatory in 2007. The garden, appropriately labelled *The Abilities Garden,* has become not only a destination for park visitors and people of all abilities (the front room, as it were, for the Conservatory) but also the home of some rather spectacular educational programming.

The Abilities Garden is bordered by three freestanding stone planter walls just over a meter in height. This planter wall is home to a varied collection of seasonal sensory plants which boldly announce the garden. The standard Rosemary always turns heads, begging visitors to smell its foliage. The billowing chartreuse sweet potato vines soften the edges of the planters and offer extreme contrast for the scented geraniums. The concept of this area is to stimulate as many senses as possible: visual, aromatic and tactile. The fuzzy foliage of the *Plectranthus* are inviting to touch, both for the sensation of feeling and to the fragrance that results – as are the many Lav-

The Abilities Garden
(Bonnie Tulloch)

ender plants. On a nice sunny day the entire garden smells of Southern France or other such exotic regions of the world. In 2008 the planters spilled over with brightly coloured *Lisianthus* which generated incredible numbers of comments. The intern student assigned in that garden eventually just told everyone who passed what the plants were as he knew that they would ask anyway. As it turns out, this was excellent therapy for him to verbalize with different people, a skill somewhat challenging for people with autism.

Large, raised wooden planters mark the area closest to the Conservatory. Built from reclaimed timbers, these planters are designed to accommodate people in wheelchairs or with walkers, or who simply have difficulty bending or reaching. For the more able-bodied gardeners, the planters are the perfect height for most, to act as a seat. The four

large planters are typically used to grow vegetables and herbs which are part of the education programming. A pizza garden was grown by the participants in the Intergenerational Gardening Program. Heritage tomatoes, basil and onions all provided the class with ample produce to make pizzas as a celebration of their accomplishment. The lessons learned over the course of this program were as obvious as where does food come from, to the subtleties and nuances of respect and good listening skills. The planters drew a great many visitors in to the garden to examine the contents of our containers. Pole beans, snap peas, trailing squash and pumpkins all called the Abilities Garden home this past season.

The crowning glory for the pizza garden is our wood fired pizza oven. If the aroma of the herbs and flowers doesn't coax people into the garden, the wafting smoke from our oven surely does. Our oven stoked with branches of Rosemary wood, oak and birch burns along for at least two hours raising the temperature well over 600 degrees. Our pizzas, made by the program participants and staff, are typically stacked high with basil, tomatoes and the requisite cheese and other toppings. In less than five minutes, the best tasting pizzas emerge

The Pizza Garden (Bonnie Tulloch)

with drooling onlookers jealously licking their lips. Yet again the garden tantalizes the senses.

The floor of The Abilities Garden is an intricate mosaic of interlocking pavers styled in circular patterns. Local, reclaimed Tyndall stone is woven artistically into the overall mix offering a very dramatic yet tailored sense of place. Currently mosses and tiny Thyme are filling in the aged cracks and crannies of this beautiful stone plaza. Attention has been given to making the plaza smooth, so wheelchairs and walkers can manoeuvre the space with ease, as well as the raised deck behind the pizza oven. This parapet is a popular roosting area for folks to look out over the garden and the many passersby. Shaded by a clump of Hawthorn trees this patio is very popular in the summer heat and is home to an eclectic collection of succulents in terracotta containers.

The Abilities Garden is not yet finished, but to those who enjoy it, apparently, it matters not. We intend to install twig arbors over two entrance ways and finish the planting of the Thyme knoll. There are three spectacular sun sails that can be seasonally installed, providing well needed shade. These triangular sails of bright primary colours will also serve as 'markers', offering additional visual ways of finding the garden.

The garden hosts a specialized program for several populations of various abilities. For three years the Winnipeg Foundation supported The Abilities Garden through grants funding the Horticultural Therapy workshops. Throughout the summer, clients planted some of the gardens, tended what areas they could manage, and were introduced to amazing tactile and sensory experiences. Several repeat clients from St. Amant, New Directions, The Huntington's Society and numerous senior's residences participated, requesting additional time each season. The success of this program can be measured by the smiles alone that these visitors bring with them each day. What a wonderful way to enrich other's lives through exposure to and gardening itself!

The Abilities Garden was dressed in warm, rich tones for the 2010 season. Requisite Lavender and Rosemary standards will punctuate the aromatic garden walls while Myrtle and Boxwood topiary dot the inner garden.

Children, active adults, seniors, couples, singles or groups, find this remarkable garden space suitable for many activities. The Conservatory gardening staff often celebrate their many accomplishments in the garden, enjoying what is a highly energized precinct of the Park. So, when you are next visiting the Park and smell the tantalizing aromas of Rosemary and pizza, follow your nose to The Abilities Garden. We will be more than pleased to share our bounty. ❦

Kitchen Gardens, Past and Present
by Linda Dietrick

Linda is an Associate Professor of German Studies at the University of Winnipeg. She loves history and has a great interest in plants.

Our great-grandmothers would have been amused to learn about a recent fashion in gardening – the kitchen garden. Some people also call it a *potager*, which is French for "a place for growing things to put in soup" or "the vegetable and fruit garden", that is quite separate from the rest of the residential garden. To our forebearers, the kitchen garden or potager was anything but a trendy accessory – it was a necessity. There are good reasons, beyond fashion, for it to be making a comeback.

Kitchen Gardens in Europe
In Europe, the kitchen garden dates back to at least the Middle Ages. It was the monasteries' grocery store and pharmacy, as well as a deeply symbolic space for the monks. Enclosed within the monastery walls, it was usually laid out in rows of geometric raised beds. The beds were handy to the kitchen, so as to supply the table with produce, and to the infirmary, to supply the only medicines they had in those days. Botanical names with *officinalis*, which means "used in medicine or pharmacy," still remind us of the plants' earlier use as medicine: *Pulmonaria officinalis*

(lungwort), *Paeonia officinalis* (peony), *Salvia officinalis* (sage). In the cloister, at the very centre of the monastery garden, were four beds laid out in a square, divided by paths in the shape of a cross, with a fountain at their intersection. The plants symbolized God's bounty and healing. The four paths radiating out from the fountain represented the four rivers flowing out of Eden (Gen. 2:10) and, of course, the cross of Christ.

Later European gardens continued the tradition of the enclosed space with its four quadrants and a water source at the centre. From the elaborate gardens of the aristocracy to the simple cottage gardens of ordinary folk, vegetables and fruit, as well as culinary and medicinal herbs and flowers were grown for their practical uses. They were also grown for the pleasures they brought to the senses. Set within tidy hedges of boxwood (*Buxus sempervirins*) or wattle fences of willow twigs woven through stakes, colourful beds of edibles delighted the eye as well as the nose and the taste buds.

The *potager* always remained central to French garden design. In 18th century England, however, the landscape garden movement banished the kitchen garden to a separate, utilitarian area, away from the house and out of sight. Some historians think that the decline of English cuisine can be traced back to this separation of cooks from their fresh ingredients.

First Nations and Colonists

To supplement what they gathered wild, the indigenous peoples of Canada kept vegetable gardens, too. Most of us have heard of the 'Three Sisters' grown by the Iroquois and Hurons of eastern Canada: beans (which fixed nitrogen), corn (which supported the beans), and squash (which shaded the roots). Archeologists say that well before European contact, First Nations peoples here on the Prairies also cultivated gardens, growing many kinds of corn and beans as well as squash, sunflowers, and tobacco.

The French and English colonists brought their own seeds and kitchen garden traditions, but, of course, the harsh climate presented challenges. The Hudson's Bay Company records include long lists of "Kitchen Garden Seeds" that the London directors kept sending to their trading forts in northern Canada. They could not understand why those communities were having no success in producing their own food. After all, Fort Albany and Fort York on Hudson Bay were at roughly the same latitude as England and Scotland!

The earliest Prairie homesteaders had plenty to keep them busy just clearing the land and producing their cash crops. Though they grew such northern staples as potatoes and cabbage, they had no time for elaborate kitchen gardens. But as Mennonites, Ukrainians, and other experienced cold-climate gardeners arrived, they brought new seeds and gardening know-how to our region. In farmyards and the backyards of thrifty townsfolk, the kitchen garden played an essential role in feeding families.

The *Potager* Today

Today's trendy gardeners often create *potagers* more for pleasure than for food. By contrast, recent immigrants and less well off Canadians are usually eager to grow their own produce any way they can. They know what they're doing: groceries cost money, while home-grown food is generally fresher and healthier, and you can grow the species and varieties you like. Those of us with small yards who value the landscape design aspects of our gardens can still enjoy those benefits.

One option is to create a small, decorative bed, say, 2m (6 ft) square. If you want to try a boxwood hedge, a hardy cultivar like 'Green Mountain' may survive here, though probably with some tip kill. But you're pruning it anyway. We don't have the right kind of willow for a wattle fence, but as our late friend and gifted basket maker Walter Dreimanis discovered, native red osier dogwood

(*Cornus sericea*) makes a beautiful substitute. Curly parsley is a great edger, too. Put something striking at the centre, like an urn or beans on a teepee. Then plant your *potager* with colourful edibles in a geometric pattern, like a quilt, rather than in rows. By following the principles of small-plot intensive gardening, you can get high yields from a compact space. Selective harvesting and successive seedings will help preserve your pretty pattern.

The other option is to incorporate beautiful edibles into your garden design. 'Grand Rapids' leaf lettuce makes a gorgeous lime-green edging. As the heads get bigger, you can harvest every second or third one and then snip leaves as needed. Chives (*Allium schoenoprasum*) and garlic chives (*Allium tuberosum*), with their early and late flowers respectively, are excellent hardy perennials. The silvery leaves of kohlrabi look wonderful with pastel flowers. Other decorative edibles include 'Bright Lights' chard, 'Explosive Ember' peppers, baby eggplants, and the many types of basil.

Why not try your own *potager*, if you have the room, or maybe just refer to your current one with this traditional name. ❧

Is There a Difference?
by Susanne Olver

Some years ago at one of our committee meetings, we had an argument. Is there a difference between home-grown carrots and commercial ones? Some of our 'experts' insisted that there was none. So I decided to consult my own experts – three German Shepherd Dogs. I sat them in a row, and put two pieces of carrot in front of each of them – one of them home grown, one store bought. Then, I allowed them to eat. After a quick sniff, each ate the garden carrot, ignoring the store bought one. Argument closed!

(Leslie Snell)

Permaculture: Back to Nature – Back to Basics

by William Dowie

William Dowie is an independent environmental management consultant. He is a LEED accredited professional and a citizen member of the Mayor's Environmental Advisory Committee in Winnipeg.

Permaculture was 'invented' by some Aussies – Bill Mollison and David Holmgren – back in the 1970's. Since then it has been adopted by many institutions world wide, including the Kootenay Permaculture Institute in British Columbia, where my permaculture mentor taught, and who was brought in to help facilitate a course that the University of Manitoba was offering to its summer students in a sleepy rural town called Clearwater, MB. It was there that I was first introduced to new concepts in environmentalism and ethics. It also helped me develop a more balanced approach with my mind, body, and spirit. Now, some readers may already be asking "where were the drum circles and the herbal teas?" Trust me, they were there, but I am not of that world. I was a business-oriented environmental consultant who happened to stumble on some native plants and started a small garden plot in my yard. I wanted to take this course to expand my expertise, but little did I realize how much more was in store for me many years later.

The word permaculture may provide a clue: it is a hybrid of the words 'permanent' and 'culture'. And it is indeed a culture. Rest assured I said culture – and not cult. In my mind, I take all the environmentally responsible things one may do around the house and yard (and in my case in the city) – and do it! That is the system of urban permaculture.

Now, for my permaculture friends, it is not that academically simple (there are zones and principles and relevant international examples that should be learned), but operationally, I believe that permaculture is a system-mindset for the betterment of life in general. For the readers of The Prairie Garden, I submit my urban journey as food for thought.

So, if you are recycling, you are practicing a part of permaculture. If you are composting, covering and shading the southern and western walls of your house (in the northern hemisphere of course) with deciduous plants, you are practising a part of permaculture. If you just can't stand throwing out anything – or buy used stuff at a garage sale – you are practicing a part of permaculture. And it goes on and on. Now, please realize that I said it was a *part* of permaculture. If one is only practicing one or another of these tasks, this is not permaculture. Permaculture is a system; an all or nothing approach to environmental responsibility.

Doing the right things – *all* the things – *all the time* is what permaculture is preaching. The cynical will say that it is not practical or realistic to do all the right things all the time. To them I say they are not thinking of approaching permaculture as a system; they are thinking of the myriad of tasks and are getting caught up in the overwhelming details. Once you are in the permaculture groove – the system – then it all makes sense – and with little effort.

Just think if you were required to break down being a mother or father to a little child (and, just for fun, make it analogous to the gardening world): the nutrition requirements (soil and water); the rest, work, and play needed for proper development (the dynamic seasons of nature); the constant health care (pruning and disease); the on-going learning that must be encouraged (reading and researching about our gardens); the balancing of the needs and wants of all stakeholders such as mommy and daddy needing a break

(wives and husbands and children envision different uses for a yard); the interaction with other children and pets (varieties and species of plants and the non-plant kingdoms). This analysis makes parenthood – and for that matter gardening – sound forced, complicated, impractical – just an unreasonable thing to do. But we know, both as parents and gardeners, once we have a naturally feeling system in place, and we are in sync with how everything works, the task becomes inherently easy. The same goes with permaculture. With time and practice it becomes natural to us – natural in the most denotative way: you are one with the natural world. Permaculture helps us get there. Let me tell you how I found permaculture.

My journey in the garden, and eventually to become certified in permaculture design, started in 1999 when I took on the project of repairing my basement foundation. As I needed to eliminate water leakage through the cement walls, I learned that the forces of our clay soils were the cause of the cracking – and so I replaced the soil from the newly dug trench with river stone – a sort of 'bag of marbles' approach to keeping the walls pressurized but with some give. Now what to do with the soil? I added some soil amendments and planted some pansies and thought the renovated pile of dirt looked pretty good and I was done. But now, more than ten years later, the gardening bug hasn't bitten me – it is in my blood stream. For instance, my home and yard library collection has grown from a few books on deck building to over 200 books on everything about plants, design, and ecology. I met John Morgan, Shirley Froehlich, and David Young – native plant retailers – and I tried to have every plant they offered in my new natural backyard. I met great teachers at the U of M, like Ted McLachlan of architecture and Steph McLachlan of environment (no relation), and Nazim Cicek of engineering. Because permaculture is about people, too, I was inspired to be a better consultant *and* landscaper through my new academic, professional, and gardening friends – in real-life and in literature, and since that time, my family property has been certified by five different naturalization programs.

There are a few common themes I would like to share with you to move your garden towards a more sustainable place in nature – and ultimately help you create an exemplar in urban permaculture:

There is always a creative tension between form and function. In other words: making something look good while it performs what it should be doing for us. Extremes of this idea would be our western judgment of an ugly slum-shack housing a small family, though it keeps them fairly warm, dry and sheltered. A mansion, on the other hand, may be an architectural wonder; but it may also cost twice the mortgage to

heat the vastness of its interior. With permaculture, there should be many form-functions working in harmony with nature. A garden sheltered by a rose and raspberry hedge melds the form of biodiversity in a hedge row with the function of an edible barrier to pesky rabbits.

There are lessons to be learned from nature. Whether you are designing a garden, a skyscraper, or a car, nature is the universal teacher. For example, why do you think leaves fall in the autumn? This is to fertilize the ground for roots to absorb nutrients in the spring to sustain the tree. Why do we rake away our nutrients? This is counter to nature and at a minimum, leaves should be composted and spread by the homeowner every season – there is no waste in nature!

We must move beyond the Three Rs. There is a way of re-thinking and re-purposing almost everything we use as consumers. I have old tires as planters, discarded wood as a new deck, broken patio furniture fixed to be new structures for a temporary gazebo, and decades-old brick as newly renovated sitting areas, paths, and retaining walls. Everything can have a new purpose – but we must use our imaginations and not let the laziness and ease of discard be our mantra.

We must know our sense of place. You needn't subscribe to far-out theories of Gaiaism (a hypothesis that the earth can be viewed as a vast self-regulating organism) to know that we must share this earth – as we are a guest, not the host. This holds true for your garden. If you enjoy butterflies, grow something the caterpillars can eat. If you hate aphids, provide cozy homes for ladybugs to overwinter. If you want squirrels and rabbits to visit, do not be annoyed with the chatter or winter browsing soon to unfold.

Start with the soil. The so-called dirt under our feet is the foundation of life. We must protect and blanket it with mulch – natural and man-made. We must allow and encourage the free flowing cycles of oxygen, water, nutrients, and all of the microscopic life processes necessary for a healthy plants and animals. The soil is the structure that holds our plants in place. Soil is home to many organisms in the beneficial animal, bacterial and fungal kingdom, and is what our houses rest on – we must admire and respect its versatility and, when undisturbed, how it works seamlessly with all the elements of nature.

The right plant in the right place. Do your research and place the plants you love in the proper environment. Don't forget about essential considerations such as pH, porosity, soil type, micro-climate, plant zone limits, snow cover, shelter and protection, bio-regionalism and true native species, as well as sun and water requirements. It may sound like a lot of work—and it

is—but you will be rewarded with a healthy and beautiful landscape with an incredible biodiversity that will attract animal and plant visitors from far and wide.

The system of permaculture is a gateway into the very important concepts of landscape ecology. For more information on these and other concepts, investigate authors like McHarg, Van der Ryn, and Forman. As members of society we can all help by contributing to the web of life through our gardens.

I will close with a rarely quoted passage from Henry Davis Thoreau's *A Week on the Concord and Merrimack Rivers.* The words sum up the spirit of permaculture nicely, that of being one with the land and being patient with Nature's plans:

"In summer we live out of doors, and have only impulses and feelings, which are all for action, and must wait commonly for the stillness and longer nights of autumn and winter before any thought will subside. We are sensible that behind the rustling leaves, and the stacks of grain, and the bare clusters of the grape, there is the field of a wholly new life, which no man has lived; that even this earth was made for more mysterious and nobler inhabitants than men and women."

Wet Ground
by Paul Henteleff

(Retiree Paul and his wife Nel have established park-like grounds in Winnipeg, MB, utilizing composting methodologies. He wrote The Downpour of 1993 *in* The 1995 *Prairie Garden.)*

Manitoba is a semi-arid zone; getting enough water for a garden is our typical concern. However, there are locations and circumstances where the ground is not dry, but too wet. Five different approaches to this problem have been useful in our experience: raised beds, gravel beds, flood tolerant plants, underground drainage and a bog garden.

Raising a bed is the most applicable. Basically, it means building up soil until the bed is a plateau. Warning: because fresh soil settles substantially over time, the plateau should be made at least twice as high as the desired end result. (The plants will settle with the bed; have no fear of exposing bare roots).

A gravel bed, or gravelly bed, is suitable for plants that can't tolerate wet roots. They need irrigation from time to time but must drain well or drown. I have experienced this problem with sumac and New Zealand flax (*Phormium*). When I saw sumac thriving in a gravel wash draining into the Grand Canyon—I had the sudden insight that gravelly soil drains better,

of course, but also evaporates better than the heavy clay soil we call Red River gumbo. Raising beds by digging in quarter inch sized gravel to about 50% content has helped the sumac. (I gave up on New Zealand flax because of initial cost and the necessity to over-winter plants indoors).

Flood tolerant plants can cope with intermittently wet ground. In our experience, the outstanding survivors are daylilies, Siberian irises and peonies. Flooding can be handled with underground drainage. A trench is needed, sloping gradually down from the wet area to a spot where the run-off can drain away. For example, a downpour of rain overwhelms the eavestroughs of our house; an underground drain below our porch can now handle it. The trench has a perforated plastic pipe (weeping tile) running its full length to a lower area away from the house. The drain pipe is buried in gravel to improve water flow to the pipe. Then the trench is filled with soil to ground level. If a prohibitive length of trench would be needed to carry flood water to an area which drains, a sump can be created. That is, arrange drainage to collect in a pit with a sump pump. The pump can be protected against the pit caving in by installing a strong plastic housing wrapped in nylon screen on the bottom and sides. The top must be open for an electric cord and hose. I used a plastic case from milk cartons. Water is delivered from the sump pump by a hose to the final drainage area. Of course, you must have a place for the water to go eventually; in our case we have a ditch. An outdoor sump pump needs a ground fault inhibitor electric outlet. The pit needs protection to prevent people accidentally stepping into it, such as a lid or fence.

Finally, a bog garden could turn the problem of wet ground to advantage. In our experience it has been necessary to create boggy wet ground; we have not had ground wet enough or in the right location to simply plant. Creating a bog garden has required preparing suitable soil (about 50% peat) and arranging for seepage from a pond or for irrigation. The range of available bog plants for sun or shade is wonderful.

Wet ground can have varying outcomes – rewarding gardening is always possible. 🦐

Flood Survivors

Anthemis spp.	Golden Marguerite
Bergenia spp.	Bergenia, Elephant ear
Campanula glomerata	Bellflower
Nepeta cataria	Catmint
Clematis integrifolia .	Clematis
Symphytum spp. . . .	Comfrey
Hemerocallis spp. . .	Daylily
Aster spp.	Fall asters
Filipendula rubra . .	Meadowsweet
Paeonia spp..	Peony
Phalaris arundinacea	Ribbon grass
Limonium spp. . . .	Sea lavender
Sedum spp.	Sedum
Iris sibirica	Siberian iris
Valeriana spp.. . . .	Valerian
Achillea spp..	Yarrow
Rosa spp.	Shrub roses
Cornus spp.	Dogwood
Viburnum spp. . . .	Highbush cranberry
Euonymus spp.. . . .	Winged euonymus

The Organic Lawn
by Ken Land

Ken Land is co-owner of St. Mary's Nursery & Garden Centre. He has 25 years experience in the lawn and garden industry.

A healthy, vigorously growing lawn can provide its owner with many benefits. It can result in a 30-40% reduction in noise levels, a natural cooling effect, the capacity to trap and filter 15 times more rainfall than a poor lawn, combined with the aesthetics of a recreation area. With provincial and municipal governments across the country believing they know what is best for a person's yard, the number of options to help maintain a vigorously growing lawn may be severely limited in some parts of the prairies.

Weed control in lawns is perhaps the most controversial aspect of lawn maintenance. There are those who say there is nothing wrong with having a few dandelions living in your lawn. If they would stay there I might agree, but they will move from your lawn and into your perennial garden or strawberry patch. Following dandelions will be thistles, creeping charlie, clover, and a host of other unwanted plants.

The best way to keep the weeds out of your lawn is to maintain a full, thick turf grass area. Seedlings of any kind have difficulty competing and establishing themselves in an environ-ment full of healthy grass plants. You can improve this competitive advantage by applying products made with corn gluten to your lawn in the spring and fall. Besides containing nitrogen, usually about 9%, which will help thicken the lawn, corn gluten suppresses root development of seedlings. With limited root development, the weed seedling has difficulty surviving. After application of the product, moisture is required to activate the corn gluten and encourage weed seed germination. Following this, a short period of drying improves the results. To achieve this root suppression requires a significant amount of corn gluten to be applied, about 8kg per 1,000 square feet of lawn. A number of fertilizer products made with corn gluten are available on the market, but almost all recommended coverage rates fall well short of the rates required to inhibit seedling root development. Those that do are typically labelled as bio-weed-n-feeds.

Dealing with already established broadleaved weeds without the use of chemicals can prove to be more difficult. There is a relatively new selective broadleaf herbicide, that is organic, available for use in removing broadleaved weeds from the lawn. It is a 'lettuce fungus' that is most effective when applied in the spring or fall when conditions are more likely to remain cool and moist. The down side of this product is its relatively short shelf life and the need for refrigeration for storage.

Early summer 2010 has seen the introduction of an iron based (Fe-HEDTA) selective, lawn weed killer. Its label lists a relatively small number of broadleaved weeds that are controlled, however, the list does include dandelions. Established dandelions can, of course, be removed from the lawn by digging them out. Keep in mind that they will regrow from whatever part of root is left behind. The smaller the piece of root remaining, the weaker the subsequent plant will be. Continued digging eventually eliminates the dandelion.

Insects in a lawn can be both a nuisance and cause damage to the lawn – ants are good example of this. Ants will invade your home and can compromise food supplies. The hills and tunnels they dig in the lawn can kill the grass by smothering the leaf blades with soil or drying the underground root system. The uneven surface they leave behind can make the lawn uncomfortable or even dangerous to walk on. Fortunately, control of ants can usually be accomplished fairly easily. The sugar baits containing borax provide a very good way to control ants. Place the bait on a non-porous surface close to the ant

hill. An old bottle cap makes a good bait station. The ants will find the bait, collect it, and carry it back in to the colony as a food supply for other members. Make sure the bait station is kept full for a week or so, until the ant colony or colonies have been eliminated. Diatomaceous earth can also be applied directly to ant hills to provide control of these insects. A few days after the first application, you should check the area to see if the ants have established new entrances to their colony below, and dust those down as well. The larger the colony, the greater the number of applications that you will be required to make.

Nematodes (*Steinernema glaserie*) microscopic worms, are available to help in the control of white grubs and sod webworms. These insects can quickly decimate a lawn if left untreated. An application of nematodes can be effective in bringing this problem under control.

Powdery mildew and snow mold are two of the more common lawn diseases. With the right weather conditions, powdery mildew can quickly spread throughout the lawn, as it can be spread by your lawn mower. While usually not lethal, the disease can weaken the grass, making it more susceptible to winter kill and weed infiltration. Garden sulfur can be applied to infected areas to help correct the problem. Snow mold can devastate a lawn during the winter months. It is usually worse when the snow accumulates on top of a damp, longish, actively growing lawn in the fall. Keeping the grass a little shorter in the fall and allowing the lawn to go dormant by not fertilizing too late in the season, will reduce the impact of snow mold.

As with all plants, lawn grass requires nitrogen, phosphorous, and potassium. Phosphorous and potassium are relatively immobile in soil, remaining there until taken up by plants. Some jurisdictions have restricted the use of lawn fertilizers containing phosphate. Older lawns, that have regularly had the clippings removed and not had any phosphate added back, can sometimes become deficient in that nutrient. A soil test can determine if that is the case. Nitrogen can be subject to leaching and is often the limiting nutrient in grass growth. Removing grass clippings also removes nutrients that the plants have used in their growth. Leaving clippings behind results in nutrients being released back into the soil when the grass clippings decompose. With leaching, and removal of nutrients by trees, shrubs, and other plants, lawns will require a replenishment of essential nutrients. A wide range of organic fertilizers are available to satisfy this requirement. Products made with bone meal, blood meal, fish, alfalfa, corn, feather meal, wheat shorts, kelp, turkey manure, and a number of other organic sources can be utilized here. Many of these products are also rich in micronutrients which are essential, but often are not added to inorganic lawn fertilizer blends.

Topdressing your lawn with a thin layer of organic material will usually improve its moisture holding capacity. Peat moss, manures, or compost all help improve the soil structure of the lawn. Do not add topsoil to your lawn. While it may help to improve the soil structure, it may contain weed seeds. Peat moss, good compost and manures should be weed free. Since peat moss is generally nutrient free, top dressing with this product may require the addition of supplementary nutrients. Good quality compost and manure should be weed free, but their nutrient content can be quite variable depending on what products went into their production. Testing compost for its nutrient levels will help in determining if additional fertilizer is required. When applying a top dressing, care should be taken to avoid applying too thick of a layer, thereby smothering the grass underneath. Generally anything under a .6 cm (¼ in) is ideal.

With any lawn, the goal is to give it a competitive advantage by keeping it growing actively. A thick, strong lawn can withstand traffic and resist the pressures of insects, disease, and weeds. It also does not serve as a source of problems that can invade your flower and vegetable gardens. With the new weed control products available, maintaining that picture-perfect organic lawn is definitely attainable, without the need to spend long hours on one's hands and knees. 🍂

10 Tips for a Healthy Lawn...
from Canada's Doctors
by the Canadian Association of Physicians for the Environment

1. Spread a blend of grass seed every Spring or Fall.

2. Use a lawn aerator to help soil breathe. Aerators can be rented at garden centres or equipment rental locations.

3. Leave grass clippings on your lawn. They provide valuable nutrients and conserve moisture.

4. Raise your lawn mower to a height of 7.5 cm (3 inches) and make sure the blades are sharp. Longer grass with deeper roots crowds out weeds.

5. Water your lawn once a week with 2.5 cm (1 inch) of water unless it has rained. Use a tuna can or rain gauge to measure the amount of water your lawn receives.

6. Pull weeds by hand when the soil is moist. Drop some grass seed in the hole to discourage weeds from returning.

7. Spread compost or manure on your lawn each year to restore valuable nutrients and build soil structure.

8. Apply natural fertilizer in late Spring and Fall. Don't overfertilize – follow label directions carefully.

9. Match plants and grasses to your soil type and sun conditions. Choose native plants where possible.

10. And remember... over 90% of insects in a lawn are beneficial.

cape
Canadian Association
of Physicians
for the Environment

(416) 306-2273
www.cape.ca

Organic Solutions to Garden Problems
by Hugh Skinner

Hugh Skinner grew up in the nursery business and now manages Skinner's Nursery near Roblin, MB. He has written many horticultural articles; teaches in the Prairie Horticulture Certificate program at the University of Manitoba and is a judge in the Communities in Bloom program.

We are becoming aware of some of the downsides of our reliance on chemicals to keep our lawns green and to protect our trees, shrubs, flowers, fruit and vegetables. The long-term effects of these chemicals to the environment can be a reduction of nature's biodiversity. We use vast amounts of fossil fuel and energy to manufacture chemicals and fertilizers to keep our lawns green and our plants free of blemishes. As a result of the use of these chemicals and fertilizers, we produce vast quantities of grass clippings and other organic wastes that we haul to the landfill where it ultimately breaks down to release methane—a potent greenhouse gas—into the atmosphere.

In addition, we expose children and animals who play on our perfect lawns to these chemicals; we track them into our houses on our shoes. While toxicologists and government regulators will tell us that these chemicals are safe if used as directed, scientists who study the long term effect of chemical pesticides have shown that persons who are regularly exposed to them may have increased risk of diseases ranging from cancer, leukaemia, non-hodgkins lymphoma, birth abnormalities and fertility problems. Even if these risks to any individual are small, we should look for ways of mitigating these problems.

Some organic pest control methods focus on plant health and growing well adapted varieties. Other methods include tried and true older techniques along with new products such as biological controls or those derived from plants, fungi or bacteria.

Plant health and pest control

Some of the ways to lessen the impacts of pests that focus on plant health include:

1. Maintaining healthy soil by addition of organic matter in the form of compost, composted animal manures, blood meal, bone meal and other organic supplements.
2. Selecting the 'right plant' for the 'right place'. Plants that prefer full sun should be planted in sunny locations in the garden while those that prefer shade should be planted in shaded spots. Plant those that prefer moist soil, together with other plants that are mois-

ture lovers. Plants that are drought tolerant should be planted where the soil is well drained.

3. Using mulch to conserve moisture, reduce stress from freezing and thawing and extreme cold soil temperatures, in order to prevent germination of most weed seeds and to provide a home for beneficial organisms.

4. Maintaining plants in a healthy condition by providing adequate nutrients and water, pruning to develop good structure and to remove damaged or diseased wood. Also control weeds to lessen competition and control insects, diseases and animals that damage them.

5. Controlling pests when they are small or few in number. Weeds are much easier to remove when they are small: insects are easier to control at the beginning of an outbreak; and diseases are much better controlled if remedial measures are applied early.

Traditional weed control methods include pulling, cultivating, hoeing or tilling. These methods are still useful to control weeds close to valuable specimen plants and in gardens that are planted to annual flowers or vegetable crops. In tree and shrub beds and in perennial gardens or mixed borders, mulching will reduce weed seed germination. In tree and shrub beds or rows, use coarse materials such as bark chips or post peelings. In perennial beds it is preferable to use finer materials such as lawn clippings or mulched leaves. These can be covered with a thin layer of peat moss to make it more attractive. The mulch layer should be 10 to 15 cm (4 to 6 in.) deep to be fully effective against weeds. If you can maintain the bed by pulling the few weeds that come up through the mulch and avoid cultivating it, maintenance will become easier and will only require additions to the mulch every second year or so.

Several new weed control products have recently been approved for use in organic culture:

1. Corn gluten meal has been widely studied and has been accepted as a pre-emergent control for dandelions in turf. To be effective, it should be applied early in the spring, about two weeks before the dandelions produce their seed. Then, applied again in mid-August. If it is applied for two years in a row it will significantly reduce dandelions, but will not kill established weeds. Other weeds controlled by corn gluten meal include lamb's quarters, purslane (portulaca), redroot pigweed and plantain. If applied according to recommendations, corn gluten meal will supply approximately half of the nitrogen requirements of turf.

2. Sarritor is a strain of the disease-causing *Sclerotinia* fungus that has been developed for spot control of dandelions. Sarritor granules are applied directly to the crown of

the dandelion plant. Sarritor must be refrigerated during storage and has quite a limited shelf life. Care should be taken not to get it on desirable broadleaved plants as it may damage them.

3. Fiesta is a chelated iron product that controls a variety of broadleaved weeds in turf, including: dandelions, white clover, black medic, Canada thistle, common chickweed and narrow-leaved plantain. The product has very low mammalian toxicity and reports suggest effective weed control comparable to multipart chemical herbicides (2-4D, mecoprop and dicamba).

4. Horticultural vinegar is 20% acetic acid compared to 5% acetic acid for culinary white vinegar. It is used to burn top growth on pathways and other areas where it won't damage desirable plants. It is effective against seedling weeds and annuals but will only burn off the tops of established perennials.

A wide variety of insects attack plants in our gardens. Some cause superficial damage to their hosts but others can cause devastating damage or even death. If we discontinue the use of chemicals for insect control in our gardens, beneficial insects that are natural control agents will again assist us in controlling most outbreaks. Cultural methods that are useful in controlling insects include:

1. Squashing, picking or pruning out and destroying infestations when found. This can be messy and the squeamish may want to wear gloves but this can be quite effective against minor infestations of soft bodied insects. (Do you remember picking potato bugs and dropping them into a can of water?)

2. Syringing with a strong spray of cold water. Insects such as aphids or early stages of pear sawfly can be dislodged by the water and knocked off the plant where they're feeding. You may have to repeat this treatment every two to three days to minimize damage but populations will be reduced over time.

3. Clean up the garden in the fall, especially if you have an insect problem. Remove leaves and debris and bury or destroy this litter rather than adding it to the compost pile. Cultivate the garden in the fall to expose overwintering larvae or pupae to cold and predators such as birds. (see Autumn—Endings and Beginnings on page 16)

4. Using sticky traps to capture and monitor insect pests. These can be homemade or purchased. In the case of some pests such as canker worms, this can be an effective control method.

5. Using floating or hooped row covers or other barriers (old pantyhose, biodegradable mats, plant collars or netting) to protect plants from insect feeding and egg laying.

Some less toxic alternatives for the control of insects include:

1. **Insecticidal soaps** penetrate the outer shell of an insect and disrupt cell membranes – causing death. They are most effective against small soft bodied insects such as aphids, leaf hoppers, thrips, white flies and spider mites. They do not usually harm flying insects such as honey bees.

2. **Diatomaceous earth** is a finely ground powder made from the fossilized remains of shelled algae. The product is literally sharp and will cut the cuticle of insects, causing them to dehydrate. It's most effective against aphids, slugs, ants, and early stages of sawfly larvae. It is not as effective when wet.

3. *Bacillus thuringiensis* **(Bt)** is a soil bacteria. A number of different strains have been isolated that are effective against specific insects. Bt kurstaki is effective against caterpillars and is used for control of tent caterpillars, cankerworms and other *Lepidoptera* species; Bt israeliensis is effective against mosquitoes and black flies and is used as a larvacide against these pests; Bt tenebrionis and Bt san diego are effective against beetle larvae such as white grubs.

4. **Spinsoad**, an insecticide derived from the fungus *Saccharopolyspora spinosa*, is effective in controlling caterpillars, leafminers, thrips, Colorado potato beetles and fire ants. Susceptible insects cease feeding on contact. It has relatively little impact on predator insects.

5. **Dormant oils** can be sprayed on trees during the winter to control overwintering insects and their eggs on trees. Dormant oil combined with lime sulphur is often used as a 'clean up' on fruit trees to rid them of overwintering mites, scale insects and aphids, as well as reducing the inoculums of diseases such as fireblight and black knot. Summer oils can be used to control scale insects.

6. **Ferric phosphate** is a fertilizer and food additive that, when used with cereal as bait, is an effective control for slugs.

7. **Ants** can be controlled with baits that are a mixture of sugar and borax or boric acid. The ants carry the bait back to the colony where it is spread and can destroy the colony. It is not effective against carpenter ants.

Plant diseases can be controlled by a combination of good cultural practices, certain traditional mineral products and new biological controls. Cultural practices that help to reduce disease problems include:

1. Choosing only healthy plants from the nursery or garden centre. Choose the 'right plant' for the 'right place'. Give plants good growing conditions – adequate moisture and fertilizer and good drainage.

2. Planting disease resistant varieties. If you've had a disease problem, plant different varieties or species that are less susceptible to that problem.

3. Protecting plants from winter

injury. Plant winter hardy varieties. Protect young evergreens by shielding with burlap from late winter sun. Protect trunks of vulnerable trees with plastic or burlap wraps to shield them from sunscald. Making sure plants have had good growing conditions, but don't over-fertilize in late summer or fall.

4. Protecting plants from damage by insects, rodents or deer. Injury leaves plants vulnerable to invasion by disease-causing organisms.

5. Pruning to develop good structure and remove dead or diseased wood.

6. Protecting the roots of trees and shrubs. Half of a tree is underground, and it needs a healthy, sound root system to be vigorous and thrive.

Less toxic alternatives for control of diseases include:

1. Copper based fungicides – Fixed copper fungicides (50% copper oxychloride), Bordeaux mixture (copper sulphate and hydrated lime), and copper hydroxide have been used for centuries for the control of mites, certain fungal disease and bacterial diseases. Fixed copper is easier to prepare and use than Bordeaux mixture but Bordeaux mixture is more persistent, particularly during winter rainy periods. While these compounds are accepted for organic production, they are poisons and must be handled with appropriate precautions.

2. Microscopic sulphur (finely ground sulphur) and lime sulphur have long been used to control certain fungal diseases, bacteria and mites. Both are corrosive, and one needs to take appropriate precautions when handling them. Recommended uses include treating *Botrytis*, powdery mildew and rust.

3. Baking soda and Potassium bicarbonate can be used to control downy mildew.

4. Hot water treatments are often used to eliminate diseases from seeds.

5. Biological disease control products work by competing with or parasitizing pathogenic organisms with beneficial bacteria or fungi. The bacterium *Bacillus subtilus* strain QST 713 (Serenade) will protect a variety of ornamental plants from powdery mildew, botrytis, and leaf spot diseases. *Trichoderma harzianum* T-22 (Rootshield) protects plants against soil borne diseases such as damping off.

6. Manure tea is a way of applying a variety of beneficial organisms to turf. A caution – don't use this on food crops because of the risk of transmitting *E. coli*.

This partial list of organic pest control techniques illustrates that there are less toxic alternatives to manage weed, diseases and insects in your garden. Continuing research should lead to more and better alternative control methods in the future. 🦋

The Real Dirt on Organic Growing
by Lori Ann Regnier

Lori Ann is a passionate gardener who has retired from teaching elementary school and nurturing young children and is focusing all her energy into nurturing as many varieties of fruits, herbs and vegetables as our prairie climate permits.

Organic farming is all about the dirt, the real dirt. My dictionary defines dirt as "mud, dust, soil, anything unclean." Unclean? Why does that sound like something bad? Dirt is the matrix of life on earth and is very much alive. A handful of soil has copious amounts of microorganisms in it, vital to keeping our biosphere together. Only nature can make dirt, or our preferred name, soil. The top ten inches of soil are teeming with life but in the last 100 years we have lost some of our topsoil. The prairies were once a biodiversity of grasses and herbs that sequestered carbon and nourished the life in the soil.

Man tore up the grass and planted a monoculture of annual grains. Some of the topsoil blew away and by the 1930s the prairies were a dustbowl.

At Blue Lagoon Organics, a certified organic family farm located in St. Francis Xavier, Manitoba, our options for fertility and pest management are restricted. Our mandate is to grow food without the use of pesticides or synthetic fertilizers. We don't have animals so we need to buy manure and we have to get it from a certified organic farm if we want to use it right away. If we use any mulch or manure from a regular farm, it has to be composted until it heats up to a high temperature in order to kill any unwelcome organisms.

Planting squash into alfalfa (Lori Ann Reginier)

Is certification necessary? If you're growing for yourself, no. If you're growing for others in Manitoba, then yes, because it assures the consumer that our product meets the required standards set by the Organic Food Council of Manitoba. Why? Because it maintains the integrity of the product.

What does 'organic' mean? If I'm paying for an organic product, I want to be sure it meets the national standards. I want a healthy product that's free of chemical residue and other additives.

Studies done by the French Agency for Food Safety conclude that organic plant products contain more dry matter; that is, they are more nutrient dense. They have higher levels of minerals, and contain more antioxidants such as phenols and salicylic acid professed to protect against cancer and many other health problems. It is generally felt that they taste better. Conventional produce, on the other hand, may be bred with the importance of having an extended shelf life over flavour. It is picked green and travels great distances. Organic produce has a shorter shelf life and is therefore best grown and purchased locally.

Organic gardening is sustainable gardening. You think of your plants as part of a whole system within nature that starts in the soil and includes the water supply, people, wildlife and beneficial insects. An organic farmer strives to work in harmony with natural systems and continually replenishes any resources the garden consumes. We are 'soil keepers', vested with the responsibility to keep the soil alive and healthy.

On our farm, we have 10 acres in production and we have to replenish the nutrients we use up, not by leaving the land fallow but by planting a green manure which is tilled in to add nutrients and organic matter. We have 17 acres of alfalfa which has deep roots and breaks up the hardpan while fixing nitrogen in the soil. We will plough some of that down and plant our vegetables into it.

A lot of herbs are perennials so they stay in the same place year after year. Our herbs grow in the open, surviving a cold north-west wind. We cover them with alfalfa hay in the winter. The parts that break down add some organic matter and nutrients to the soil before we rake it off and put it on the compost pile.

A compost pile is a must. By using compost, one mimics nature's cycle of birth, decay and rebirth. You can have just a lazy pile in a corner of the yard or use a neat and tidy bin. The tiny microorganisms that convert plant and animal residue into soil organic matter also need food, water and oxygen in order to do their work. They require nitrogen and carbohydrates. Nitrogen materials, called 'greens', include green grass clippings, produce trimmings and garden waste. Manure or at least living soil is a good thing to toss in to provide microbes. For carbohydrates, called 'browns', look for straw, dried leaves, sawdust, wood chips, shredded newspaper and cardboard. These are called browns. You need 1 part greens to 3 parts browns.

In our greenhouse we have a worm farm of red wrigglers. We feed them organic carrot pulp, the residue of our morning carrot juice and organic coffee grounds. We also give them crushed up eggshells to help them digest. We add handfuls of worms and this vermicompost into our container pots or planting beds. The worms produce castings to feed the soil. The liquid collected at the bottom of the bins can be used as compost tea.

Sometimes your soil needs more of a boost than even compost can provide. We use alfalfa pellets or fish emulsion for additional nitrogen, rock phosphate for phosphorus and kelp meal for potassium.

One unpleasant reality in organic farming is what urbanites call weeds. We call them volunteers. Some of them are edible and quite welcome, such as lamb's quarters, purslane and round-leaved mallow. We have eaten some delicious dandelion fritters and salad greens, but the truth is – they are too plentiful. We plant as much as we can into plastic (polyethylene film) mulch in order to not give weeds any place to grow. Direct seeded crops like carrots don't go into plastic mulch, so we have to rogue (manually remove) the weeds in the rows. On a small garden plot, we lay sections of wet newspaper in the walkways and cover them with straw mulch or grass clippings. The beauty of this is that the grass clippings deteriorate and can be tilled in at the end of the season, thereby adding organic matter to the clay. Wet newspapers prevent weeds from growing and attract earthworms to the surface. In large areas we mow the walkways.

Insect pests are a big problem. We plant a numerous flowers to attract beneficial insects. They are our best defence. The only significant pests we have are potato beetles and flea beetles. There have been years where we spent a lot of time removing potato bugs manually by picking them off or spraying the plants with diatomaceous earth.

Some years we have a lot of canola growing around our farm. This monocrop hosts tremendous amounts of flea beetles and when the farmer cuts it down, the flea beetles come to our garden and decimate our brassicas. We have to cover our cabbages with a row cover to lessen their impact. We also spray our cabbages and kales with *Bacillus thuringiensis* var. *kurstaki* (Btk) which is a bacteria that makes cabbage loopers sick so they can't eat. We always have to make sure that whatever we use is specific to pests and doesn't target the beneficial insects.

The unpredictability of climate change affects our food security. Growing organically has become our mission since we believe it is the solution to many of society's health problems.

Besides giving better taste and health benefits, working in tune with nature can heal the earth. Some ecologists predict that the window of time for homo sapiens to exist is 120 years. If we don't buy more time, the earth will survive and continue to evolve without us. At

Blue Lagoon Organics (and anyone who tries to grow organically) we are trying to reduce our carbon footprint and leave the life-giving soil in better shape than we found it for the generations to come. 🐾

See page 92 for a colour photo.

Organic Gardening – *A viable alternative or simply 'Yuppie Chow'?*
by Allan J. Murphy

Allan is a horticulturalist with a background in plant physiology living in Winnipeg, MB.

Any discussion of what constitutes a healthy garden seems certain to bring up the subject of 'organic gardening', exactly what it is and what it may or may not provide in the way of improved nutrition. At this time, given the level of consciousness regarding the use of synthetic chemicals in horticulture, it is almost certain that most home gardeners will be using an organic approach to some extent. This article attempts to trace the evolution of organic gardening from both a sociological perspective and a scientific one, examining some of the claims made by its proponents and what evidence may be available to validate these claims.

Let me say at the outset that I have always been skeptical about the claims made for the benefits of organic agriculture. When I was invited to write this article, I thought it would be a simple matter to review the literature available on the subject and find some definitive studies that would justify my beliefs. But it wasn't all that simple. There are studies galore to be sure, but upon reading them one finds the writers divided into two camps, each attempting to invalidate the claims made by the other. That approach really wasn't much help. I am therefore presenting some information, the reliability of which I am comfortable with, in the hope that it will provide at least some information that the reader will then be better equipped to engage in the debate.

One might say that until about the end of the 19th century, all agricultural products were produced 'organically' since the use of synthetic fertilizers and pesticides[1] was not yet widespread. At that time, the earth's population stood at approximately 1.6 billion but since that time, it has grown to almost 7 billion today. Regardless of whether or not one regards this as a desirable development, it is certain that it could not have occurred without the development of what is termed 'industrial agriculture', which through the use of machinery, large scale farming practices, and using the most advanced scientific techniques, production is rationalized in order to obtain maximum yield per given area. In the 1940's an added boost was given to food production with the development of what was called the 'green revolution', spurred on by the outstanding breeding efforts of Norman Borlaug. But he himself, in an interview recorded shortly before his death, stated that this was only a stop-gap measure and that sooner or later mankind would be faced with serious food shortages.

What people eat is not a matter of chance, but is closely tied to cultural values, social status, education, income level, availability and so on.

1. In this context, an umbrella term which is understood to refer to insecticides, fungicides, and herbicides.

Because organic food costs more than traditionally grown food products, the term 'organic' now equates with expensive and seen by some as little more than a self-indulgent fetish by members of a more affluent western society. An entertaining account of the industry's development has been written by Julie Guthman (Guthman 2003) who traces the development of organic food from one of its main focal points, California, in the 1970's. Alice Waters of Chez Panisse fame is given credit with introducing salad greens or 'mesclun' to the public and the term 'Yuppie Chow' also appears about this time. While in the beginning small, artisanal-type producers (read 'hippies') were the sole suppliers to local restaurants, but it was only a matter of time before larger scale farms appeared, owners realizing the large profits that could be made from this new development in agriculture.

Of the many claims made for the organic approach, the most important seem to be (1) that organically grown food is more nutritious (health benefits, appearance, taste)and (2) that organic practice is less damaging to the environment than current large scale agricultural practices.

If we examine the health claims first, we must first deal with the issue of synthetic chemicals. The major claim here is that the pesticides used in large-scale crop production remain on the product after it leaves the field and if consumed by humans, serious consequences may result, chief among them being cancer. One could say a great deal about this issue, but I could find no firm evidence to back up this claim. It is agreed by most authorities that any residue remaining falls well below critical limits for human health. With regard to nutrient status, it is claimed that organic products are inherently superior inasmuch as their own nutrients are supplied 'naturally'. There is invariably a moralistic, nostalgic tone to this line of reasoning and these claims are difficult to reconcile with what we know about the chemistry of nutrient uptake by plants.

Plant Nutrition

Before plants can be used to feed us, they must first feed themselves and knowing just how they do this should give us some insight into whether or not the claims made on either side of the organic/inorganic debate may be valid.

The requirements for healthy plant growth are straightforward and fairly well understood. Green plants need energy from the sun to drive photosynthesis, a supply of carbon dioxide (as a source of carbon) and oxygen for respiration, particularly during periods of darkness when oxygen is not being produced by the plant, and, of course, minerals from the soil. It is only then that the highly complex intracellular machinery can incorporate these nutrients into com-

plex organic molecules viz. the amino acids, vitamins, fats, starches and the many other compounds, upon which higher animals are ultimately dependent. We should remember that these products are not produced for our benefit even though they are used by us, but for the plants own requirement for growth, reproduction, and energy storage. Plants belong to a class of organisms termed 'autotrophs' which means they are capable of manufacturing their own food (organic compounds), from the raw materials just mentioned, and are thus the critical link between the organic and inorganic worlds. Of the large number of minerals present in most soils, only certain ones are necessary for plant growth. Through careful experimentation going back at least a century, most if not all of these have been identified. We say 'most' simply because the limits of detection using the most sophisticated instruments presently available cannot be relied upon with absolute certainty to detect certain elements which may yet be found to be essential, albeit in extremely minute quantities.

The soil, as well as providing mechanical support for the root system, is also the source of water and nutrients, the latter being necessarily present in the water or 'soil solution' which bathes the roots. Critical to this discussion is an understanding of the exact mechanism by which plants obtain these nutrients from the soil solution. In the presence of water, certain chemical compounds are capable of breaking down into subunits called 'ions'. By way of example, common table salt or sodium chloride, when dissolved in water, disassociates into individual sodium and chloride ions. The substances typically found in chemical fertilizers eg. ammonium nitrate, calcium phosphate, etc., behave in exactly the same way, forming ammonium, phosphate and numerous other ions. What is important to understand is that this is the only form in which these minerals can enter the plant root.

This process requires energy on the part of the plant and hence is referred to as an 'active' process. Plants are highly specific with respect to their nutrient requirements, and, by and large, nutrients are transported into the plant's cells more or less in proportion to the plant's needs.

The relevance of this process in any discussion of organic agriculture lies in the fact that regardless of the manner in which nutrients are supplied, ie. as mineral fertilizer or in some organic form such as compost, the ultimate process is exactly the same. Just as mineral fertilizers must be broken down into their constituent parts, so too in the case of fertilizer applied organically. There are some differences: in the case of mineral fertilizer, it will be available to the plant much more quickly and can be applied in precise formulations appropriate to the needs based on soil or tissue analysis. Organically

applied material must first break down, a slow process taking several weeks or months and possibly more. There is, however, no question as to the benefits to long-term soil health from this latter form of application. The incorporation of organic materials greatly increases the overall health of a soil, whereas mineral fertilizers tend to be inefficient in that a good portion of the material applied is not taken up by the plants but is leached out of the soil by water movement. It eventually ends up in larger water bodies where it can create serious environmental damage by upsetting the balance of aquatic organisms.

If, then, a crop that is grown organically breathes the same air, uses the same energy source (the sun) and (assuming it is grown in the same type of soil as industrial crops), takes up the same nutrients in the same way, what basis might we have for maintaining that one is intrinsically 'healthier' than the other? Or tastier, more appealing aesthetically, etc.? If the above points are conceded, then we must look elsewhere for the source of differences which may or may not exist. A number of arguments have been advanced by the organic lobby but only one is examined here (possibly the most important, however).

One of the chief benefits of organically grown produce is said to be the absence of pesticide residues other than that which may have been transported by wind. There is the direct harm that these chemicals are thought to do, but there is another line of argument that centres around their effect on plant metabolism. This involves that group of compounds known as anti-oxidants, a term that should be familiar to anyone who has kept up on health issues in recent years. These substances which are produced in various quantities by different plants, are capable of reacting with 'free radicals', reactive chemicals produced during normal metabolism. In sufficient quantities these free radicals are capable of damaging our DNA, potentially leading to serious health problems. Part of the rationale for eating those 5 – 9 servings of fresh fruits and vegetables is based on the assumption that since these foods contain large amounts of vitamins C and E, beta carotene, lycopene as well as a group of compounds known collectively as polyphenols, all of them powerful anti-oxidants, we can thus avoid serious diseases such as cancer and some forms of heart disease.

It is known that these polyphenols are produced by plants in response to attack by insects and other forms of stress. The argument goes then that since pesticides prevent insects from attacking plants, and since it is only when thus attacked that polyphenols are produced, then by holding back the application of these chemicals, the plants will undergo insect stress and produce these compounds capable of providing benefits to human health.

After reading several authors on this subject, I began to feel we were dealing with an ideology in search of a scientific rationale. As I said at the beginning, it was impossible to come to any conclusions based on current research literature. The logistics of conducting bona fide research on human nutrition are overwhelming. The number of variables one has to contend with make up an astronomical number of possibilities. But in my own research for this article, I found that I modified my own views somewhat. That is, I'm not so quick to dismiss the organic option, nor would I accept the industrial model without reservation. The ideal, of course, would be to incorporate the best features of both in some way and that indeed will likely happen, but in a world of expanding human population, and the attendant increased requirement for food, a truly sustainable model for crop production remains a long way off.

But either approach has serious limitations, such that regardless of what we choose to do, with human population continuously expanding, it appears that ultimately humans will be faced with some very difficult choices and a truly sustainable method for crop production is a long way off. &

Reference:
Guthman, J. (2003) Fast food/organic food: reflexive tastes and the making of 'yuppie chow', Social and Cultural Geography 4 (1): 45-58.

Corn Gluten Meal
by Sara Williams

Sara Williams, retired as the Horticultural Specialist with the University of Saskatchewan. She is the author of a number of gardening books. She gardens near Saskatoon, SK.

Corn gluten meal (CGM) is an organic, non-toxic byproduct from the manufacture of corn syrup and corn starch. Long used in pet, cattle and chicken animal feeds, it gained a new life about two decades ago as a pre-emergent herbicide with the added advantage of nitrogen. That means it will prevent weed seeds from developing into plants, but has no effect on the established weeds already in your lawn or garden. It can be applied to lawns, flower and shrub beds as well as vegetable gardens.

The great advantage of CGM is its non-toxicity. Lawns can be used by

Apply corn gluten meal with a fertilizer spreader (Laura Brandt)

people and pets immediately after application without the wait time advised for chemical herbicides. (Caution: if members of your household have an allergic reaction to corn, it's best to err on the side of safety and not use it.)

Developed by Nick Christians of Iowa State University, it was patented in the United States in 1991 and has since been registered in Canada. The United States Environmental Protection Agency considers it a "minimum risk pesticide", exempt from registration requirements.

CGM consists of 60% protein. The protein, dipeptide, inhibits the root growth of seedlings by breaking down the cell walls of the emerging roots. This reduces the ability of the tiny seedlings to absorb water, causing their death.

A broad-spectrum herbicide, CGM does not differentiate between grasses (monocots) and broad-leafed (dicot) plants. Nor does it affect established garden plants or established weeds.

It is effective for about six weeks after application. The downside of this is that you cannot over-seed your lawn for at least six weeks after application of CGM as it also inhibits the germination of lawn seed. With flowers or vegetables that are directly seeded, do not apply CGM until the seedlings are well established.

Because corn gluten meal contains 10% nitrogen, in a slow release form, it is also a fertilizer. The label should read 10-0-0.

Two formulations are available. It can be purchased as a fine yellow powder, or in a pelleted form that is golden brown in colour. The pelleted product is easily applied in a fertilizer spreader. The powder form is not as easy to spread, and may cake or blow away. Store unused CGM in a dry place.

To be effective as a pre-emergent herbicide, the product must contain 60-98% corn gluten meal. If other nutrients have been added to make it a broader-based fertilizer, ensure that what you buy still contains at least 60% corn meal gluten.

Consumers should be aware that too much moisture, and the associated increased microbial soil activity, can reduce the effectiveness of CGM. This problem has sometimes been experienced in the Pacific Northwest where precipitation is considerably greater than on the prairies. As well, it may be slightly more costly than conventional chemical herbicides. Up until recently, availability has also been problematic, although it can generally be found in larger centres. Or, simply ask your local garden supplier to bring it in.

Corn gluten meal should be applied twice a year, in spring and in fall.

Spring application should be a few weeks before the time that weed seeds begin germinating. This usually coincides with the bloom time of forsythia and (of course!) dandelions. The fall application to controls 'winter annuals' (weeds that germinate in the fall but put on full growth the following spring) should be made between late August and mid-September. For both applications, timing is important: just before weed seeds begin to germinate.

Using a fertilizer spreader, apply the meal at the rate recommended on the package (generally 5 to 10 kg per 100 m2 or 20 lbs per 1000 square feet). For even coverage, spread half of the required amount in an east-west direction, and the other half in a north-south direction. In order to activate it, water it moderately into the soil.

Proteins will be released whenever it rains or the lawn is irrigated until the pellets are decomposed. It is most effective if the soil is allowed to dry out after weed seedlings have germinated as that puts added stress on them.

Corn gluten meal needs three or four years of consistent application. In this respect, it is no different from conventional chemical herbicides. Each consecutive year should obtain better results.

Among the weeds controlled by corn gluten meal are dandelions, knotweed, lambs quarters, red root pigweed, plantain, purslane (portulaca), foxtail, annual bluegrass, shepherd's purse and chickweed. ❧

Food Matters
by Izzy Goluch

*Izzy Goluch was an intern for Food Matters Manitoba through the Red River
Creative Communications Program in the Spring of 2010. Food Matters
Manitoba is a registered charity that engages Manitobans towards healthy,
sustainable and fair food for all.*

Manitoba has a long history of action and coalition around building food security, going back as far as the 1992 document from The Nutrition and Food Security Network of Manitoba, entitled "An Action Plan for Food Security for Manitobans".

Today, the movement is stronger then ever, with a provincial organization spear-heading work towards a more food-secure future. Food Matters Manitoba is a registered charity that engages Manitobans towards healthy, sustainable and fair food for all. This is accomplished in a variety of ways: cultivating community food skills, public education and awareness, as well as partnerships and networking.

As a grassroots not-for-profit organization, Food Matters helped develop The Manitoba Food Charter. You may see the recognizable logo swinging on reusable bags on the shoulders of those who shop at farmers' markets. Through more than 70 public consultations, the Manitoba Food Charter set out to identify what Manitobans believe our food system should look like. These consultations led to a final document, the Food Charter itself, as a vision of how things should be and a goal to work towards.

In order to sign the Charter, you must identify the action steps you will take as an organization (choosing healthy foods for staff meetings) or in your own life (shopping for local food) towards achieving food security in Manitoba. Becoming a signatory is a statement of goodwill that you are working towards a just and sustainable food system in Manitoba.

Food Matters Manitoba really does mean food security for the entire keystone province, not just Winnipeg. Buying local food is a great first step towards supporting food security in Manitoba and lowering everyone's ecological footprints. Food Matters has developed the "Buy Local Manitoban Grown" labels that are (hopefully) placed in your local supermarket to indicate which foods are Manitoba-based.

Food Matters believes there should be more options to choose sustainably produced local food versus foods that produce high amounts of greenhouse gas emissions during their production. Food Matters works on food projects across Manitoba, including northern, rural and urban communities. Following are some local food champions and their stories.

Father Forrest

In the northern community of Berens River, Father Forrest has utilized the benefits that go along with having goats and chickens; not only because "these animals are very easy to tend to, and everyone likes them" but also because they fertilize the soil. Father Forrest hasn't let the short growing season or poor soil stop him from producing his own food in an area where a highly processed diet prevails due to lack of options.

"It doesn't take much grain to feed the chickens, and they produce one egg a day, which is an excellent source of protein" says Forrest.

Father Forrest has been in the north for 12 years where he ministers in communities such as Berens River, Little Grand Rapids, and Poplar River, in addition to gardening. The longer daylight in these northern areas accelerate the growing process of garden produce. Most of his vegetables are frozen or preserved for the winter months. He strongly encourages the use of organic matter as a fertilizer, and anyone who walks

by his impressive garden can understand why. From his small, animal-manure powered garden, Father Forrest is able to grow a delicious variety of veggies (sometimes raided by local children): corn, cabbage, potatoes, lettuce, chard, beets, kale and carrots.

Those who want to get involved with farming up north will need some training and raw materials to properly care for the animals, notably fencing, feed and shelter. Father Forrest is a strong advocate for local food production which can solve some of the challenges facing residents who live in remote, northern communities.

Jim Beckta, Immigrant and Refugee Community Organization (IRCOM)

Food Matters Manitoba is encouraging urbanites to also lean in a healthier direction as well. One option is to create balcony gardens. Residents of IRCOM started growing their own food in the IRCOM apartment building after volunteer Jim Beckta got involved as the Greening Coordinator.

Jim is a self-proclaimed old hippie who organized Earthshare (a workers co-op with the idea of bringing fresh veggies to the city) out of IRCOM in the early '90s.

He explained both the practical and healing effects of balcony gardens for those who live in IRCOM's building, where newcomers can stay for up to three years after they arrive in Canada. "There are a lot of programs, language programs, a lot of stuff for kids and youth, helping people find jobs, and integrate into the community" explains Beckta. "They come here as refugees, some have been in refugee camps for 15-17 years or have horrific backgrounds. No wonder they love to get onto balconies and garden."

What is balcony gardening exactly? Jim explains that container and balcony gardening are the same – essentially creating a garden with fruits, flowers or veggies (or all three!) in a container or a pot. It's a great way to keep things local, utilize limited space and supplement your grocery bill, as you can grow almost anything with shallow roots in a container garden: "You want to grow things that give you more 'bang for your buck'. You don't want to grow broccoli or cabbage because you'll get one head of cabbage. Stuff like kale, spinach or swiss chard will grow high and you don't have to replant. You can just break the leaves off and keep going."

Best of all, balcony gardening is relatively easy if you have the right conditions.

"First, you have to have a good southern exposure. Light is absolutely necessary. It's also nice to have a bit of protection because of our height, it gets windy."

IRCOM has about 1,000 feet of space on a south-facing balcony which Jim says is "absolutely fantastic. The first summer, four years

ago, we tried out a few containers to see how people would respond and people were really taken by the idea. They grew tomatoes, salad greens, green and hot peppers."

Jim claims there is no such thing as a green thumb and that, "the great thing about working with that bunch is, they're farmers, they really know what they're doing. The whole idea is they own their production, they decide what they grow and they do it. I'm in the background if they need any support."

Landless Farmers Collective

If you don't have a south-facing balcony, but are still interested in local, organic veggies, meet the Landless Farmers Collective (LFC). Self-described as local, urban and pedal-powered (they deliver produce with human powered cargo tricycle and bicycle trailers, virtually eliminating CO_2 emissions) they "create landscapes of seasonal veggies on under-used urban land." They define 'organic' as: "to grow food in a manner that minimizes the degradation of the ecosystems that sustain us while supporting a community dedicated to this goal."

The LFC grow a variety of veggies and culinary herbs, as well as some medicinal herbs and cut flowers. Their farm site is located in the Pan Am Forest, north of the Pan Am Pool on Grant Avenue in Winnipeg. The food is grown on public land where everyone is welcome to explore at their leisure. The LFC formed in 2008 when a group of city slickers wanted to farm together as a group. They rented about eight acres of land for Community Shared Agriculture (CSA). This space provided 85 shares of organic food for urbanites. Nationally, the number of CSA farms increased from four in 1992 to more than 40 in 2010.

The small group of farmers state, "Food is what keeps us alive. It's important because it's part of being a mindful person. It's important to make informed decisions about what we buy, and what we put into our bodies. It's important because it builds relationships that help us better understand the world, and how our actions affect it."

The LFC have three beliefs that they farm by:

1. Organic farming methods that create long-term sustainable practices for food production. They don't use any synthetic pesticides, herbicides, fungicides or fertilizers.

2. Urban food distribution without fossil fuels. Their deliveries are human powered by human on bikes!

3. The importance of the farmer-eater relationship, i.e. knowing your farmers. They believe it's imperative to know where your food comes from, the impact of what is eaten and how it's grown and how much you should pay for it.

Here is how it works: sharers pay ahead for a portion of veggies etc. that are planted in spring. Depending on climate conditions, the buyer in turn is delivered 13-14 weekly boxes of produce that will feed 2-4 people. They also provide a weekly newsletter. "We wanted to encourage other people to grow their own food by making agriculture visible to the public. We also wanted to transform the under-used spaces that we see in this city, into something more productive and interactive," say the urban farmers. "We farm because it is direct action against a corporate system that exploits natural resources, and the economically marginalized who are forced to work for sub-par wages. We farm in solidarity with the workers of the world who provide the essential services of life – food."

These are merely three stories of local Manitobans who are changing the way we think about food and our local food system. To learn more and become involved please visit www.foodmattersmanitoba.ca. See the link **Other Food Security Groups** for other Canadian groups. 🐾

See page 100 for a colour photo.

Interested in starting your own urban garden? Here's Jim Beckta's advice for you:

Container Gardening With Urban Waste Material

Growing Medium

The growing medium must drain well. I prefer my own compost made from vegetable trimmings, grass clippings and tree leaves. I have the lazy man's way of composting. I layer the materials and let them sit a year. I turn it once, or twice if needed. I tried waste hay bales once and was plagued by weed seeds.

I found last summer that a top-grade topsoil mix will work well too. Any amount of clay in the mix will only harden it after repeated waterings. Straight compost is too rich for growing beans and parsley. I prefer a mix that is 50% compost and 50% sand.

Containers

I like using urban waste materials, such as" kitty litter pails, plastic processing containers from the food industry and 20-litre pails, etc.

I also make larger containers from steel mesh and landscaping cloth for tomatoes, zucchini, cucumbers and muskmelon.

I will continue to harass the food-processing industry for their leaky plastic containers.

Fertilizers

Fish emulsion, Epsom salts (Magnesium sulphate or $MgSO_4$), worm compost, bone meal, fermented nettles and comfrey.

Watering

Containers with loose soil do not hold water well. Repeated watering is necessary. I use drip irrigation on my containers lined up in rows.

Bottom watering works well. I make trays from bread delivery containers lined with plastic. This will hold two inches of water. I then put 4 square kitty litter pails in one bread container.

Vegetable Varieties

Green Onions: Set and seeds.

Lettuce: Minimum 3-gal pot. Oak leaf best. Can pick leaves over long period of time. Resists bolting.

Greens: Spinach, Chard, Kale, Italian Dandelion. Any container deeper than nine inches. Kale will do better in deeper containers.

Tomatoes: Tiny Tim, Tumbler, Window Box Roma in three-gallon containers. Larger tomatoes need something two-feet wide and 20 inches deep. I continue to experiment with the larger varieties but my favourites are Celebrity, Viva Italia and a cherry called Sungold from West Coast Seeds. I use re-bar for staking.

Green Peppers: North Star and Early Prolific. Kitty litter pail. Hot Peppers grow well in Kitty litter pails.

Cucumbers: Straight 8. I have had disappointing results with 'container' cucumbers. On the other hand, I had great results growing Straight 8 in an orange plastic garbage bag. Two foot containers.

Zucchini: I like Ambassador Hybrid and Golden Dawn. They need a two-foot container.

Canteloupe: Any early variety. Two-foot container.

Eggplant: Victoria hybrid in Kitty litter pail. Would probably do better in 2 foot containers.

Ground Cherry: Kitty litter pail.

Herbs: Basil, Fern Leaf Dill, Cilantro, Parsley, Thyme, in at least a three gallon pot.

Footnote: This is an ongoing experiment for me. This year, I hope to learn a good deal about growing Asian and African vegetables in Winnipeg. If anyone would like to share their knowledge of container or raised bed gardening with me, my email is jbeckta@mts.net.

Ten Tips for Canning
by Patti Eilers

Patti is a registered dietitian who presents 'how-to can and freeze' workshops in northern Manitoba. She is an avid gardener and berry picker and has been canning for most of her life.

Canning your own food is making a comeback! There are still many 'mature' canners who never quit for a variety of reasons such as tradition, taste, knowledge of ingredients, food security and gratification.

There is a great deal of information to share on the subject of canning. Here are just some key tips for successful and safe canning:

1. Jars should be clean, chip-free and sterilized.
2. Lids consist of two parts: a metal screw band and a one-use metal lid (this has a rubber seal that you sterilize with boiling water poured over them but **do not boil** these lids as the rubber seal will deteriorate).
3. Wipe the jar rim clean before placing the lid on the jar.
4. All jams, jellies and pickled products should be processed in a boiling water canner for 10 minutes. Water should cover top of jars.
5. Most vegetables, except for sauerkraut and pickles, are low acid and therefore must be processed in a pressure canner. Due to consumer demand, tomatoes have become lower acid by selective breeding.

To each pint (500 ml) of tomatoes, add ¼ teaspoon citric acid and 1 tablespoon of bottled lemon juice, double this amount for quarts (1 litre). Again, tomatoes and most vegetables have to be processed in a pressure canner.

6. Use only good quality vegetables and fruit. Wash carefully.
7. When filling jar, leave ¼ inch headspace for jams and jellies and ½ inch for fruit, pickles and relish. For processing vegetables and tomatoes in a pressure canner, leave 1 inch (2.5 cm) headspace.
8. After processing in a canner or pressure canner, remove the jars without tilting them.
9. Cool jars upright and **do not move** for 24 hours. Do not tighten screw bands after processing.
10. Test for a perfect seal after jars have cooled and before storing in a cool dark place. The sealed lid should curve downward (as the lid has 'popped' inward when cooling) and not move when pressed with a finger.

The book ***Bernardin Guide to Home Preserving*** is a good reference for more complete step-by-step instructions.

Willow Creek Community Garden
by Denise Sarauer

Denise has a certificate in Horticultural Therapy and co-ordinates the Willow Creek community garden in Meadow Lake, SK.

"Gardens, scholars say, are the first sign of commitment to a community. When people plant corn they are saying, let's stay here. And by their connection to the land, they are connected to one another."

ardening columnist Anne Raver may not have been referring to community gardening when she wrote those words, but connection to the land and each other is especially evident in community gardens where people and plants grow together on common ground. No one gardens alone, as participants share the weeds, the weather, and the rewards. A sense of belonging builds as gardeners take

Young gardeners, Stacey, Katherine & Joelle sharing zucchini with Janice (Denise Sarauer)

pride in shaping the brown earth into rows of green.

Many community gardens have sprung up across the country in recent years, and one such garden is alive and well in Meadow Lake, Saskatchewan. The garden started in 2005 when a group of single-parent families, linked together by a local health program, expressed an interest in growing their own vegetables. Town council approved the use of a neglected piece of land on the town's east side and the patch of quack grass was transformed into a productive green space.

The packed earth was cultivated and the heavy clay soil was supplemented with a special blend of dirt from a pasture down the road. Working on a shoestring budget, the group was happy to accept any free or inexpensive gardening resources that came their way. A request put out on a popular local radio program called Swap and Shop, yielded pails of potato eyes, enough to plant a football field. With a few borrowed tools, digging and planting began and the garden soon took seed.

Each family was assigned their own plot, which they personalized with a hand-painted sign. With space to spare, participants from the local Community Living group were also invited to join. The wide-open location proved to be an ideal setting for the garden. A gully fed by rain and runoff at the north end of the site was convenient for filling water buckets. Along with plots of vegetables, there are rows of raspberries, strawberries, and rhubarb for everyone to share. In spite of a late start, our first harvest was enjoyed that same fall. The project was named Willow Creek Community Garden after the willows along the gully.

Inch by inch, row by row—as the garden grew so did interest in community gardening. At the start of the 2010 season, the participants numbered over one hundred. The tilled space has been expanded several times for more fruit trees, as well as for more gardeners who came from all corners of the community. Families from the Health Region's programs and the Community Living group, continue to be involved and are now joined by participants from various non-profit agencies as well as from the neighbourhood and town population in general. Our most recent partner is a group of enthusiastic Junior Forest Wardens who joined us for the first time this spring.

Our garden is a meeting place for a diverse group of people, ranging

in age from infants to eighty, who bring different skill levels and gardening experience. A community garden is a great tool for community development. The garden has worked its roots into the community and also into the hearts of Willow Creek members. One gardener talked about how much more rewarding it is to be gardening together, chatting over the peas, rather than spending time alone in her yard. Cultural and economic differences are transcended and people, who may never have met before, are now exchanging seeds and stories in a space they collectively call their garden. Even the children have staked their claim to the space, and often cry in protest when it's time to pack up and go home. The gardeners learn from and support each other and all skill levels are respected. A few rules and expectations are worked out at informal meetings. Participants are responsible for their own plot for

A very happy harvester about to fill his wheelbarrow (Denise Sarauer)

which a small fee is collected. The strength of the group grows out of positive shared experiences, and an increasing commitment made to support the collaborative green space.

We get by with a little help from our friends—for whom we are very thankful. We are fortunate to be surrounded by a generous community spirit and a strong circle of volunteers. As the garden grows, so has our town, which in 2009 was declared a city. City status hasn't changed the support from council, as they continue to lend a hand with area improvements such as tree planting and a supply of wood chips for mulch.

Various partnerships create further stability. The Communities in Bloom, heritage committee and the health region have been sources of support. We've been fortunate to receive some funding for new tools, a shed and a water tank. A few raised beds and planters have been built, as well as a large, well-used sandbox for the children. Dedicated individuals help out with tilling, water delivery and carpentry skills. And then there are the plants – parsley, sage, rosemary and thyme. Bedding plants donated from the local greenhouses are also very much appreciated.

The benefits of gardening are many, and in a community garden, these benefits are multiplied by the combined inspiration of more people and more plants. Research shows that working with plants can enhance your physical and men-

tal health by lowering stress levels and providing an excellent physical workout. Gardening has been used for centuries for physical and emotional therapy. Such benefits provide the basis for the field of horticultural therapy, a therapy that involves the use of plants and nature to simultaneously restore a person's mind, body and spirit. Being with plants allows us to connect with nature, and in a community garden, the plants also connect gardeners to one another. Access to healthy connections in the garden and in the community grow year after year. The community garden offers a place for many opportunities to enrich lives of both the young and the elderly. Author Wayne Winterrowd writes, "It often happens to children, and sometimes to gardeners, that they are given gifts of value of which they do not perceive until much later." Those gifts are multiplied in a community garden, where there is more to be gained than a crop of vegetables or an extra zucchini. ❧

See page 102 for colour photos.

Books cited and suggested reading:
Lewis, Charles A. Green Nature Human Nature: the meaning of plants in our lives. University of Illinois Press, 1996.
Simson, Sharon P. and Straus, Martha C. Horticulture as Therapy: Principles and Practice. CRC Press, 1998.

Growing a Healthy Community at the Yara Community Gardens

by Sarah Varey

Sarah combines her experience with community development and urban gardening as the Project Coordinator for the Yara Community Gardens. Sarah is a certified Master Gardener and currently lives in Moose Jaw, Saskatchewan with her husband, Jordan.

The garden gate swings open after a long, quiet winter. As I step inside, the street noise of passing cars fades to the background. This space, once a vacant lot, now shows signs of deep-rooted life. Despite winter's harshness, our expectant perennial border grows in quiet confidence. The air is sweet with moist, decomposing earth. It is Saturday morning and it seems I have arrived early. Soon this calm and peaceful place will be busy with the excited chatter of community garden members. Soon these empty garden plots will overflow with sun-ripened, local produce.

Ever since 2005, the Yara Community Gardens have been growing in the southern Saskatchewan community of Moose Jaw. Administered by the local community development organization Connecting As Neighbours (CAN) and sponsored by Yara, the gardens program began with a year of careful planning and grant applications. Pioneering the way in 2006 with eighteen members, the gardeners and CAN worked in tandem to clear the land, mark out plots and spread anticipation through the neighbourhood. Since those humble beginnings, the Yara Community Garden has expanded twice and currently has over 100 active gardeners. We now work alongside many like-minded organizations such as Food Secure Saskatchewan, Hunger in Moose Jaw, local schools and clubs. Truly, the gardens are a flourishing centre for healthy community life.

Whether in a private backyard, in a classroom experiment or in a community garden, the activity of vegetable gardening promotes and

Gardener Lloyd Grigg examines his heirloom pumpkin (Sarah Varey)

empowers participants towards greater health. However, our typical definition of 'health' – a static concept referring to physical wellness or nutrition – may be insufficient. Indeed, the act of planting a vegetable garden engages our holistic being and promotes a greater, more substantial form of health, rather than simply nutrition.

Despite age, nationality or financial situation, the act of vegetable gardening connects us to a collective humanity as we plant with age-old seeds and techniques. This form of gardening connects us to our heritage and geographical region as we grow culturally appropriate produce. We develop a keen sense of the passing seasons, an awareness of weather patterns, and the patience needed to wait while our garden grows. We learn how to slow down and see, really see, the small wonders of the natural world around us. It is undeniable that vegetable gardening provides us with physical recreation and healthy, local produce, thus enabling us to become more physically active. However, it must be noted that planting a vegetable garden, no matter how small, promotes personal, mental, environmental, emotional and social health.

As we look more particularly at the act of community gardening, the health benefits expand outward from the individual to envelope the health of an entire neighbourhood, community and city. Community gardens bring unlikely people together to share in a common goal – to grow healthy, local food together. Perhaps unknowingly, seniors, new families, immigrants and teenagers grow together as individuals and collectively grow the community. They come together to learn and to teach, for sanctuary and for inspiration, for social networking and for social acceptance. We learn how to care for one another in simple acts of service as we replace common tools after using them and offer rides home after membership meetings. We contribute to environmental health as we return our vegetable tops to the compost bins, conserve water and practice integrated pest management. Welcoming neighbours into our gardens, we host educational workshops. We grow vegetables for worthwhile charities in an effort tto look outside of ourselves and help others. Gardeners share seeds, stories and time for the empowerment and beautification of the neighbourhood. All of these actions and attitudes are signs of deep-rooted life. Again, I say that truly the gardens are a flourishing center for healthy community life.

For the last three garden seasons, I have had the privilege of participating in this thriving community project. I have witnessed and heard testimonies of gardeners living healthier, fuller lives. We are all drawn together because of food; yet we come back, year after year, because of the rich holistic living that the community gardens foster. Contact your local community garden to see how you can be involved. It is better for you than you might think. ♣

Crop Rotation Reduces Problems
by Sara Williams

Sara is a respected horticulturalist and architect of the Master Gardener Program at the University of Saskatchewan Extended Education. Sara Williams and Hugh Skinner will release **Gardening Naturally, A Prairie Gardener's Chemical-Free Handbook** *in the spring of 2011.*

Growing your own vegetables can be an extremely satisfying endeavor. Nothing beats digging for those first new potatoes or brushing off the soil and eating a freshly pulled carrot in the garden. But an infestation of Colorado potato beetles or cut worms can make the experience less satisfying, more stressful and the outcome less bountiful. Many of these problems can be reduced through the use of rotation.

Crop rotation is a planting schedule in which different vegetables are planted in different parts of the vegetable garden each year. The rule of thumb: "Don't plant the same veggies in the same spot every year." Rotating vegetables has two major benefits: less depletion of soil nutrients and reduced pest and disease problems.

Vegetables differ in their nutrient or fertilizer requirements. Corn and members of the cabbage family (cabbage, cauliflower, broccoli, Brussels sprouts) require a great deal of nitrogen. If they are planted in the same area of the garden year after year, they soon use up soil nitrogen. By grouping together vegetables with similar nutritional needs, and planting them in a different area of the garden each year, less depletion occurs.

Plants also differ in the extent and distribution of their root systems. Some are shallowly rooted (lettuce and radishes), while others (potatoes, tomatoes, parsnips, carrots, turnips, and beets) are deeper rooted. Those with shallow roots absorb nutrients from the soil's upper layer; those with more extensive root systems absorb minerals from lower depths. These types of plants should also be rotated.

If some vegetables are 'depleters' and use a lot of minerals, others are 'replenishers.' Peas and beans are members of the legume family. Due to a unique relationship with certain soil bacteria called *Rhizobium*, legumes are able to 'fix' nitrogen from the air, utilize it for their own growth, and still produce some in excess for the crops to follow.

The second major advantage of crop rotation is that it discourages the build-up of pest populations. Vegetables in the same family are generally infested by the same insects and infected by the same diseases, and therefore rotated by family.

Among these groupings are:

- Cabbage family: cabbage, cauliflower, Brussels sprouts, kale, broccoli, radish
- Legumes: peas, beans
- Vine crops: squash, pumpkin, cucumber, cantaloupe, watermelon
- Corn
- Onion family: onions, shallots, garlic, leeks, chives
- Potato family: potato, tomato, green pepper, eggplant
- Goosefoot family: beets, chard, spinach
- Carrots, celery, and parsnips are added to the rotation which is most convenient in terms of space

The basic approach is to grow plants susceptible to a particular pest or disease only once in a period of four or more years in a particular place in your garden. Rotation is more effective in controlling insects than disease. It's most effective when the organisms causing the problem live in the soil for only one or two years. In the absence of their host plants, most root-dwelling fungi (such as *Fusarium* of tomato, potato, and strawberry) tend to die out. Crop rotation is less effective against potato scab fungi, which may persist in the soil for many years.

Crop rotation works well in controlling insects that feed on only one type of vegetable and do not move very far or very fast – such as the Colorado potato beetle. These insects will die soon after they emerge in the spring if their food plants are absent. Conversely, insect populations tend to build up in soils repeatedly planted with the same crops. It's like providing them with a guaranteed annual grocery basket.

In a smaller garden, crop rotation is less effective in controlling insects simply because some (like cabbage butterflies or flea beetles) are far-ranging. It is sometimes argued that if members of the cabbage family are scattered here and there throughout a garden, insects might not find them and damage will be less. But in a small garden the scattering technique is less likely to be effective.

How do you manage the rotation? Depending on the size of your garden, vegetables may be divided into either four or six major groupings. If your garden is small, try the following four groups: cabbage family members; legumes; carrots, beets and onions; and vine crops. Divide your garden into four areas and plant a different group in each area every year, beginning the rotation again at the end of 4 years.

If your garden is larger, divide it into six areas, rotating on a six-year basis, with the following groupings: cabbage, vines, legumes, corn, onions, and potatoes. Carrots, celery, parsnips and herbs may be added to whichever group is convenient. Perennial vegetables such as rhubarb, asparagus and horseradish are not rotated. 🦂

How to Enjoy Gardening
When you have Outdoor Allergies
by Melanie Mathieson

A.K.A. The Gardening Guru. Melanie is an Ontario Registered Professional Forester, former Ontario Certified Master Gardener, and has over 30 years gardening experience in Fort Frances (zone 4) and Thunder Bay (zone 3), Ontario.

Gardeners with allergies or those with environmental allergies want to be able to enjoy being outside in their yard without prompting an allergy attack. The following information provides tips and techniques to assist the allergy sufferer in enjoying the outdoors, whether it is to garden, landscape or simply breathe in the fresh air.

Seasonal allergies can stop some people in their tracks with sneezing attacks, watery eyes and runny noses or an inability to breathe comfortably. The onset of spring marks the beginning of the allergy season with the pollen of ash, birch, elm, hickory, and other trees. Late spring and summer brings allergy problems with grasses. Summer and fall continues the allergy misery with numerous weeds such as burdock, ragweed, goldenrod and amaranth.

Pollen and moulds are some of the most common causes of human and pet allergies. Unfortunately, it can be very difficult to visually confirm if mould and pollen are present in the air each day. Of course there are times of the year when allergy symptoms may be worse, but the pollen index calcu-

lated for your area on a daily basis is a reliable source to determine whether the pollen counts in the air may affect your allergies. Some parts of Manitoba, including the city of Winnipeg and northwestern Ontario, often have higher pollen index levels, especially in the spring, because of the large areas of treed and forested land. This is not good news for allergy sufferers. Although you cannot do anything about the pollen in the air across the region, you can reduce the pollen levels right in your own yard and garden, which may lessen your symptoms.

People who are unaware of their particular allergies often want to blame plants with bright, fragrant flowers, even though these may not be the culprit. The plants that often cause allergies are those whose pollen is windborne and have inconspicuous flowers. Brightly coloured, fragrant flowers have heavy pollen that need insects, not wind, for the transfer of their pollen. You can usually identify these plants because they attract bees, hummingbirds and butterflies. Unfortunately, though, some people with high sensitivities still may be affected by insect pollinated plants as well. These plants usually have strong fragrances and this can also prompt allergic reactions that are not necessarily related to pollen.

The first step in gardening with allergies is to identify those plants which cause problems. Allergies can change over time, as can sensitivity, but by knowing what triggers your allergies, you can begin developing avoidance strategies. Altering your surroundings can significantly reduce your exposure to your allergy triggers. The microenvironment you create for yourself may not help much on windy days at the peak of your allergy season, but it should help at other times. Use plants throughout the landscape that do not aggravate your allergies. If you have allergies to tree pollen, you may consider planting shrubs or flowers instead. If grasses cause problems, avoid large expanses of lawn. Wind-borne pollen can collect on anything and it sometimes gives other plants a bad rap. Many ornamental shrubs, annuals and perennials are safer or less irritating. Fruit trees that are pollinated by insects are also, generally, less irritating. You may also want to consider planting perennials that are known for their decorative foliage instead of their flowers such as hosta, lamb's ear (*Stachys byzantina*), bugleweed (*Ajuga*) and silvermound (*Artemisia schmidtiana*). Some of these perennials still produce flowers but the spikes can be cut off as soon as they appear. The other advantage of this is that the energy the plant would have used on

producing flowers and the subsequent seed set, is instead directing at producing a larger plant. Look for varieties of trees and ornamental shrubs with the emphasis on decorative foliage rather than on flowers as the focal point.

Tree pollen is the number one allergen and is supplied in large quantities by oak, birch, most maple species, elm, ash and alder, all of which are common in this region. Surprisingly, the clouds and layers of pollen we see from pine and aspen trees are usually not allergy-provoking.

Weed and grass pollens are the next most notorious pollen-producing plants – this includes the weeds from the ragweed family. The season for weed and grass pollens begins in late spring and continues into the fall. Chrysanthemums, daisies and marigolds are members of this group, as well as goldenrod, burdock and amaranth. Most common turf grasses do not produce pollen if kept from producing seed. To prevent your lawn from producing seed, keep it mowed to a height of two to three inches (five to eight centimetres) throughout the season. Remember, wild grasses at the edge of your property that are allowed to mature, can also be large pollen contributors. Keep all grasses trimmed to prevent seed production, whether lawn, ornamental or weed species.

The good news is that there are thousands of plants that are just fine for the outdoor allergy sufferer. The pollen season starts in late winter/ early spring and lasts until the first

frosts in the fall. Short of never going outdoors, here are some things a
gardener with allergies can do:
• Native plants are advantageous for
  people with allergies because they
  require little effort, withstand
  climate extremes, do not need
  fertilizers, are more drought tolerant and insect resistant. Check
  your local nursery for plants
  native to your region.
• Plant insect-pollinated plants in
  your garden. Check your local
  library or the internet for a list of
  plants suitable to your growing
  region.
• To reduce your contact with
  pollen, wear a mask and sun or
  safety glasses. Wear a hat, gloves,
  long-sleeved shirts and pants
  (instead of shorts). Long hair
  should be pinned up to prevent
  it from collecting spores and pollen. Avoid taking pollen-covered
  clothing into the house. Wash
  these clothes frequently and do
  not dry them outside on the
  clothesline.
• Shower immediately after outdoor
  exposure, making sure to wash
  thoroughly, including your hair,
  and then change into clean clothing. It can also be helpful to not
  bring indoors the clothing that
  you wear while gardening. Washing your outdoor clothing in hot
  water will kill all of the spores.
• Avoid gardening in the early hours
  of the morning as pollen levels
  are usually at their highest at this

time, especially when the weather
is hot and calm, or windy.
Garden in the late morning or
afternoon when pollen is carried
higher in the atmosphere, or, on
cloudy, rainy or cooler days when
it is not as prevalent.
• Keep grass and weeds in check by
  vigilant mowing, pulling and
  mulching, or by planting ground
  cover. Use ground covers instead
  of organic mulches.
• Replace hedges with fences or walls.
• Install a water garden instead of a
  garden with plants.
• Check the local pollen count. The
  pollen count monitors pollen
  levels in the air and can help
  you when planning outdoor
  activities. Rain or a change in
  the weather can remove a lot of
  pollen from the air. However,
  moisture from rain can also
  prompt new blooms on some
  troublesome plants and increase
  mould spore counts.
• Avoid 'seedless' or 'male' varieties
  of trees or shrubs. These are typically wind-borne pollen producers, 'unlike' the female or seed
  producing trees. This designation
  may not appear on the plant tag,
  but it doesn't hurt to check.
• Mould spores are also a cause of
  distress for many allergy sufferers and can occur in dry or wet
  weather. During wet springs,
  clouds of spores can actually
  be seen rising like smoke from
  mouldy twigs or fruit.

• If you have allergies to moulds or fungus, take care to rake up and compost fallen leaves from your yard. Allowing piles of leaves to sit undisturbed on your lawn only encourages disease organisms to thrive. Leaves that are visibly diseased should not be added to your compost bin. Re-duce mould spores by eliminating organic mulches such as bark mulch or chips.

I hope these tips will help you to enjoy your yard or garden or at the very least help to lessen chances of allergic reactions. 🦃

The Whys and Wherefores of Green Manure
by Sheryl Normandeau

Sheryl lives in Calgary, AB and is a Graduate of the Prairie Horticulture Certificate program and long term work experience in retail garden centre. She also volunteers for Calgary Horticulture Society.

Soil health is critical to any growing endeavour. It is no secret that, although some plant species may survive in poor conditions and require very little in the way of moisture or nutrition, most would flourish in the best possible soil that can be provided. Achieving a carefully-balanced combination of organic matter, textural composition, water and air in soil is essential for the optimum success of any plant, and has the further benefit of discouraging certain occurrences of pests and diseases.

An often under used method of improving soil condition and introducing a rich food source is to grow green manures. As the term suggests, green manures are crops grown for the specific purpose of eventual incorporation into the soil, to increase organic matter and fertility. The use of green manures is often associated with large-scale farming operations, where entire fields are grown over with cover crops and rotated regularly, but the method can be highly effective on a small scale as well, especially in vegetable gardens. If it is possible, portions of the beds can be sown with green manures while the rest of the beds remain in food production, and the whole process can be rotated in successive years.

The primary focus of green manures is to provide organic matter

and some of the macronutrients and micronutrients that the soil may be lacking due to depletion, erosion, or other factors. (Other cover crops may be strategically planted to combat compaction, erosion, or run-off, or perhaps to prevent weed growth). Increased organic matter in the soil will also improve its physical properties, which will in turn enhance its water-holding capacity, a boon in dry areas. In the Prairies, green manures are usually annual crops, planted as soon as the ground can be worked in the spring, so that they will grow during the warmest months of the year. Perennial crops are used as well, in less arid areas.

Sowing green manures is simple: broadcast green manure seeds evenly over partially worked soil and rake in. There is no need to create rows, except if the seeds are large. If possible, select crops that will not require excessive moisture throughout the growing period, as it is always preferable to direct water to the food crops instead of the green manure. Green manures are naturally low-maintenance and they will consume space that weeds may ordinarily overrun, making the job of the gardener even easier. Nitrogen-fixing crops in the legume family will require inoculation with the appropriate Rhizobium bacteria. This will require some research to determine the correct match of Rhizobia to plant species, and the proper time and method for use. As for fertilizing green manures, a light application of nitrogen may be used for legume crops until they are

fully rooted, after which additional supplements are no longer required. For grass species fertilization with nitrogen is recommended.

There are many suitable crops that can be used as green manures in the Prairies. With the renewing interest in this practice, smaller quantities of seed than would be required for large agricultural purposes is commonly available. The table at the bottom of this page is by no means exhaustive, but includes many leading crops.

Incorporation (tilling or digging in) of green manures is nearly always done once the crop has begun flowering, although this task can be performed earlier during the growing period, without as many benefits. A flowering crop will produce the most organic matter as well as the balanced carbon and nitrogen levels that promote rapid decomposition. If incorporation is not desirable at the time the crop is in bloom (i.e.: the crop is perennial), the flower heads should be trimmed to prevent it from producing seed. Many of these crops, such as the clovers, are considered marginally 'weedy'. Manually till in green manures when the soil is warm (and ideally, moist); this will make the physical effort somewhat easier and it will promote more rapid decomposition. Tall or dense plants may be cut before digging in, but the clippings should be allowed to rest a couple of days to facilitate incorporation. Green manure crops should not be tilled in too deeply, as this may slow decomposition; as it

is, if the crops are turned too late into their bloom time, when they contain more carbon than nitrogen, they will be slower to break down. As well, woody or fibrous plant species will take longer to decompose. For fall sown green manures, two or three weeks should pass before their incorporation and the sowing of production crops.

Although incorporation is somewhat laborious, and there is the cost of seed and possibly legume inoculants to consider – as well as the temporary loss of space for production crops – there can be benefits to growing green manures. Store bought fertilizers and

amendments are usually costly, and the chemicals they contain may not be desirable, especially in vegetable gardens. By giving over portions of garden beds to green manures and rotating regularly, overall soil conditions – including physical properties and the amount of organic matter – are improved, and there may be lower risks of incurring diseases or pests. Using green manures is an alternative environmental approach to improving soil structure and fertility and can replenish and revitalize this growing medium over a season or two. 🪶

Annual Green Manure Crops

Field Pea (*Pisum sativum*)	Legume; fixes nitrogen	Sow in spring, or 'dormant' in the fall to be incorporated the following season; grows quickly	Grows well in clay soil
Lentil (*Lens culinaris*)	Legume; fixes nitrogen	Sow in early spring; till under as soon as it flowers	
Annual Ryegrass (*Lolium multiflorum*)	Grass	Sow in spring; do not allow to set seed, but incorporate frequently throughout season; can also be sown 'dormant' in the fall for growth during the following spring	Will grow under many diverse conditions
Winter Rye (*Secale cereale*)	Grain	Seed in late summer and allow to overwinter; incorporate the following spring	
Buckwheat (*Fagopyrum esculentum*)	Annual	Excellent supplier of potassium and phosphorus, which make it a good green manure to use preceding potato crops; grows very quickly and will need to be trimmed regularly to prevent seed set	Tolerant of poor soils

Perennial and Biennial Green Manure Crops

Alfalfa (*Medicago sativa L.*)	Legume; fixes nitrogen	Plant in the spring and allow to sit over winter, till under the following year; slow to establish; must be trimmed before seed sets, usually a few times per summer (leave the cuttings on the ground or compost)	Drought-tolerant, will not perform in acidic soil
Alsike clover (*Trifolium hybridum*)	Legume; fixes nitrogen	Sow in spring and cut periodically when blooms emerge; may be left on ground over winter and incorporated the following season; slow to establish	Does not mind clay, acidic soils
Red clover (*Trifolium pratense*)	Legume; fixes nitrogen	Plant in spring and allow to grow through one season or more (trim flower heads frequently to prevent seed set)	Tolerant of shade
Sweet clover (*Melilotus officinalis*)	Biennial legume; fixes nitrogen	Sow in spring; do not allow to set seed as it can be problematic in the garden (trim frequently); slow growing	Not tolerant of acidic soil

Rocks!

by Susanne Olver

Rocks, stones and gravel have a beauty all of their own. A garden needs the help of these inanimate components of nature - on paths, seating areas, as accents and of course, rock gardens.

As a child I loved playing with the 'pretty' stones on the paths of our old-fashioned, 19th century garden. I even found 'gold' (fool's gold), which I proudly collected. Rocks, from small gravel to the towering Alps and Rocky Mountains, all hold a fascination for me. Their shapes, colours and, as witnesses to our geological history would be worth a lifetime of study.

However, even the most beautiful stone in our garden is an inanimate object which has to be used judiciously.

There is a very disturbing trend in landscaping known as 'hardscaping'. Lawns, trees, shrubs and flower beds are being displaced by gravel, woodchips, bricks or concrete!

Newly created, this looks very smart. Neat lines, colours, enlivened by a few shrubs and/or planters. No weeds, no grass, no more boring lawncare, no re-planting of flower borders. It sounds, and at first, looks good. This type of design seems to be encouraged by certain people in the landscape business, who impress their clients by creating an instant, perfect yard.

Is this type of landscape really maintenance free? If executed properly, landscape cloth will be placed under the inert materials, which certainly retards the growth of weeds, but does not prevent it in the long run. The easy answer, then, is to spray with potentially cancer causing chemicals, or weed by hand.

Then, just try to plant anything through a layer of rocks over landscape cloth. Not an easy job!

Now to the real problems. Rocks and gravel, or concrete, do not absorb water, thus adding to the water load of our sewer system after a heavy rainfall, or even flooding. A second problem is that inert substances absorb far more summer heat than plants, which are able to create a certain cooling effect by evaporating water through transpiration. It might not be much in a small yard, but added to a city's vast areas of houses, roads and parking lots, it does have an impact.

The third, and biggest problem is that these dead substances do nothing to prevent the build-up of carbon dioxide (CO_2) in our environment. Plants, however, from the smallest blade of grass to the biggest tree (not forgetting algae in the water) are the only living things on our planet able to convert CO_2 to Oxygen (O_2) and sugar through photosynthesis. All life on our planet depends on this marvellous ability of our plants. Why replace them by stones and concrete, thus, bit by bit, destroying life on earth? &

A Healthy Garden Includes Insects

by Ian Wise

Ian is a biologist at the Cereal Research Centre of Agriculture and Agri-Food Canada at the University of Manitoba.

What constitutes a healthy garden? Most would claim it is a garden with vigorous growing plants that are free of weeds, disease, or insects. Disease is often a sign of plant weakness, caused by soil infertility, fungal or bacterial pathogens, or inclement weather, and weeds a sign of grower neglect. A garden devoid of insects is neither healthy or in balance with nature. It is unrealistic for any gardener to expect to have a fruit and vegetable garden that is completely free of insect pests without resorting to an endless cycle of insecticide sprays. Besides, insects are the most ubiquitous form of life on earth, and serve a vital role in nearly every important terrestrial niche, including many which are necessary for a garden to flourish.

Gardens are unique ecosystems. They are like small ecologically rich islands that pose significant challenges for any insect intent on exploiting its bounty. Unlike large scale commercial operations, gardens do not provide pests with a bountiful enough supply of food to enable most pests to build up large sustainable populations. With a bit of work, gardeners can minimize the possibility for pest populations to establish.

One easy method is to rake the leaves in the yard in the fall, particularly around the bushes where leaves provide an effective insulation barrier for overwintering flea beetles and lygus bugs. However, not unlike other remedial measures which can be helpful in some ways but harmful in others, gardeners without these insect problems may not want to be overly zealous in removing all leaves lest they reduce beneficial lady beetle and spider populations.

A second method is to collect any cutworm pupae in the fall when the garden is turned. Do not discard the pupae, but rather place them in  *Cutworm pupae* a plastic container with a bit of soil and then plant the container in the garden. In the spring, unearth the container, gently empty the contents into a glass jar (making sure the pupae remain covered by soil) and place the jar in a shaded spot where it can be readily observed each day. And then see what happens. This can be a great educational tool for anyone, particularly children, as the result can be quite surprising. Cutworms in Manitoba are frequently parasitized by various species of wasps, and often what emerges is not a moth but a colourful parasite. The moths can be allowed to die, but the wasps should be released back into the garden to parasitize anew.

Parasitic wasp

Another way to prevent pests from establishing in your garden runs counter to the mostly beneficial strategy of mulching your crop residue and adding it back into the garden. If you have had problems with the European corn borer damaging your corn, discard and destroy all stalks and cobs to prevent the borer from over wintering in your garden and recurring at even higher populations next year.

Most of the insects that find their way into a garden live right next door. They are the colonizers or visitors that contribute to the health of the garden by assisting in such important functions as plant matter decomposition, insect predation, and pollination. There should not be a garden in Manitoba without a rich array of ants, beetle and fly larvae, as well as springtails that beneficially assist in the bacterial and fungal breakdown of plant matter. These insects are natural colonizers and are an early season indicator that the garden is healthy. Also, while we all recognize bees as primary pollinators, much of the later pollination of fruit-bearing vegetables in gardens is done by flies and beetles from nearby plants.

A garden's ecological isolation poses the most difficulty for those few insects that all gardeners hope to avoid. Isolation means insect pests like cutworm and flea beetles are out of luck unless they find the garden right away because vigorous plants quickly outgrow the ability of these insects to cause damage to vulnerable seedlings. Other insect pests like aphids and diamondback moths need to colonize plants early in the growing season in order to be able to produce multiple generations. This gives added emphasis to the importance of checking cruciferous crops like broccoli, cabbage, kale, or cauliflower for the telltale signs of leaf skeletonizing by diamondback larvae early in the season, and to remove any small green wriggly larvae to prevent subsequent generations from greatly increasing the populations. For aphids, frequent watering to maintain high humidity levels in crops like lettuce will weaken the aphids by diluting the sap on which they feed, making the aphids more vulnerable to fungal disease, while at the same time improving the ability of the entomopathic fungus to produce spores and disburse.

In Manitoba many vegetable crops such as cucumbers, tomatoes, carrots, parsnips, peppers, squash, and beans, can be grown by gardeners without much fear of damage by insect pests. This does not mean these plants will not get fed upon by insects, but only that damage is usually very superficial and can largely be mitigated by simple vigilance.

Other crops, however, can face significant damage from pests. Onion maggot flies can fly long distances and have a great ability to detect developing onion plants and completely decimate them. For gardeners who have not grown onions in the past, it is worth the effort to see if maggots are found in your area, because once established, maggots are very difficult to eliminate. Avoid growing onions for at least one or two years until they are no longer present.

Corn and cole crops (refers to waxy-leaved *Brassicas*) like broccoli and cauliflower also cannot be grown without the expectation of insect pest presence. While commercial growers are required to produce these crops nearly pest free, gardeners should be less concerned because in most situations the presence of the insect is more of a concern than its damage. Corn is attacked primarily by the European corn borer and cole crops by the imported cabbage moth, also known as the white cabbage butterfly. Both of these insects

are excellent fliers and one can almost guarantee they will find most gardens with these *Brassica* plants. With a slight change in philosophy and a willingness to remove the offending larvae at harvest by vigorous washing or extraction, a gardener can happily produce these crops without having to potentially upset the health of the rest of the garden.

One method for a gardener to get an early check on the status of pest insects is to consult the Manitoba Agriculture website. Diamondback moths, the imported cabbageworm, and some aphid species do not overwinter in Manitoba but disperse north on southerly winds. Manitoba Agriculture keeps a watchful eye on these and many other insect pests which may alert you as to which pests you should be checking in your garden at any given time.

So the bottom line is to know what crops you can grow and what plants you should avoid based on the history of your garden. Good cropping practices like residue management, soil fertility, crop avoidance or rotation, plant inspection, and timely watering are as important to maintaining low pest problems as they are to maintaining good crop growth and a healthy garden. 🐾

All pictures courtesy of the Cereal Research Centre, Agriculture and Agri-Food Canada.

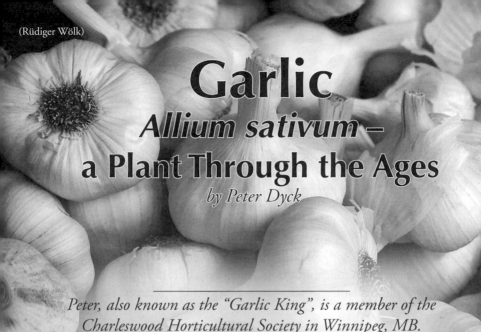

(Rüdiger Wölk)

Garlic
Allium sativum –
a Plant Through the Ages
by Peter Dyck

Peter, also known as the "Garlic King", is a member of the Charleswood Horticultural Society in Winnipeg, MB.

Garlic is believed to have originated in Central Asia, and it was also found later in Egypt and Mesopotamia. The Roman Empire later spread the use of garlic for cooking and dietary purposes. A number of medicinal properties became associated with garlic in Europe, Africa and other areas.

In more recent times, research has attributed a host of benefits and many believe that it lowers cholesterol, blood sugar levels, blood pressure and that it has anti-cancer properties if used regularly.

General Usage Suggestions
1. Crushed fresh with orange juice in the morning.
2. Use in all meat dishes for excellent flavour, whether the dish is cooked on top of the stove, in the oven or a slow cooker.
3. Garlic adds flavour in soups such as squash, vegetable, bean or meat and vegetable mixtures. It can serve as a substitute for hot peppers.
4. Sauté or roast.
5. Use in pickles with cucumber, such as dill pickles.

Planting
My favourite varieties are Red Morada and Manitoba Prairie Purple, which have strong flavour. Milder ones are White (silverskin) and Elephant garlic (*Allium ampeloprasum* var. *ampeloprasum*). Seed catalogues offer softneck garlic (*A. sativum* var. *sativum*) and stiffnecked, (*A. sativum* var. *ophloscorodon*).

Garlic does well in fertile, well drained soil high in organic matter with a slightly acid pH and adequate amounts of nitrogen and phosphorous. Weeding regularly is required and the best means of disease control is regular crop rotation.

Under prairie conditions the best results for growing garlic are obtained from fall planting. This should be done about mid-September with bulbs placed about five inches apart in rows. In limited space, stagger rows 15–20 cm (6–8 in) apart. Place cloves in holes 10 cm (4 in) deep. In very early spring you will notice flat leaves popping up. A touch of spring frost will not hurt them.

Crop Care

Rain or regular watering maintains growth and prevents stress. Stiff neck garlic scapes or flower stems should be pruned before blooming occurs. This portion of the plant is edible and may be used in soup. Removing the scape will promote growth of larger bulbs. Warm weather in July will cause the plants to harden off.

Harvest

In mid-August dig out the bulbs, remove soil, prune the roots and lightly wash. Dry for two to three weeks in a well-aired place with very limited amounts of sunshine. Do not peel away any of the skins.

Two methods of storage are common. Netted bags are excellent for long term storage but some people leave stems and leaves in place for braiding to store hanging braids. Either way the storage place should be airy, dark and semi-dry. If possible it is best to maintain at temperatures of 5°–0° C (41°–32° F) or even -2° C (28° F).

Sort bulbs into sizes before storage, leaving the largest for later use. Very small garlic bulbs or seeds are very useful for planting with flowers susceptible to aphids, such as roses. The small garlic plants may be left in one place for two years before removal to a spot in regular garlic beds.

Tips and Recipes for Using Garlic

Squash and Garlic soup

1 medium squash or small cooking pumpkin

2–3 onions

8–10 cloves of garlic

2–3 sprigs of thyme

1–2 stems of parsley or a piece of parsley root

2–3 chopped stems of parsley leaves for garnish

A single medium clove of garlic contains	
7 calories	.07 mg iron
.31 gm protein	.9 mg sodium
.01 gm fat	26 mg potassium
1.5 gm carbohydrate	.01 mg Vitamin B1
1.4 mg calcium	.004 mg niacin
10 mg phosphorus	.75 mg Vitamin C

3 tablespoons of vegetable oil
Salt and pepper to taste
Cook squash by steaming in a large pot with a steaming basket. Place the seeds and pulp, one onion, a few thyme sprigs, parsley leaves or root in the pot and add up to 2 litres of water. Steam for one hour or till tender.

Meanwhile chop 2 onions, and 8–10 cloves of garlic and sauté in pan with the vegetable oil. Cook till tender but do not burn. Add the chopped parsley when nearly done.

Cool the squash. Scrape out pulp and place in batches in a blender with cooked onions and garlic. Strain the cooking water from the squash and add to blender. Remaining water may be used in other soups.

Almost any other vegetable may be added to this soup; chicken or beef stock may be used as the liquid. This makes a nice creamy soup that is very nutritious.

Garnish with croutons, grated cheese or parsley.

Roasted Garlic Spread

Trim garlic heads to expose tops, remove loose outer skins. Top with 2–3 teaspoons of olive or vegetable oil. Bake in a 350⁰ F (175⁰ C) oven in a covered dish until tender. Cool and remove from skins. Mix with butter and use for garlic toast.

Garlic and Vinegar for Your Dog

Small amounts of crushed garlic will assist your dog in digestion and worm elimination, as well as tick and flea control. Add a teaspoon of vinegar per litre of drinking water, and a ¼ clove of crushed garlic to the water/vinegar mixture or to their daily food. Everyone can benefit from garlic! 🐾

Garlic Quotes

"Three nickels will get you on the subway, but garlic will get you a seat."
Old New York (Yiddish or Jewish ?) Saying.

"Garlick maketh a man wynke, drynke, and stynke."
Thomas Nash, 16th Century poet

"There are five elements: earth, air, fire, water and garlic."
Louis Diat

Rain, Rain, Go Away. Come Again Another Day...

by Jan Winnik

Jan has been gardening in the St. Vital area of Winnipeg, MB for 30 years. Her current passion is growing gourmet vegetables.

We may not be able to stop the rain when our plants have enough, nor can we sing a song for it to return some other time. We can, however, save some of that rain to benefit our gardens, as the song says...on '*another day*'.

In summer, the flat prairie land heats up quickly, creating turbulent skies and bringing furious thunderstorms and more rain than we need at one time. Another thirst quenching rain for gardens may not come for many hot days. When it rains in densely populated areas, impervious surfaces like rooftops, driveways and sidewalks produce runoff that goes straight into storm sewers.

It is possible to supplement the lack of rain by watering your garden from a domestic source that has been chlorinated and treated with chemicals for human consumption, but coming from an underground source it's also cold, harsh and costly. Approximately 40% of domestic water used in summer is used outdoors.

Rain is fresh, pure and soft water, naturally low in salt and other chemicals, so it's healthy for your plants. It is always the ambient temperature, so it won't shock plants in the way that cold water from an underground source can, and remember...it's free... so you won't be billed for it!

Prairie soils generally have a neutral pH (7.0) to alkaline pH (up to 8.5) due to high clay content. Most plants prefer a neutral to slightly acidic soil (pH 5.5–7) where nutrients are more readily available. Precipitation interacts with carbon dioxide as it falls from the atmosphere, therefore rainwater is slightly acidic and

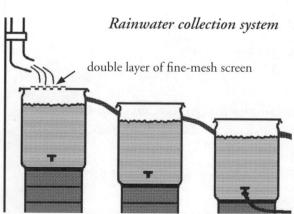

Rainwater collection system

double layer of fine-mesh screen

is much easier for plants to absorb.

A rainfall of 25.4 mm (1 inch) yields approximately 2,360 litres (519 gallons) of water for every 92 square meters (1000 square feet) of roof surface. Collected in rain barrels, this soft water can be distributed among garden plants as needed. Using some type of rainwater collection system slows the flow into a city's storm drains as well as allowing the gardener several options for distributing the water to plants. A watering can may simply be dipped into the barrel for hand watering a few planters nearby, or a more elaborate setup could include a barrel tap or spigot to which a garden hose is attached, leading to a drip irrigation system around the plants in larger planting beds. Instant soluble fertilizer can be added directly to the barrel just before doing a large amount of watering.

Try connecting several barrels together with a barrel connector, hose or flexible pipe. Excess water from the first barrel flows into the next barrel. Let gravity handle the flow of water by placing the first barrel higher than subsequent barrels. Concrete blocks work well as they are very sturdy, easy to stack and quite inexpensive. It is important to plan for an overflow tube to lead excess water away from your house foundation, as prairie storms can dump a lot of rain in a short time. This can be as simple as fitting on a rain pipe with silicone near the upper side of the barrel, or a more elaborate stand-pipe inside the barrel connected to a piece of hose leading away from the house foundation.

To make your own rain barrel, look for food-grade containers with a childproof lid made of a solid colour material to inhibit algae growth. Do not use barrels from petroleum products or strong agricultural chemicals, as even a small amount of residue can harm plants. Metal barrels are not a good choice, as rust and corrosion will harm plants. Plastic barrels can come from many sources. Check out food stores that may import olives, pickles etc. Seek out beverage manufacturers and health food stores as they sometimes get food supplements in large containers. You could also search for plastic barrels online, narrowing the search by also entering your city. If you don't care for the bright blue colour, make the barrels as inconspicuous as you wish by spray painting with aerosol paint for plastics. Choose a paint colour close to the exterior colour of your home, and the barrel will hardly even be noticed.

Openings can be cut with a jigsaw and hole saw to accommodate downspouts and overflows. Adding a barrel tap or brass spigot allows the gardener to fill a watering can, hook up a soaker hose or drip line. Check out online hardware and gardening catalogues for spigots and flexible tubing to connect barrels.

Standing water can be a haven for mosquitoes, an important thing to keep in mind when setting up your rain collection system. Keep mosquitoes and debris out by filtering the downspout flow through a double layer of fine plastic screening before it enters the barrel. As an added precaution, a few tablespoons of kitchen cooking oil will form a thin film on the top of the rainwater and prevent mosquito eggs from hatching. Even a few drops of liquid dish detergent on the top of your stored rainwater will kill mosquito larvae, but won't harm the plants when it is time to water. Check the overflow pipe for openings where it attaches, and block small openings with non-rusting curly stainless steel (silver colour) pot scrubbers available at larger grocery stores.

Clean your eaves troughs regularly! The dust and leaf sludge that builds up can block the flow of water from your eaves and give mosquitoes a place to lay their eggs.

Is creating your own rain barrel not for you? There are many commercially designed rain barrels on the market available at home improvement stores and garden centers, or by ordering from online suppliers. Some are flat at the back, and can be placed up against the house if you have limited space. Look for the shape, size and price range to suit your needs. Shop around for the ones that have a top that can be lifted so a watering can may be filled by dipping. Although the initial cost is considerably more than creating your own from repurposed con-

tainers, the commercially designed barrels often include childproof lids, overflow hardware, connector hoses, spigots and clamps.

Even if commercially designed, consider adding a piece of fine mesh plastic screening on the top in addition to the strainer that may have come with the purchase. Often this type of rain barrel is designed and manufactured in another country, where mosquitoes are less of a problem than on the prairies. Purchase a small squeeze tube of silicone at a home center, squeeze a line of silicone around the opening and press the mesh into it. Be sure there is an overflow outlet to move excess water away from your house.

At the end of the season, drain the barrel and hose it out. Re-connect the original downspout to bypass the rain barrel. Store the disconnected barrel with the spigot open and the lid on, or ideally, upside down. In the cold climate of a prairie winter, the freeze-thaw cycle could damage the spigot or crack the barrel.

Many communities are now encouraging residents to use rain barrels to decrease the demand for domestic water in which irrigation can account for almost half of summer consumption. Short-term or long-term water shortages have meant that some areas have begun to limit outdoor water use or limit water use to specific days and times.

Your community may now have rain barrels for sale on the same day as compost bin sales, often held for one day only, in late spring. Cities subsidize the purchase price of the compost bins to lessen the amount of grass clippings being hauled to landfill sites. They are now also realizing the benefits of rain barrels and are starting to subsidize the cost. Watch your community billboards and newspaper ads for 250 litre (55 gallon) rain barrels offered at subsidized prices.

More information is available on the internet by searching 'rainwater', 'rainwater collection', or 'rainwater systems'. You can search online for 'plastic barrels' and insert your city, or even try the free online classified ad sites. Online gardening/woodworking catalogues carry the barrel taps and connectors. Yes, there are even a few how-to videos out there—some better than others!

On a bigger scale than a rain barrel, here's a great tip for owners of in-ground swimming pools. Many pools have a solid winter cover, on which late fall leaves and winter snow accumulate. When spring arrives, and warm temperatures melt the snow and ice, what's left is a dark brown unappealing mess of 'leaf tea'. Don't just pump it down the drain – it's melted snow, the same as soft rainwater! By the time the ice has melted on the winter cover, the ground has warmed and thawed several inches below the surface, and is ready to absorb moisture. Place a few large plastic plant pots (the type used for shrubs and small trees) around the edge of the pool. Using your long-handled pool leaf skimmer, skim the slimy brown leaves out of the pool and deposit them into the plant pots. The wet mess will drain through the holes and later can easily be tipped into your compost bin. Those leaves have already got a head start on decomposing and are wet, forming a 'brown layer' in your compost bin.

Next, use a small pump (a spare sump pump is ideal) to get the snow melt off the winter cover. Place the pump in a plastic pail with holes drilled in it, to keep any stray leaves from jamming the intake on the pump. Pump the brown leaf tea, which contains nutrients from the decomposing leaves, onto your trees and lawn. The force of water from the pump will be strong, so you may want to place the end of the pump hose into another plastic pail with holes drilled in it, to diffuse the force. Just move it around the yard every few minutes.

Don't throw away your old blue vinyl pool pump hose! Simply spread it on the lawn, punch holes in it with a screwdriver, and attach it to the pump with a clamp. Secure the far end with a knot. You now have a large soaker hose that can be laid in planting beds! That brown water may look ugly, but it's soft, natural and full of nutrients for your garden, trees and shrubs.

If you want your garden to be healthier and more beautiful, give it a treat of rainwater! 🌑

Nurturing an Inter-generational Community at Assiniboine Park Conservatory
by Karen Lind

Karen Lind is an Education Co-ordinator with the Assiniboine Park Conservatory. Karen thoroughly enjoyed facilitating APC's first inter-generational program with fellow Education Co-ordinator Melissa Scouten.

For years the education team at Assiniboine Park Conservatory (APC) has been hosting a variety of popular programs geared towards school age children. More recently the APC has been delivering a wide range of programs specifically to seniors. For the first time, during the summer of 2009, the APC launched a program linking these two age groups together through a series of inter-generational gardening workshops.

Why Inter-generational Gardening?

Introducing inter-generational programming appears rather straightforward, defined as the "bringing together of different generations in on-going, mutually beneficial, planned activities, designed to achieve specified program goals (Generations United, 2007)." The outcome of this work can be quite profound.

Focusing our program on plant based activities combined the health benefits from inter-generational socialization with the health benefits from horticulture.

Coming Together

Working with a group of six youths from the Ryerson Boys and Girls Club and three senior volunteers, we met once a week throughout the month of August. As a pilot project we decided to work with a smaller group. Our program consisted of four workshops with hands-on garden projects designed to high-

(Karen Lind)

light the benefits that plants have on our health and well-being. A key element built into each workshop was the opportunity for social interaction and relationship building amongst the participants.

I distinctly remember feeling quite anxious when we all met for the first time. While the aim of our project was to connect youth and seniors together, I couldn't help but be concerned that the group may have no genuine connection with one another. But, almost immediately, the participants discovered a common thread that linked them all – none of them were born in Canada. This multicultural element provided an additional level of learning and sharing for both age groups. Throughout the month I was privileged to watch the group further discover their commonalities and differences by sharing their experiences, both past and present.

The limitation to starting this project in August was that we missed out on the opportunity to plant a garden bed together at the APC. However, this challenge soon turned into an opportunity by introducing many members of the group to indoor gardening, which can be done all year round. For the first workshop the participants were asked to bring their own container, the more creative the better, with which to create an indoor herb garden. For most of the youth this was a new experience altogether, and

the experienced senior gardeners provided excellent mentorship.

The second workshop was designed to explore different ways to use herbs and enjoy some new culinary treats. Together we made herbal butters, cream cheese, vinegar and punch using the fresh herbs grown in the Abilities garden. This workshop provided a new and delicious experience for everyone. Our third workshop took us from the edible to the aesthetic benefits of gardening. In an excursion to the English Garden, the participants broke up into smaller groups and created their own floral arrangements. The final workshop was more of a celebration using our newly installed outdoor pizza oven. Together we harvested, prepared and enjoyed a tasty outdoor lunch of pizza and salad.

We spent our last day together sharing what we had learned from one another and providing suggestions for future programs. Although it was a lovely way to end our program, I couldn't help but feel a little sad that it had ended so soon. I remember thinking how amazing it was that after just four meetings there were genuine bonds formed between and amongst the generations. I could only guess what sort of relationships would have developed had there been more time together.

What we learned

Although our first program was small, we certainly took away some big lessons. Immediately we discovered that our role as facilitators had to be kept to a minimum so as to allow the participants, both youth and seniors, to take leadership roles. Also, there was a unanimous desire to see the program start earlier in the season, and continue throughout the growing season in order that both interpersonal relationships and plants had the necessary time to be nurtured and mature.

The APC looks forward to hosting other inter-generational programs and eventually incorporating inter-generational programming year round. 🦐

Suggested Reading:

Generations United. 2007. The Benefits of Intergenerational Programs. Washington, DC: Generations United. Accessed online August 24, 2009 at:

http://www.gu.org/documents/A0/IG_Benefits_2007.pdf

Seedsman, T. A. (2006). Viewing participants as resources for one another, communities and societies: Intergenerational solidarity toward a better world. Journal of Intergenerational Relationships. V. 4(1):23-39.

Generations United. 2002. Steps towards a society for all ages. United Nations: Programme on Aging. Accessed online August 31, 2009 at: http://www.un.org/esa/socdev/ageing/society_steps_fostering.html

Participants at Inter-generational workshop (Karen Lind)

An inviting walk
past the hostas to
the echinaceas
and lilies
(Frances Wershler)

Creating a Beautiful and Beneficial Garden
See page 1

Echinacea purpurea
(Darlene McPherson)

Bumble bees on
Gaillardia aristata
(Sarah Coulber)

Eastern bluebird
(Larry Kirtley)

Page 91

Carnivorous Plants
See page 162

Sarracenia minor
(Darlene Stack)

Sarracenia 'Judith Hindle'
(Darlene Stack)

Rainbow carrots
(Lori Ann Regnier)

The Real Dirt on Organic Growing
See page 46

First place vegetables
(Valerie Denesiuk)

Cabbage
(Frances Wershler)

Zucchini
(Valerie Denesiuk)

More Than Just Another Pretty Garden
See page 21

Recently emerged monarch butterfly
with abandoned chrysalis
(Darlene McPherson)

Tools to assist the gardener who
doesn't want to 'over-do-it'
(Darlene McPherson)

Highbush cranberry fruit
(Sarah Coulber)

Healthy Trees, Gardens and People
See page 18

Well managed Manitoba Maple
Acer negundo L
(Michael Allen)

Rooftop Gardening
See page 123
(Valerie Denesiuk)

Classic vegetable garden
(Valerie Denesiuk)

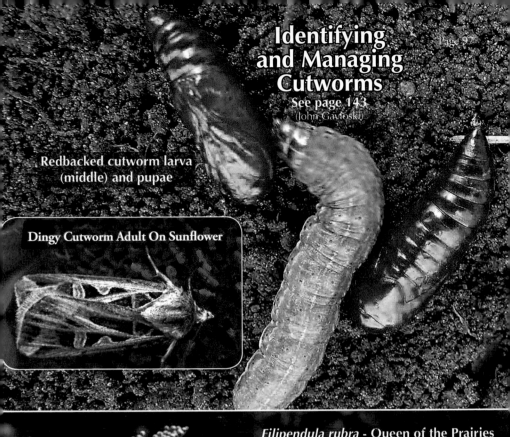

Identifying and Managing Cutworms

See page 143
(John Gavloski)

Redbacked cutworm larva (middle) and pupae

Dingy Cutworm Adult On Sunflower

Filipendula rubra - Queen of the Prairies
(Darlene McPherson)

Bee on native sunflower -
Helianthus spp
(Sarah Coulber)

The fruits of canning
(Valerie Denesiuk)

Ten Tips for Canning
See page 61

Heuchera
See page 111

Heuchera collage to show varieties
Note: not all shown are hardy
(Terra Nova Nursery)

Invasive Species
See page 175

Yellow Flag Iris

Himalayan Balsam (Jan Samanek)

Oxeye Daisy
(Steve Dewey)

Showy
ladyslipper
(Eugene Reimer)

Native Orchid Conservation
See page 138

Anemone vulgaris
(Sarah Coulber)

Container gardens on balcony
(Jim Beckta)

Food Matters
See page 56

Monarch butterfly on echinacea
(Darlene McPherson)

Firecracker
Chrysanthemum
Showbiz (Philip Ronald)
See page 120

Matthew and Memori mingling in the Cosmos

See page 62
(Denise Sarauer)

Preparing the plot for the season

WiLLow Creek
Community Garden

The healthy harvest

With Fronds Like These...
See page 131

Japanese painted fern
(Valerie Denesiuk)

Contrasting succulents against rocks
(Frances Wershler)

Bee on purple prairie clover
Dalea purpurea
(Sarah Coulber)

Yellow coneflower
Ratibida pinnata
(Sarah Coulber)

Hoar frost one mile south of Indian Head, SK at the Shelterbelt Centre
(Dan Loran)

Tuberous Begonias
by Susanne Olver

I love begonias – from the little, miniature eyelash begonia to the big cane-stemmed varieties, the colourful rex begonias to masses of wax begonias in the garden. The outstanding ones for blossoms are the tuberous begonias (*Begonia tuberosa* hybr.) and the newer hybrid, the pretty non-stop, which was discussed in the 2010 issue of the Prairie Garden.

While the pretty non-stop begonias are not usually carried over from year to year (although it is possible), the older, larger, tuberous begonias get bigger and better with age.

Their cultural requirements are similar to their smaller cousins. They like a light, humousy soil, good light but not strong sunlight. Hot mid-day sun will burn their foliage to a papery white, but too much shade will result in poor flower production.

Let's start at the beginning – I start my tubers in March. When buying them, I look for nice, plump ones with at least one or two 'eyes' showing. It sometimes happens that even a fat tuber will not sprout, and valuable time (and money) is lost before one realizes that the plant is not growing. Before planting, I soak the tubers overnight in tepid water to plump them up, then plant them concave side up, either in a tray with moistened (not wet) peat, or directly into pots with a light potting soil. It is important to keep the planting medium slightly moist, not wet, to avoid rotting. If planted in flats they should be potted up when both foliage and roots are growing, and before they crowd each other. At this point – as well as later, if necessary – extra shoots should be removed to avoid the branches crowding each other. If extra large blooms are wanted (for flower shows, for instance), all but one strong shoot can be removed, as well as all the smaller male flowers which flank the larger, female flower. Otherwise, three to five stems are sufficient to give good growth, except when the bulbs get very large. In that case, some more stems can be left on the plant.

Susanne with her begonias
(Valerie Denesiuk)

It is easier to buy plants already started, from a nursery. This saves time and space. One drawback is that these plants are grown in a warm and moist environment and may develop mildew and stem rot. In that case, all affected plant parts should be removed and the plants treated with a fungicide, as recommended by your nursery or garden centre. Cinnamon is a natural fungicide; commercial products come and go. The foliage has to be kept dry at all times while growing indoors. This goes for the non-stop begonias, too. Outdoors this is beyond our control, so care has to be taken during periods of inclement weather that mildew or stem rot doesn't occur.

I fertilize my begonias with a 15-30-15 fertilizer while growing. When I put them outside I sprinkle some slow-release fertilizer on the soil and give them a "Bloom +" fertilizer for increased flowering from time to time. This, when given throughout blooming time, seems to increase the number of blossoms. If extra large blossoms are required, now is the time to pinch out the smaller male flowers which sit, one on each side, next to the larger female flower. I just leave them on.

In fall it is important to prevent the tender plants from freezing, and they should be moved to a cool storage room for the winter – with their foliage intact. This can be removed when completely dried up. The nutrients in the green parts of the plant will go back into the bulb to help carry it over the winter. Do not fall into the temptation of keeping the still flowering plants in your living area – the extra light and warm temperature will prevent dormancy, weaken the bulb – or even prevent it from forming, so that next year's growth will be affected. If the plants have been planted in the ground, they should be dug up with plenty of soil adhering to the roots, placed in a box or other container with the spaces between the plants filled with peat (moistened) or soil. I follow the same routine as with the potted begonias, removing the dry foliage mid-winter, and check sometime in January-February to make sure the bulbs are not drying out too much. Then I give them just a slight watering which helps them to keep plump until March.

By the time the bulbs are 2–3 years old they have usually grown quite large and can be divided. I cut them in half, dust the cut surfaces with powdered wood charcoal and let them dry off for a day or two before restarting.

Using this method I have kept my begonias for over ten years and they have repaid my efforts by growing into bigger and better plants, with up to 80 blossoms at a time, blooming all summer right into fall. Not only do I save money not having to buy new plants, but I get a lot of pleasure seeing my begonias reappear and getting bigger and better year after year. ❧

From Seed to Table a Practical Guide to Eating and Growing Green

Review by Jean I. Pomo

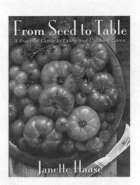

Janette Haase Insomniac Press - Toronto, Ontario. Canada ISBN 978189717875 245 pages .

This garden book was written by a Canadian author who grew up in Montreal but now lives and gardens in Sydenham, Ontario. Janette Hasse planted her first garden in 1984 while she and her family were living in Newfoundland. She became friends with a family who were 'living off the land.' These friendly folks filled her fridge with the fresh produce from their garden and farm - fresh goat's milk and garden vegetables. The author remembers well the quality and taste of their produce, and she wondered 'why' such a difference existed between the food from the grocery store and food from the garden. Hence her reason for this very well thought out book.

The section "Getting Started" - provides a wonderful introduction for all those people who have never bought a package of seeds but who would love to know how to grow a successful garden and have the joy of eating fresh vegetables from their very own garden.

Hasse, in the "Getting Started" section, goes into very easy to understand detail about *'a few things you should think about if you are going to try a garden out yourself.'*

Beginner gardeners will also be interested in the author's description of composting facilities and basic equipment as well as information on fertility, climate and an explanation of zone numbers. There is also a wonderful description of Seed Types and Definitions, and a good list of Seed Companies found across Canada.

Ms Hasse has set up the 'Contents' page, to show how gardening can happen from January right through to December, giving you many suggestions on how to plan your garden even when you can't get out digging because it is winter out there.

I was very impressed with this book and would like to quote a short note from the 'press release' which sums up very nicely my thoughts on Janette Hasse's book "From Seed To Table".

"Hasse takes the home gardener through the tasks of the gardening year, giving clear and helpful instructions for the work to be done at each time, from planning to planting to harvesting and storage. And she doesn't forget the best part of growing your own food - eating!"

Healthy Birds

by Sherrie Versluis

Juvenile and adult red-headed woodpecker
(Jennifer Howard)

Sherrie is the owner/operator of The Preferred Perch Wild Bird and Speciality Store in Winnipeg, MB

To those who feed wild birds, there is no question it's a hobby that is part of their lifestyle and even their health. In today's world, stress is the leading contributor to many illnesses - it's a fact that feeding birds is a source of relaxation. When watching the antics of birds flitting about and singing in the yard, it's easy to let go of the troubles of the day and just enjoy nature at its best. Mental happiness leads to total relaxation and watching birds is a fabulous way to achieve this. Feeding birds has become one of the most popular hobbies in North America, second only to gardening. The presence of wild birds in the garden provides a natural source of pollination, insect control, and even lawn aeration, reducing the use of man-made products.

Unfortunately, songbird populations are declining very rapidly. Numerous species are being added to lists of concern or as being endangered every year. To aid in the preservation of these amazing creatures, there are things you can do in your own backyard to nurture visiting birds and enhance your enjoyment of them.

At The Feeders

When choosing a birdfeeder, look for important qualities like: small feeding ports to reduce spillage; drainage; material that is long-lasting such as UV resistant polycarbonate; and one that's easy to fill and clean. Using a quality food at birdfeeders will reduce any messes on the ground. Seed mixes may contain fillers that many birds will not eat. The undesirable seeds that are uneaten, end up germinating and producing undesirable patches of wheat, barley, and other grains that the unhappy gardener will spend hours plucking. The seeds can also be an attraction to mice. Seed mixes sometimes contain low-grade seeds that have mould which is very unhealthy. Using proper foods, like black-oil sunflower seeds, white millet, or shelled sunflower for a total mess-free experience, will reduce waste and prevent rodents. Washing feeders at least twice a year helps prevent the spread of diseases like salmonella, which can be a problem when wasted seed is left to rot either on the ground or in feeders.

In The Yard

History has shown that chemicals and birds are a combination that do not go together. Toxic concoctions to eliminate insects and weeds are harmful to wild birds. Even though the days of DDT have passed, there are still many products on the market that can harm birds and are unhealthy for humans as well. In fact, it is believed that the increase of albino and partial-albino wild birds is linked to chemical fertilizers and weed control products. Many of the birds showing these signs are ground feeders like American Robins, Dark-eyed Juncos, and grackles, to name a few. These birds don't just walk through lawns that may be laced with chemicals, but they eat insects that may also have been con-

taminated. Earthworms and other burrowing insects can absorb traces of these toxins which the birds then ingest. Avoid products containing 2 4-D, Captan, Diazinon, Dursban, Dacthal, Dicamba, and Mecoprop. Instead, choose products that are organic based – for your own health, the health of your pets and the health of your feathered friends.

Offering Water

With the threat of West Nile Virus now an annual reality, many are hesitant to have birdbaths in the event they may be a contributor to hatching mosquitoes. Stagnant water that has been left for seven days can certainly provide the perfect breeding habitat for mosquitoes. It is important to replace the water on a frequent basis, preferably daily, to keep the water clean and fresh. Birds don't just wash themselves, they also drink the water. After a robin has been digging for worms you will may your birdbath a complete mess by the time they are done cleaning up. Many birds even defecate in the water, so changing it is important. Circulating or moving water discourages mosquitoes, so consider a fountain type birdbath, now available with solar power, or Water Wigglers (also solar-powered), that keep the water agitated and are even more attractive to many birds.

Feeding Summer Birds

Hummingbirds and orioles are a very desirable visitors to birdfeeders from spring until late fall. Their amazing colours and songs make them both very desirable birds to attract. However, there is much inaccurate information about the proper ways of feeding these special birds. The fascination of hummingbirds makes people want to do just about anything to attract them. The study of hummingbirds over the years has brought much new information to light about attracting them to birdfeeders. Some of the things you may have learned from parents and grandparents could very well be outdated information today.

When it comes to hummingbird or oriole feeders, be sure to look for ones that are bug-proof to avoid attracting wasps and ants. They should also be leak-proof, and most importantly, easy to clean. The nectar nourishes bacteria and mould, so it is imperative you are able to easily clean the bottle and the base. Feeders should be cleaned a minimum of once a week, but two to three times per week is preferable, especially in hot, humid weather. I often remind people to think of their own sweet drink left outside for days and whether they would drink it. Plants provide fresh healthy nectar and so should we.

There are many recipes for nectar, and in many cases these recipes are harmful to these delicate little birds. Products like honey, jello, Kool-aid, fruit juice, and even rum have been found in some recipes. Honey and juices ferment and spoil very quickly;

the others have artificial flavours and colouring, and, of course, it is irresponsible to add alcohol. The proper recipe for nectar is four parts water to one part white sugar. Boil the water, turn the element off and stir in the sugar till it dissolves. You can make a larger batch and keep it in the fridge for up to two weeks, making it easier to quickly wash and refill the feeder more often. The feeders are designed to attract birds, so **never** add harmful colouring to the nectar. Always use the ratio of four-to-one. Some recipes suggest a sweeter concoction in spring – but plants do not change their sweetness and neither should you. Stronger solutions are more difficult to digest. After a long migration it is important that birds ingest and absorb needed calories. Offering properly prepared, fresh nectar will provide hummingbirds and orioles with a much needed healthy source of food.

Including wild birds as part of your backyard sanctuary is a wonderful way to bring nature into your life. Enjoying the harmony of trees, flowers, and birds, is a wonderful path to a healthy, stress-free lifestyle. The addition of colourful, active, and entertaining birds adds quality to the life of your garden and the choice of proper feeders and foods will make the experience that much better. Wishing you a season of health in your garden, enjoy it! 🐦

Heuchera

by Barbara-Jean Jackson

B. J. Jackson is a Master Gardener who also holds a Horticulturalist Certificate from the University of Guelph. A self-proclaimed plant addict, she lives in Brandon and recently retired from Brandon University. She is also an accredited iris and lily judge.

Heuchera, coral bells, alum root: whatever you call them, these perennial plants have experienced an explosion in popularity in recent years. Although no one is quite sure how to pronounce the name (the supposedly correct pronunciation is HOY-ker-uh, as well as hew-CHERR-ah (the way you'd say 'chair'), hyoo-KUR-a, hew-KUR-a, hoo-CUR-ah), this plant is one of the most hybridized plants in the garden today. One of the few exclusively North American species, heucheras come from western Canada, the mid-western United States and Mexico. There are about 50 species in the plant family, however, few are being used in hybridization; the most popular being *H. sanguinea, pubescens, pulchella, villosa, brizoides* and a few others.

Once thought of as just for the shade garden, heucheras have recently moved out of the dark and into the light. These new sun-tolerant varieties generally have lighter-coloured foliage, although several of the bronzy and dark purples do quite well in part sun.

Pioneering hybridizers of heucheras over the years include the Morden Research Station in Manitoba. The program, initiated by Henry Marshall and later passed on to Lynn Collicutt, resulted in several cold-hardy, tough-as-nails varieties including Brandon Pink, Brandon Glow, Northern Fire and Ruby Mist. All but Brandon Glow are in my garden and if anyone knows where that one can be obtained, I would forever be in your debt.

Then self-proclaimed 'hortaholic', Dan Heims of Terra Nova Nurseries in Canby, OR, got into the act and the hybridizing effort literally took off! Other notable hybridizers whose creations seem to do wonderfully in my gardens are Charles and Martha Oliver of The Primrose Path in Scottdale, PA. In 2008, Dr. Wilbert Ronald of Jeffries Nursery in Portage la Prairie, MB introduced his own creation, Arctic Mist, to the mix with a wonderful variegated green and yellow leaf colouration.

There is foliage in every colour of the rainbow and some with significantly larger flowers. There are ruffles and deep lobes, tall sprawling open forms and small mounding compact forms.

But, are all heuchera suitable for northern gardens? In my garden in the city of Brandon, MB, the answer would be an emphatic – NO! I have, therefore, for your consideration, compiled a list of the most hardy varieties, those that have survived at least three zone 2b winters. (See the box at the end of this article). I can't tell you how many times I have succumbed to the temptation of the newest varieties acquired at sometimes staggering costs, only to see them languish and not even make it through the first winter. Of course, this would be the one you most wanted to survive. For me, believe it or not, it was Palace Purple. After trying without success to over winter this one many times, I went searching for answers and was told I must not be growing it right. Well, excuse me, I have more than 50 varieties, most that perform well. Therefore, it is not I who is at fault. What I finally tracked down was that the cultivar Palace Purple was now being propagated via tissue culture (as most heucheras are nowadays) but at one time there was an inferior clone being used. I located a grower who only propagates via division and not tissue culture, and obtained the plant again. I am very pleased to report that it is now a most vigorous grower that is strong and healthy.

I have nothing against tissue culture for the most part, except when things like this happen. My advice is, in order to obtain the ones you really, really must have, buy it from someone who grows field grown plants rather than someone who just brings in plugs and pots them up. My all-time favourite, though, is a child of Palace Purple by the name of Molly Bush. Given to me many years ago by my dearest friend on earth, this variety is far superior to its parent. Described as a vigorous, clump-forming cultivar, it features a dense basal mound to 38 cm (15 in) tall and as wide, of large, crinkled, maple-like, dark purple leaves 15–20 cm (6–8 in). Tiny bell-shaped greenish-white flowers appear on slender stems rising above the foliage mound to 76 cm (30 in).

As to culture, heucheras like a rich, well-drained soil growing in sun, part sun, shade or part shade. They do not take well to sitting in water, but what plant does? In containers, they grow well in regular potting soil and will tolerate some inattention. You can't ignore them all summer, but if you miss watering a couple days, they do not seem to mind. There is nothing more beautiful than a planter full of H. 'Amethyst Mist'. One culture tip I gained from Jim Hole of Hole's Garden Centre in St. Albert, AB was to periodically dig and reset the plants. They need to be dug completely out, the hole enlarged and the plant reset every 3 to 5 years. So far this technique has worked for me. This prevents the heaving caused by spring freezes and thaws.

In the garden, some heucheras can get to a fairly large size rather quickly. For that reason, these larger types, including Green Spice or Dale's Strain, are not suitable for the edge of the border. Some of the smaller varieties, most notably Petite Pearl Fairy, Petite Marbled Burgundy, and those that have a compact mounding form would be more appropriate.

Heucheras can be difficult to divide. The first time I saw a friend slicing through the crown of a single plant with no obvious increases, then plunking the division into a small pot, I thought it was toast. To my surprise, however, the division survived after initially wilting down totally. Plants divided in this way can take several weeks to perk up and you may think they are dead, however in most cases, they do survive and thrive when planted in the garden. I would not try this on a special variety, new to the garden, but to an established clump. This method is not for the faint of heart. Usually you can find a natural division point and remove it from the main stem with or without roots attached. This is definitely much easier on both you and the plant itself.

Another excellent and easy way to propagate heucheras is from seed. I currently have several attractive seedlings growing that were started from seed, collected by myself or purchased from many friends and commercial growers. The nicest of these is one to whom I have given the garden name 'bronze maple leaf'. This plant is in its third year and is still being evaluated. In order to do it right, below are the directions for growing heucheras from seed.

Harvest heuchera seeds after the seed pods become dry but before the pods have opened. Heuchera seed pods are so tiny they are difficult to see, but it is easy to strip off the seed pods by running your fingers up the flower stalk. You will end up with a lot of fine dry chaff and seeds mixed together. I never try to separate them, but I do remove any large pieces of seed pod. Another way I have had success gathering the seed is to break off the bloom stalk from the plant and shake the stem inside a small paper bag (sandwich size). When you have bashed the heck out of it, remove the pieces of the pods and store in a coin envelope in the fridge until spring.

Plant seeds in a good seed starter mix that has had an equal amount of perlite and/or vermiculite mixed in to 'lighten' the soil. Moisten the mix until it is damp but not wet. Fill the seed trays with the seed-starting mix and sprinkle the seed and chaff thinly and evenly over the top. Each little seed pod has copious amounts of seed, so over-planting can be a problem. Do not cover the seeds as heuchera seeds need light to germinate. All you need to do is to spray the surface lightly with water. To prevent the possibility of damping off (infection with a fungus), sprinkling cinnamon (a natural fungicide) on the soil may inhibit damping off (the commercial product No Damp is no longer available).

Cover each seed tray with a clear plastic bag or plastic cover and place under plant grow-lights or a sunny window. Do not allow the tray to dry out; misting regularly is recommended. Germination will occur in about ten days to two weeks. As soon as the seedlings appear, remove the plastic bag or cover and start watering the trays from the bottom. Again, you may want to sprinkle cinnamon on the soil.

Heuchera seedlings grow fast and should be transplanted for the first time as soon as the seedlings have grown a second set of leaves. Continue to use the same soil mix with the added vermiculite and/or perlite and water seedlings from the bottom. As the seedlings grow, transplant them to larger containers as you would with any other seedling. When all chance of frost is past, plant them outside in the garden or in containers. Those in containers can be moved at the end of summer to the garden for over-wintering and will be bigger and better in the containers next year!

Give heuchera a try – you will enjoy this marvellous addition to your perennial collection. 🍃

See colour photo on page 99.

Top Heucheras in Barbara Jean Jackson's Gardens

Dale's Strain - Silver-blue marbled leaves. Flowers are pale white, but insignificant.

Green Spice - Clump-forming featuring silvery, gray-edged leaves with purple veins (in cool weather) and conspicuous but not showy whitish flowers. Leaves turn orangey in autumn.

Black Beauty - Attractive crinkled lobed leaves emerge burgundy in spring, turns deep purple the rest of the year.

Dolce Licorice - Glossy, near black foliage with vigorous habit.

Peppermint Spice - Foliages comes in shades of green, red and gray. Rose-pink flowers

Petite Marbled Burgundy - Bronze leaves with strong silver markings. The plant has large, light pink and white flowers. It is compact, with sturdy stems.

Petite Pearl Fairy – The plant has dark green and silver marbled foliage with gray veins. It is miniature and compact.

Molly Bush - Large leaves of shiny reddish turning to bronze. The new leaves are a little redder and the old leaves are greener and bright light brings out the bronze.

Magic Wand - Large wands of showy coral-pink flowers. Leaves are green with a silverfish cast.

Frosted Violet - In the spring the leaf coloration is a wonderful pink-violet with deeper veins. Light pink flower clusters.

Strawberry Swirl - Ruffled green leaves overlaid with silver veining and tall, arching stems of tiny, bell shaped pink flowers with a slight fruity scent.

Hollywood - Scalloped leaves are silvery with a patterning of darker veins. The plant has spikes of large bright coral-red blooms.

A. P. Stevenson Commemorative Award Presented to Prof. Louis Lenz

by Linda Pearn and Hugh Skinner

Louis Lenz (Tena Kilmury)

The Manitoba Horticultural Association (MHA) recognizes conspicuous achievement in the field of horticulture by presenting the A. P. Stevenson Commemorative Award.

Mr. A. P. Stevenson was one of Manitoba's early horticultural pioneers. He settled in the Morden, MB area in 1874 and planted fruit trees from his native Scotland. He tried to acclimatize trees from the British Isles, Eastern Canada and the Northern United States but found that plant material from Russia performed better in Manitoba's climate. Many of his early introductions are still in use as breeding material. His work encouraged the Canadian Federal government to establish the Morden Experimental Farm (later an Agricultural and Agri-Food Canada Research Station). This institution promoted much horticultural research in the Northern Plains and Prairie Provinces.

The Stevenson Gold Medal (later to be known as the A. P. Stevenson Commemorative Award) was initiated to honour Mr. A. P. Stevenson. It is the highest award for horticulture breeding in the Prairie Provinces and Northern States and it was first awarded in 1932 to Dr.

Frank Skinner. More recent winners include Dr. Henry Marshall, Dr. Wilbert Ronald and Dr. Dale Herman. More details on the award and winners can be found at http://www.icangarden.com/uploaddocuments/d7672+stevenson.pdf.

Professor Louis Lenz is the 21st recipient of this prestigious award. The award was presented at the Manitoba Horticultural Association Convention in January, 2010 by MHA president Hugh Skinner.

Professor Lenz joined the Plant Science Department at the University of Manitoba as an Assistant Professor of Horticulture in 1964 and was promoted to Associate Professor in 1976. Louis' first commitment was as a teacher. Throughout his career at the university he had a reputation for fairness and consistency. His door was always open to students and they knew what to expect. His courses were popular with students. Over the course of his tenure he taught many who have made significant contributions in Horticulture. Among the graduate students that he advised are Wilbert Ronald, Campbell Davidson, Martha Barwinsky, Lynn Collicutt, and David Vanstone.

Beyond his teaching of University courses, he offered short courses at the School of Agriculture, through the Continuing Education Division and developed a course for the Prairie Horticulture Certificate Program. Many of us have attended field days at the All America Selections Annual Flower Trials or at the extensive Perennial Flower Trials that Professor Lenz conducted.

Louis took an active part in the activities of the MHA during his tenure at the U. of M. He judged home grounds competitions and was a frequent presenter at its annual conventions. For his contributions he was made an Honorary Life Member and was presented with a Lifetime Achievement Award.

Professor Lenz served for many years on the Planning Committee of the International Peace Garden, was a founding member of the Friends of Assiniboine Park Conservatory, an active member of the Western Canadian Society for Horticulture and a frequent contributor to conventions and programs of the Manitoba Nursery and Landscape Association.

For his outreach work in the community, Professor Lenz was awarded the University of Manitoba Outreach Award in 1986 and the Dr. and Mrs. Ralph Campbell Outreach Award in 1990.

Professor Lenz shared a strong knowledge of ornamental plants and throughout his career he avidly collected perennials, tree and shrubs. We've already mentioned the perennial flower trials that he carried out. As well, he worked on the development of a systematic arboretum. When the original site along Bison Drive at the university proved prone to flooding, he began the development of a landscaped arboretum on the Point.

He frequently spent time collecting native plants from across Manitoba, including the northern regions around Churchill and Thompson. He developed a test site at the golf course in Thompson and tested trees and shrubs for hardiness and suitability for growing in the climatic and soil conditions there. He was a regular visitor to the Morden Research Station where he frequently took students; and for many years he was a regular visitor at the Skinner Nursery property. During the summer he regularly visited North Dakota State University and colleagues Don Hoag, Neil Holland and Dale Herman.

Professor Lenz set up a remote test site for evaluation of chlorosis resistance in plants. This trial focused particularly on Amur maple. As a result of these trials, 'Royal Crown' Amur Maple was introduced.

Professor Lenz's greatest contribution to our prairie gardens has been the development of his potentilla cultivars. (For more details about this program see page 65 in the 2009 issue of The Prairie Garden.) You'll find examples of his double flowered cultivars, 'Sundance', 'Yellowbird' and 'Snowbird' in gardens across Manitoba, Saskatchewan and Alberta as well as the rest of Canada and the northern United States. 'Mango Tango' with its unusual orange and yellow blend and 'Pink Beauty', a double pink variety with outstanding colour stability, are widely grown around the world. Royalties from these cultivars bring the University ten's of thousands of dollars in royalties each year.

Louis was chairman of the Prairie Garden Editorial Committee for nine years following a few years as an associate editor. The Prairie Garden congratulates Louis Lenz on his achievements in horticulture and on receiving this Award. 🍂

Back to Basics
by Frances Wershler

The title 'Back to Basics' brings thoughts of the ways my grandfather used to plant his garden and the ways its produce nurtured us. When I was a child I used to watch as Grandpa planted a huge vegetable garden to be used to feed our farm family, the hired workers who assisted with harvest and hay, the visitors who dropped in unannounced, or the repair men required when machinery broke down.

Our garden supplied vegetables to can, and later on, to freeze. Rhubarb, strawberries, raspberries, crab apples and currents were used for pies baked for noon dinners as well as the jams, jellies and canned fruit we consumed in the winter.

There were few fancy hybrids to plant, but reliable old varieties were sought out for their dependable appearance each year. There was a time when the moon was right and the soil temperature appropriate for planting each vegetable. Hoeing, picking when the beans were dry, watching for cabbage butterflies, covering the maturing cauliflower and picking potato bugs were all necessary and basic routines.

The cutting garden was a regular part of the garden as well, holding cosmos, mallows, gladiolus, sweet peas, and sometimes sweet-scented stocks.

To me, that was a basic garden. Necessary plants, sensible procedures for planting, care and harvest that resulted in nutritious vegetables and fruit for a healthy family and translated into the basic necessities of life.

Master Gardener Program for Manitoba

by Mary Petersen

Mary is Program Coordinator, Agriculture Extension, School of Agriculture and Environment, at Assiniboine Community College.

In response to a growing demand for a locally delivered Master Gardener program in Manitoba, Assiniboine Community College (ACC) is pleased to announce that it is in the process of brokering the Master Gardener Program from the University of Saskatchewan. Delivery of the program will be through ACC's Agriculture Extension with an initial target date of October 2010.

Local horticultural groups such as the Friends of the Assiniboine Park Conservatory and Steinbach Area Garden Club as well as Master Gardeners throughout the province have been instrumental in spearheading support for the program. ACC will continue to work together with local hort groups to promote the program and to encourage others to participate in becoming a Master Gardener.

The Master Gardener Program is open to anyone interested in gardening. Graduates of the Master Gardener program are very enthusiastic about becoming involved in learning, working and sharing with fellow gardeners. Once they have completed the program and become a Master Gardener, they hold their certificate with pride and continue to share their knowledge with others in their community.

The gardener begins by registering in the program with ACC and receives a book to begin their home study portion. Use the term 'home study' as an educational term. Gardeners who receive their book will have a hard time putting it down. Even experienced gardeners will keep on learning and growing with each page.

Overview of the Program

The program consists of 7 core courses:

1. Garden Fundamentals (includes Soils for Horticulture and Applied Botany for Gardeners)
2. Botanical Latin
3. Communications
4. Identifying Insects in Your Yard and Garden
5. Safe Use of Pesticides and Alternatives
6. Common Plant Diseases
7. Tree & Shrub ID

These one-day courses will be delivered face-to-face in a classroom setting and will allow for activities and demonstrations to provide a practical side to gardening.

Internship

The gardening student must complete 40 hours of volunteer service within his/her community. Opportunities abound and range from volunteering in a community garden to delivering presentations, writing articles – a whole range of diverse and interesting activities. Keeping a record of the number of hours committed is important.

To become a Master Gardener, you must register, complete the 7 core courses, write a final exam based on the manual and complete the requisite 40 hours of volunteer service.

Assiniboine Community College is committed to making the Master Gardener Program avail-able to Manitoba gardeners. The Master Gardener program covers comprehensive subject matter that is vital to Manitoba gardeners. The strength of delivering the program in Manitoba is reflected in its ability to provide an excellent avenue for gardeners to come together to share their knowledge. Master Gardeners are part of a valuable volunteer base that assists large and small communities throughout Manitoba to enhance their communities through their gardening knowledge.

A true gardener never stops learning – they just keep on growing! 🌿

If you are interested in becoming a Master Gardener please contact:
Mary Petersen
Program Coordinator
Assiniboine Community College
1-800-862-6307 Ext 6683
PeterseM@Assiniboine.net

Sharing Backyards

One of the biggest barriers to growing food in the city is access to land - despite the fact that many yards, lawns, and backyards have plenty of room to spare. Sharing Backyards links people with unused yard space with those looking for a place to grow food. If you have a garden and want to share it with someone, or if you are looking for a space to garden, Sharing Backyards is for you.

Visit <www.sharingbackyards.com> and look up your city.

Sharing Backyards is a project of LifeCycles <lifecyclesproject.ca>

LifeCycles
cultivating communities

The Firecracker Collection of Chrysanthemums
by Philip Ronald & Rick Durand

Philip is the current Research and Development manager at Jeffries Nurseries near Portage La Prairie, MB. Rick is the retired manager of Research and Development at Jeffries Nurseries.

Frost represents a challenge to prairie gardeners at both ends of the growing season. An early fall frost can bring a sudden end to the dazzling blend of colour associated with fall-blooming perennials. As plant breeders, our challenge is to manipulate the plant germplasm to better fit the growing conditions. In the case of chrysanthemum, that translates to selecting for early-blooming genotypes that will reach their peak floral display before they are touched by the icy fingers of frost.

In 2000, Jeffries Nurseries Ltd. of Portage la Prairie, Manitoba took up the challenge of developing a new series of early-blooming, cold-hardy chrysanthemums for the prairie gardener. Rick Durand hybridized several of the famous Morden Mums with 'Centerpiece', a superior cultivar from the University of Minnesota program. Evaluation, selection and propagation over several years produced six new cultivars with a profusion of colours and textures – the Firecracker Chrysanthemums.

The release of Dreamweaver and Suncatcher in 2004 marked the passing of 20 years since a new prairie hardy mum had been introduced. Tigertail, Firestorm and Showbiz were released in 2005, followed by Stardust in 2006. All six Firecracker cultivars have large flowers with fluted petals that amplify colour in the landscape. These mums were selected for their cold-hardiness and consistent, early flowering in the fall. Firecracker cultivars flower from late August to early September, and often bloom fully before a killing frost. The early flowering also allows the plants to harden off sooner in preparation for winter.

Dreamweaver was derived from a cross between 'Centerpiece' and 'Morden Fiesta'. Its large sized flower is a soft mauve colour with fluted petals. A hint of the yellow centre is evident. This plant has a broad globe shape (75 by 120 cm / 30 by 48 in) with a neat and compact appearance. The attractive flowers blanket the plant at full bloom.

Suncatcher was developed from a cross of two Morden chrysanthemum cultivars ('Fiesta' and 'Canary'). The bright yellow flowers, with fluted petals, are a real standout in the landscape. The plant has an open and lanky appearance. This cultivar attains a height of 75 cm (30 in) and a width of 120 cm (48 in).

Tigertail was also derived from a cross between 'Centerpiece' and 'Morden Fiesta'. Its dazzling flowers radiate different shades of yellow and rust. The plant is very compact and neat (75 by 120 cm / 30 by 48 in) and the abundance of multi-coloured flowers totally covers the rich dark green leaves during peak blooming season.

Firestorm is a 'Fiesta' x 'Canary' hybrid. The bright yellow eye (center) is encircled by the striking red petals. This cultivar has an upright plant form that is dense and tidy. The mature size of the plant is 55 by 100 cm (22 by 40 in). Firestorm appears to be slightly less cold hardy than the other Firecracker cultivars.

Showbiz is a cross between 'Fiesta' x 'Canary'. This petite plant (45 by 75 cm / 18 by 30 in) produces large, eye catching purple-pink coloured flowers that look like pompoms.

Stardust is a hybrid from the cross 'Centerpiece' x 'Morden Fiesta'. The attractive flowers are presented as a soft pastel blend of purplish pink colours complimented by a bright yellow centre. The plant form is dense and orderly and the size is 55 by 100 cm (22 by 40 in).

Planting Time

Firecracker mums can be planted throughout most of the growing season, once the danger of spring frost is past. The small plants that a gardener obtains from divisions and rooted suckers should be planted out only in the spring.

Soil, Site and Fertilizer

Firecracker mums perform best in full sun on fertile, well-drained soil. The planting site should be somewhat protected by larger plants or buildings to ensure best growth and flowering. The addition of compost

Firecracker Chrysanthemums at a glance

Cultivar Name	Parentage	Flower Colour	Plant Size (HxW) cm (HxW) in	Year
Dreamweaver	'Centerpiece' x 'Fiesta'	Soft Mauve	75 x 120 30 x 48	2004
Suncatcher	'Fiesta' x 'Canary'	Bright yellow	75 x 120 30 x 48	2004
Tigertail	'Centerpiece' x 'Fiesta'	Peach-orange	75 x 120 30 x 48	2005
Firestorm	'Fiesta' x 'Canary'	Deep-red	55 x 100 22 x 40	2005
Showbiz	'Fiesta' x 'Canary'	Purple-pink	45 x 75 18 x 30	2005
Stardust	'Centerpiece' x 'Fiesta'	Dusty Rose	55 x 100 22 x 40	2006

provides nutrients all season long and also helps to moderate the soil temperature. A well-balanced, slow release fertilizer such as 12-12-12 can be added to the soil in spring and liquid fertilizer, such as 20-20-20, can be applied until late July. No fertilizer applications are suggested from August onwards when plants have less than two months to develop before a killing frost.

Water

Chrysanthemums prefer to have an even distribution of water during the growing season. Periods of drought will severely reduce the ability of the mum to grow vegetatively and produce a profusion of flowers. A rule of thumb is one inch of rainfall per week, from natural precipitation or hand watering. It is best to water in the early morning so that the plant can prepare for the hot afternoon temperatures and also to allow time for the foliage to dry before the evening, in order to prevent foliar diseases from developing.

Pruning and Staking

The only Firecracker mum that requires staking is Suncatcher. Due to its lanky stems and open crown, this cultivar is more susceptible to blowdown. A support unit such as a tomato cage would work well to stabilize a plant in the landscape. Occasional removal of spent flowers is also recommended to promote further flowering and keep the mum looking its best.

Dividing

Eventually Chrysanthemum plants grow outwards, leaving a dead area in the center of the clump. It is recommended to divide Firecracker mums every 2-3 years so that the plant can be renewed and kept vigorous and strong.

Over-wintering

Firecracker mums may need some protection to survive the winter. Allow the mums to finish their full growing cycle in the fall and then cover with dry leaves or branches. Retaining the mum stems until spring will help to prevent desiccation and allow snow to be caught and held by the remaining plant material. An application of water may be required in the late fall if there is a delay in snow cover and warm temperatures persist.

Firecracker mums are available at garden centres across prairie Canada as well as the northern United States. Plants are sold in a wide variety of container sizes, from 3 ½ " pots to 2 gallon containers. Often they will be predominately displayed in a branded yellow pot associated with the series.

See page 99 for a colour picture.

Rooftop Gardening
by George Shirtliffe

George is a retired science teacher who became interested in horticulture while living on his family farm as a boy. He and his partner have developed many fine gardens. He now lives in one of the penthouses in the Nokomis Bldg. in downtown Winnipeg.

The need to work the soil and grow things has been with me from childhood. Having been raised on a farm just outside of Winnipeg provided me with the experience, the knowledge and the love of seeing things grow. Today, I find myself in a rooftop apartment in Winnipeg's downtown. What attracted my partner and me to this place was the outdoor space available. When the owner showed us the apartment and we viewed the roof, he told us that we could plant trees out there. We didn't need any urging. Both my partner and I had visions of a lush garden where we could spend our leisure time enjoying the outdoors in a beautiful setting. We had been active in the development of the gardens at the Brentwood Lodge Apartments in Crescentwood, and were no strangers to horticulture. This was to be a new challenge for us.

We have a northwest patio and another one facing south. In all, there is likely more outdoor space available to us than for people who have houses. We are talking about a lot of roof.

The first summer involved getting soil and planters. We chose large pots and a few whiskey barrels

for the most part, and used bagged soil from gardening stores. We needed a lot of soil.

We had started dahlia roots and calla lilies indoors, so that when the planting season began, we would have

Even the cat enjoys the rooftop garden!
(Valerie Denesiuk)

a good start. The rest of the plants were annuals. We found our favourite annuals grew well in this space. Watering became a major job everyday. The drip pans one often finds with the pots were for the most part too shallow. We needed something deeper that would hold a lot of water. A visit to the Dollar Store remedied the situation, although the pans we bought did not match the planters. Later, we invested in hoses and installed a valve to run water from inside the apartment.

One learns a lot in the first few years with experimentation. Virginia Creeper, chives and Hens and chicks readily survive winters. However, only one dwarf Alberta spruce out of four also survived. But, for the most part, other perennials did not.

The garden, always a pleasure to behold, came with a lot of responsibilities. Winnipeg is often windy, and larger plants, no matter how healthy they appeared, needed to be staked. Then there were the heat waves. Plants needed to be watered daily. If one ever decided to accept an invitation to go to a friend's cottage, major watering had to take place before you left and the deep drip pans filled to overflowing. Longer absences meant testing friendships to ensure someone would come and water the plants.

In the summer of 2009 we got into vegetables. I made a trip to one of the local lumber yards and had them cut an industrial sheet of ¾ inch plywood into four pieces to build a structure that was 8 feet by

four feet and 16 inches deep. Bagged soil would have been too expensive, so, a borrowed half-ton truck and a trip to the nursery solved that problem. The next challenge was to get that amount of soil up to the roof via the elevator. That took an entire Saturday of hard work. We had a bumper crop of Roma Tomatoes that fall, along with carrots and yellow beans. The beets were not so successful as they were planted too close to the tomatoes, and soon became crowded out. Another lesson learned.

The thought had occurred to me at the beginning that weeding would not be an issue, but elm tree and dandelion seeds did find a way to invade the garden although not to the extent they would have on the ground.

Although the work can be intensive, one cannot describe the pleasure we get from these gardens when every plant is in bloom and the vegetables are producing. To be able to walk out and pick vegetables and flowers is such a treat. I know that we are the envy of our neighbours in the high rise next to us. When they wave to us from their apartments, I know they are letting us know they appreciate what we have done to what was once a bare rooftop.

Breakfast outside, along with barbecues in the evening, are the norm. There is also the bonus of no mosquitoes to ruin the time spent outdoors. A little bit of heaven in downtown Winnipeg! 🐝

See page 96 for a colour photo.

Late Blight -
a Gardener's Potential Nightmare
and a Persistent Commercial Concern
by Andy Tekauz

Andy is a Research Scientist - Plant Pathologist of Crop Production Systems (Sustainable Production Systems) with Agriculture and Agri-Food Canada and The Prairie Garden committee.

While not always familiar with the details, most of us have heard of the 'Irish Potato Famine'. This sad and unfortunate mid-19th century event, during which some one million people died of outright starvation or debilitating disease, and another one to two million citizens subsequently emigrated to other lands, was a pivotal period in Irish history. The famine and its fallout were precipitated by the near total failure of the potato crop, beginning in 1845, as a result of a new malady, the 'potato murrain' (potato plague or pestilence). It is said to have "struck down the growing plants like frost in summer". Today we know it as 'late blight' disease.

In Ireland, by the 1830s, some one third of the population of 8 million, mostly poor tenant farmers or 'cottiers', came to rely on the potato as their sole source of food. Potato was the only crop that yielded a sufficient harvest to sustain a family on the small rented farms that ranged in size from as little as a quarter to a few acres of what was often poor land. To survive, 5–8 pounds of potato had to be consumed daily, year-round, by each individual – a 'heavy'

Late blight on heirloom tomato leaves
(Meg McGrath)

diet indeed! This reliance on a single staple by a sizeable portion of the population, and the resulting famine when the crop was destroyed, was restricted to Ireland. The disease itself affected potato crops throughout northern Europe, although general famine did not occur. Grains, some meat, and other staples were available in other regions of Europe to supplant the potato.

What is late blight and why did it result in such devastation in the 1840's, as it still can today? Late blight is caused by what was previously a 'fungus', but is currently classified as a 'fungus-like' organism, *Phytophthora infestans*. This pathogen was unknown in Europe until its sudden appearance in 1845, likely a result of travel from South America on prevailing westerly winds, and/or in infected potatoes shipped from North America to Europe (on the eastern seaboard of North America the disease appeared several years earlier). Late blight affects members of the *Solanaceae*, a family of plants that in addition to potato, includes tomato, pepper and eggplant, as well as some weedy and horticultural 'nightshade' species. The disease affects all portions of the plant – leaves, petioles, stems, fruits – and in the case of potato, can invade the developing underground roots or tubers.

Phytophthora infestans is an 'obligate parasite', that is, one that is dependent on living tissue for its development and survival. Since the potato tuber is 'alive', it provides a means for *P. infestans* to survive locally from one growing season to the next. If rotting, infected potato tubers are discarded in above-ground cull piles following storage, or otherwise scattered on the ground surface, they can act as a source of disease for newly-planted susceptible crops.

Under favourable conditions, late blight develops and spreads quickly throughout plantings of a host crop, whether in commerce or the home garden. The disease thrives under moist, cool to temperate conditions, and infection results in development of rapidly-expanding, water-soaked lesions with pale yellowish-green halos (see References). The lesions occur on the foliage and stems of susceptible plants, and quickly turn brown and become brittle. A feature that distinguishes late blight from other foliar diseases of potato and tomato such as 'early blight', 'grey mould' or 'black dot', is that individual lesions can cross the leaf mid-vein. Lesions caused by sun-scald also can do this but are not accompanied by the paler surrounding halo. Within days, the lesions acquire a white cottony growth on the leaf's under-surface, where the propagules that spread the disease develop. These microscopic propagules, or 'sporangia' and 'zoospores' (spores) to be precise, are carried to neighbouring plants and fields by wind, rain, or mechanical means. When spores from potato leaves or stems are washed onto the soil surface they can contact and infect potato tubers, which will then develop a reddish-brown discolouration just beneath the skin surface. This 'dry rot' is prone to secondary infection by other fungi and various 'soft rot' bacteria, resulting in further tuber discolouration and deformation, making these unusable. Symptoms on tomato are similar – dark, firm lesions appearing randomly on the fruit.

In Canada, the disease was previously most common in potato crops grown in eastern provinces or British Columbia and was not a major factor on the prairies. However, greatly increased potato acreage, changes in production practices, and transformation of the causal fungus, have resulted in late blight becoming the chief production concern in potatoes grown on the prairies. Late blight 'cycles' quickly when conditions are favourable, and once an infection focus is established, movement within a crop is swift and losses substantial if protective measures are not employed.

Fungicides against late blight are registered for commercial use, but to be effective need to be applied numerous times (up to 15x in a growing season favouring the disease) to fully protect the crop. Typically, 'protective' and 'systemic' fungicides are alternated to reduce the likelihood of resistance to these

developing in *P. infestans*. Late blight forecasting systems, based on weather data, are in place in major potato and tomato growing regions to assist in scheduling of fungicide sprays. This frequent, necessary use of fungicides adds considerably to the cost of potato production. Therefore, it is not surprising that commercial growers, and the industry as a whole, are vigilant in preventing an early onset of late blight. This involves following rigorous sanitation measures to ensure that infected over-wintered tubers and other sources of the pathogen are eliminated and do not contribute to the initiation of disease.

Green tomato fruit affected by late blight (Meg McGrath)

For the home gardener raising a few to several dozen solanaceous plants, the only practical option to combat the spread of late blight is to pull up any visibly affected plants (preferably during a dry spell), bag these in dark plastic, and allow the bags to bake in the sun from two to several days. This will kill both any living plant material as well as the pathogen. Affected plants should **not** be left on the soil surface or thrown onto a compost pile as they can continue to act as a source of infectious spores over several days. Of course, being able to recognize the symptoms of late blight is a necessary first step (see References).

In spring 2010, some retail outlets in the eastern prairies inadvertently sold tomato seedlings with what appeared to be incipient symptoms of late blight. It is not clear how these plants became infected, but it may have been due to airborne spores entering the production greenhouse ventilation system. As soon as noted and late blight confirmed, a provincial agricultural alert was triggered to contain the problem. Retailers were asked to remove the offending plants from further sale, while home gardeners who had already purchased the plants were advised to destroy them using the steps outlined above. This action plan was instituted to prevent the probable early-season spread of late blight to tomato, potato, and other host plants in neighbouring gardens and in particular, to commercial potato fields. Both retailers and home gardeners complied willingly, and this community effort helped to avert an early, specific outbreak of the disease. Unfortunately, the cool and wet conditions in much of the eastern prairies in spring and early summer of 2010 strongly favoured the development of late blight (as well as many other plant diseases), and late blight once again broke out in prairie potato crops. 🐛

References:

For information, including images, and for updates on late blight locally, see:

http://www.gov.mb.ca/agriculture/crops/diseases (then click on "Late Blight", in potato or tomato);

http://www.agriculture.gov.sk.ca/Production (click on "Crops-Disease", then "Late Blight") http://www.agf.gov.bc.ca/cropprot/lateblight.htm

For numerous and excellent images of symptoms of late blight on tomato, see:

http://www.longislandhort.cornell.edu/vegpath/photos/lateblight_tomato.htm

For images of symptoms of late blight on potatoes, and symptoms of other similar-appearing diseases, see:

http://www.ndsu.edu/potato_pathology/ (under "NDSU Late Blight Hotline", click on "Additional Late Blight Information - PDF")

For more comprehensive information on the 'Irish Potato Famine', see (among others): http://en.wikipedia.org/wiki/Great_Famine_(Ireland)

Prairie Gardening Memories
by Val Werier, CM, OM

Val Werier is a distinguished journalist, winning many awards for his writing, including the Order of Canada and the Order of Manitoba. For almost 70 years, he has written articles championing the environment, protection of trees and forests, social justice, civil liberties, and spending time with his family at Lake Winnipeg.

A prairie garden raises beautiful images of the mystery and splendour of nature. We witness the wonder of life, plants rising from the earth with their fruit of fascinating lineage.

I savour these pictures and perhaps, more so, in their retelling. A prairie garden tells many stories, perhaps of no great import, but delightful in the moment. I take the liberty to extend the definition of prairie garden to include the little stories that arise from any encounter with nature within the family hearth or the prairie scene.

I remember looking out of my window one morning early in March to observe a wondrous scene. The brilliant sun had cast a shadow of my Amur maple onto the thick blanket of snow. A slight breeze arose and the branches, black in shadow, floated gently in the snow. The shadow was in sufficient detail to distinguish leaves remaining from last fall, a magical moment indeed.

Plants are fertile with vignettes of our times. More than 80 years ago, pansies and tobacco plants (also known as nicotine) were favourites, certainly in our household on Aberdeen Ave. Pansies provided the colour, nicotines the fragrance.

One man who resided on Redwood and Andrews undoubtedly was the champion of tobacco plants in the city. In an era of loose zoning controls, he had a horse stabled in a barn at the rear of his domicile. He built a long wooden trough extending alongside the front of his property. He filled it with manure-rich soil and planted it with a mass of white nicotines, opening in the evening to envelop the neighbourhood with a delicate perfume.

That was during the depression when people did the most with what they had.

The Ficus ('the rubber plant' in our home and in many others) was a note of distinction in the dreary depression. Our Ficus, more than two meters high and of ample girth, occupied half of the dining room. It signalled the change of seasons in a rite of long standing. When summer came, the Ficus branches were bound close with strips of cloth. Then in a horizontal position, firmly ensconced in its wooden tub, we hauled it through the hallways to the screened veranda. The Ficus clearly loved the summer interlude. In the fall we dragged it back to the dining room to shine with a rich, glossy green, spreading oxygen and delight.

Today 75 years later, I realize my mother Manya was a fine indoor gardener. A Ficus, originally from the tropics, requires special care, sensitive as it is to water, light and location. In my mind's eye I see my mother wiping the dust off the long, oval Ficus leaves, to gleam and shine in our household.

Plants foster family ties in their wondrous exploits. In our family, the flower is the Lily of the Valley, of delicate fragrance. In the 1950's, my mother-in-law Eda dug out a clump of the flower to bless our home. The hardy flowers thrived in a border along the front of the house. Later we gave a clump to a friend living on Elm Street. By coincidence 25 years ago, my daughter Judy, co-founder of the Coalition to Save the Elms, and her husband Leon bought a house next door. And this is the story: the Lily of the Valley spread into their front yard in a happy twist of fate and dramatic turn of events. So the chronology of our Lily of the Valley now extends over 55 years and three generations of our family.

Gardens are a family tradition in Manitoba where flowers and vegetables abound.

The tomato red and round, sweet and fresh on the vine, is a symbol of family relations. Like others, I have planted tomatoes on a lavish scale to give to family and friends to celebrate our connections and the wonder of nature. I stretched the tomato season well into winter storing the green remainders under paper wrap in the basement.

One great triumph was in the cherry tomato. I had long strings of green cherries when heavy frost forced a retreat. I hung the strings on a pipe in the basement. This was my orchard, picking cherry tomatoes so rosy and sweet in the depth of winter.

My son Jonathon, who raises orchids and many other plants, has continued the family tradition. He has taken over the planting of flowers at my place, recently concentrating on a splash of marigolds which remain after the first frost in magnificent colour into November, like oranges in the snow – a remarkable sight indeed.

In my extended definition, the Prairie Garden lives in my household the year round. This is a bouquet of tall grass prairie that graced the Central Plains in the past, blue stem shimmering in the wind in a blaze of colour. 🦌

The kiss of the sun for pardon,
The song of the birds for mirth,
One is nearer God's heart in a garden
Than anywhere else on earth.

An excerpt from **God's Garden**
by *Dorothy Frances Gurney*

With Fronds Like These...
by Sara Williams

*Sara Williams is co-author (with Hugh Skinner) of **Best Trees and Shrubs for the Prairies** and **Best Groundcovers and Vines** for the Prairies. Sara gardens on 5 acres near Saskatoon, SK.*

Ferns are generally found in northern boreal forests and river valleys where they flourish in sheltered locations – in full to partial shade, and in moist, but well drained soil that is rich in humus or organic matter. In our gardens, we are well advised to imitate these conditions. Add generous amounts of peat moss, compost, or well rotted manure to the soil. If you're on a heavy clay soil or drainage is poor, consider slightly raised or bermed beds. Ensure that the ferns have shade, protection from prevailing winds, and even moisture.

Experienced prairie fern growers advise purchasing larger plants and planting them as early in the season as possible. Mulch the soil surface with organic material, or simply leave the leaves where they fall to conserve moisture. And to protect the crowns over winter, wait until spring to remove old foliage. All are hardy in prairie gardens, but may be slow to emerge in the spring and slow to establish a large clump.

Rock Polypody - **Polypodium virginianum** (Sara Williams)

Some are more difficult to find in garden centres and nurseries than others. And a few have more names than you really care to know!

Northern maidenhair fern (*Adiantum pedatum*) – Native to North America and widely available, the fronds are forked in the middle with the two parts curving backward to form a fan or horse shoe. They are tri-pinnate (3 times divided), with the smallest segments shell-shaped and slightly over-lapping. The stipes (stems) are shiny black and somewhat brittle. Northern maidenhair fern expands slowly but steadily, with attractive blue-green foliage and a mature height of about 30 to 45 cm (12 to 18 in.). Some gardeners seem to have more success with this fern than others, and for no apparent reason.

Lady fern (*Athyrium filix-femina*) – Lady ferns are native to Europe, Asia and North America. The northern lady fern (*A. angustum*, syn. *A. f-f angustum*), indigenous to North America, is found in Prince Alberta National Park and areas of Manitoba. There is sometimes confusion in the nursery trade and in books concerning nomenclature. The European species (*A. filix-femina*) has many varied forms and is more readily available commercially. Its stems (stipe and rachis) are green or red, the fronds erect, thin and feathery with a delicate lacy appearance, and a mature height of about 60 cm (2 ft.). The common name, lady fern, arises from their delicate appearance.

Among the cultivars and selections of the European lady fern are:

Tatting fern (*Athyrium filix-femina* 'Frizelliae') – The common name refers to its resemblance to tatting or hand-made lace, as the smallest segments (pinnae) are reduced to bead-like balls or rounded lobes that look like lace. These may occasionally revert to their species-like form. A dwarf plant, it has an open, arching form and is about 30 cm (12 in.) in height.

Dwarf lady fern (*Athyrium filix-femina* 'Minutissima') has been described as a 'perfect miniature'of the larger species, forming a dense rosette of only 8 to 16 cm (3 to 6 in.). In overly rich soil, it may become larger. It combines well with hostas and lungworts.

'**Lady in Red**' - A selection of *A. angustum* (*forma rubellum*) found in the wild in Vermont and introduced by the New England Wildflower Society, it has vibrant red stems and lacy, light green foliage. With an upright growth habit, it's about 60 cm (2 ft.) in height, tri-pinnate (3 times divided), and extremely hardy and reliable. An excellent fern for beginners, place it in bright shade. It's reputed to be deer resistant.

Japanese painted fern (*Athyrium niponicum pictum*; syn. *A. n.* var. *pictum* 'Metallicum') –Native to Japan, China and Korea, the triangular-shaped fronds are a soft shade of metallic silver-grey while the rachis or stems are a contrasting wine-red. Expect a height of 30 to 45 cm (12 to 18 in.). Slow to establish, the best colour is obtained in light shade. The roots are black. Selections of the Japanese painted fern include:

'**Burgundy Lace**' - A favourite of veteran Saskatoon gardener, Jeaniene Smith, she considers it 'the prettiest' of all her ferns, and recommends planting it next to blue leaf hostas. The new fronds are a rich burgundy, contrasting with the silver stipes. It's clump-forming, with arching, triangular fronds and a height of 20-30 cm (8 to 12 in.). Also deer resistant.

'**Silver Falls**'- Introduced by Terra Nova, it is largely untested on the Canadian prairies. It's a slow grower and slow to emerge in the spring. Highly silvered, it has a clumping form, and a height of about 30 -40 cm(12 to 16 in.).

There are several **hybrids of the lady fern and the Japanese fern**. Attractive and with exceptional vigour, they get their height from the lady fern and colouring from the Japanese painted fern.

'**Ghost**' - Upright and 60 cm (24 in.) tall, the silver fronds are accented by contrasting dark maroon midribs. Silvering is best in spring, with the foliage becoming more of a grayish-green by mid-summer during hot weather. It's vigorous, not fussy, and quickly forms large upright clumps. Good with hostas. Grow in light shade.

'**Bradford Beauty**' – Hybridized by Nick Nicou of Bradford, Connecticut, it has a red rachis and contrasting grey-flecked fronds and a height of 60 cm (24 in.). It's extremely vigorous and grows rapidly, forming a tight clump.

Fragile fern or bladder fern (*Cystopteris fragilis*) – Native to our boreal forests, it's found in rock crevices in Manitoba and Prince Albert National Park. Short (20-30 cm/6-10 in.) and delicate in appearance, it has light green, erect and arching bi-pinnate (2 times divided) fronds. Once established, it's spreading but not invasive. The fronds are not always where you expect them. The stipes (stems) are somewhat brittle, but are soon replaced if broken. The creeping roots are black. It's of easy cultivation in gardens.

Golden scaly male fern (*Dryopteris affinis* 'Stableri Crisped') – The species is native to Europe and Asia and 'officially' classed as zones 4 to 8. Its many selections are quite variable. *D. a* 'Stableri Crisped' has been growing happily in a Saskatoon garden for over a decade. The erect narrow fronds are leathery but shiny, 60 to 90 cm (24 to 36 in.) in height, with short pinnae (segments) and a wavy margin. The stipes and rachis (stem) appear shaggy because they are covered with golden brown scales. Easy to grow.

Buckler or robust male fern (*Dryopteris* x *complexa* 'Robust', syn. *Dryopteris filix-mas undulata robusta*) – Another fern struggling with the burden of confused nomenclature, this is probably a hybrid of *D. filix-mas* with *D. affinis* subsp. Robusta. You might find any or all of those names on the plant tag! Originating in England and an 'official' zone 4 to 8, it has nevertheless been growing in Saskatoon for a number of years. Taller than many, the gracefully arching, dark green fronds are up to 90 cm (3 ft.). The plants are vigorous, forming strong clumps, and not fussy to grow.

Autumn fern (*Dryopteris erythrosora*) – Native to Japan, China, and Korea, the bi-pinnate (twice divided), triangular fronds emerge a striking and unmistakable bronze-copper in the spring (thus the derivation of its common name), then turn a pinkish-green, and are a deeper lustrous green by mid-summer. The arching fronds are 45 cm (18 in.) in height.

Ruffled male fern (*Dryopteris filix-mas* 'Linearis Polydactyla') – The species is native to the cool, moist boreal forests of North America, Europe and Asia, including Riding Mountain National Park. *Dryopteris filix-mas* 'Linearis Polydactyla' has been growing in a Saskatoon garden since 1996. The fronds are about 45 cm (18 in.) in height and finely divided. The frond tip is fairly unique in that it is multi-forked and some of the widely spaced narrow pinnae (segments) may be missing. Easy to grow.

Oak fern (*Gymnocarpium dryopteris*) – Described variously by local gardeners with whom it is a favourite as a "lovely wee little one

that creeps around" and "lovely, and delicate; a very ferny fern", the small tri-pinnate (three times divided) fronds are a diminutive 12 cm (6 in.) in height, bright green and form broad triangles. Small round sori are found on the undersides of the fronds. Native to North America, Europe and Asia, it is hardy to zone 2. Good with spring bulbs.

Sensitive fern (*Onoclea sensibilis*) – Why sensitive? It is said to go limp or brown if exposed to severe frost or drought, but gardeners in Saskatoon have not observed this. Native to moist boggy areas of eastern North America and related to the well known ostrich fern, it is found as far west as Manitoba. Fronds are of two types. The sterile fronds are green and up to 60 cm (2 ft.) high with widely spaced segments (pinnae) on the upper half of the stem only. In contrast, the fertile (spore-bearing) fronds are club-like, emerge later, are brown and woody and persist through winter. Because of the creeping rhizomes, it tends to spread rather than form clumps. Surprisingly, under cultivation, it does better in shade gardens than in a bog garden.

Jeaniene Smith notes, "I find this one difficult to landscape with. It comes up in different places every spring, and actually seems to prefer to come up through the crowns of other plants!" Perhaps a good candidate for 'naturalization'? 🐾

See page 103 for a colour photo.

Perennial Releases from Morden Research Station

by John den Heyer

John is the propagator for Aubin Nurseries near Carman, MB

The Agriculture and Agri-Food Canada Research Station in Morden, Manitoba has a long history of development of herbaceous perennials. There have been varieties developed exclusively at the station as well as cooperative ventures.

In 1953 the first varieties of *Chrysanthemum* crosses were released. Over the next 26 years other varieties were developed and released. Of the 32 varieties released, 7 are still available in the trade.

These chrysanthemums save their best flower show for fall. The compact, mounded plants are covered with flowers. The plants will handle some frost. Size will vary depending on site but generally range from 30–45 cm in height and 45–60 cm in width.

Monarda is another perennial that has gone through a lot of development work at the station. Most of the *Monarda* developed are available in the trade.

In 1986 *Monarda* 'Marshalls Delight' was released followed in 1997 by 'Petite Delight' and 'Petite Wonder'.

In 1998 a consortium of three wholesale nurseries joined forces with the Research Station to further develop *Monarda*. The goal was to develop a wider range of sizes and colours.

'Coral Reef' was the first release of the consortium. It is 80 cm tall with hot pink flowers. The next releases were 'Grand Marshall' and 'Grand Parade'. 'Grand Marshall' is 60 cm tall with fuschia purple flowers while 'Grand Parade' is 60 cm tall with lavender purple flowers. The most recent release (2009) is named 'Grand Mum' and is 40–50 cm tall in a compact plant with soft mauve pink flowers.

The selection criteria aimed for different colours, good form, and resistance to powdery mildew. These Monarda are well adapted to our climate and are very hardy.

It appears that the work of the consortium is winding up, although there may yet be some releases of selections already in the program.

Lily development has been another successful program. From the mid-'70s to early '90s, station staff made a number of successful crosses. In the early '90s, due to a decreasing emphasis on perennial development at the station, a consortium was formed to evaluate the lily crosses.

There were three main groups of crosses. The Orienpets are a cross between trumpet and oriental lilies. The Easterpets are a cross between trumpet and easter lilies. The Asiapets are a cross between trumpet and Asiatic lilies.

The consortium finished its work in 2002 but breeding work is still ongoing in Manitoba.

Coral Bells developed at the station are 'Northern Fire' and 'Ruby Mist' in 1974 and 1994 respectively. What is most impressive about these varieties is the flower colour. Most new introductions are focused on foliage variation, with little attention paid to flowers. Northern Fire has bright red flowers on 60 cm stalks while 'Ruby Mist' is lighter in colour with shorter flower stalks. Both make colourful additions to the landscape.

The plants in the table are available in Manitoba. Some searching may be required.

Maintenance of these perennials consists of removal of spent flowers for appearance sake and removal of dead or overcrowded stems. Leaving stems on the plant over winter encourages snow collection which will help insulate the root to aid in overwintering. In spring cut the tops off and remove the trash collected over the plant.

Propagation by divisions in the spring works well for all varieties.

The herbaceous perennial program at Morden is at an end.

Here is a list of plants that are available in the trade

Chrysanthemum:
Morden Candy
Morden Canary
Morden Cameo
Morden Delight
Morden Fiesta
Morden Gaiety
Morden Garnet

Heuchera:
Northern Fire
Ruby Mist

Monarda:
Marshalls Delight
Petite Delight
Petite Wonder
Coral Reef
Grand Parade
Grand Marshall
Grand Mum

Lilium:
Orienpet:
Starburst Sensation
Northern Beauty
Northern Carillon
Northern Sensation
Northern Star
Easterpet:
Easter Dawn
Easter Morn
Asiapet:
Silky Belles
Fiery Belles
Creamy Belles
Golden Belles
Ivory Belles

At present it is unclear whether this work will continue at federal research stations in other parts of the country or be terminated countrywide.

Thanks to Marty Dykman and Suzanne Enns at Morden Research Station for their assistance with research and proofreading, and to Dr. Wilbert Ronald from Jeffries Nurseries for all things lily in this article. 🍂

The Healthy Garden
by Sandy Venton

What is a healthy garden? To me, a healthy garden is that perfect, pie-in-the-sky place where there are no invasive weeds such as Canada thistle (one of the banes of my life), loamy soil liberally amended with compost (not clay, not sand, but that dreamy soil that smells wonderful, looks like chocolate cake and retains just the right amount of moisture); no pests such as slugs (the other bane of my life), snails, cutworms, climbing cutworms or looper caterpillars (geometer moths) - those skinny little green worms/caterpillars that hang themselves from trees in the spring and early summer and manage to get into your hair, onto your clothing, and worst of all, onto flower and rosebuds, where they will sneakily sit and start to eat, so that when you come out in the morning to look to see how big a rosebud is, you will find a very fat, green looper sitting in the place where the rosebud used to be (please excuse the run-on sentence, but I am very passionate about those awful green worms!)

But I digress. A healthy garden needs neither chemical additives nor chemical pesticides. And from such a healthy garden will come healthy plants, both ornamental and edible. No hesitation about eating a vegetable from the garden and worrying about pesticides.

That being said, I have a garden that is almost pure clay that must be amended yearly with compost, has a huge slug population, ditto a Canada thistle population, and crabgrass growing with abandon. It is my plan to start amending the soil with compost, get rid of the Canada thistle, or at worst, cut off the flowers before they go to seed, and dig up as much of the crabgrass as I can.

Rome wasn't built in a day, and neither was my garden. But the older I get the more concerned I am about pesticides and other poisons which are oftentimes used in the mistaken notion that a healthy garden is being created.

New Tool Now Available for Native Orchid Conservation

by Doris Ames

*Doris is the president of Native Orchid Conservation Inc.
a non-profit group based in Winnipeg, MB*

Conservation of Manitoba's native orchid species depends primarily on habitat conservation and conservation of plant populations in the wild. Human activities such as wetland drainage, agricultural and residential development of tall grass prairie, logging, and some recreational activities are the major threats to our 37 native orchid species and their habitat. However, digging up and removal of plants for transplanting into home gardens is still a significant threat to some species of slipper orchids; notably Showy Lady's-slipper (*Cypripedium reginae* Walter) and Yellow Lady's-slipper (*Cypripedium parviflorum* Salisbury var. *pubescens* (Willdenow).

People often ask me what they can do to help protect native orchids, and I always tell them not to pick or transplant orchids from the wild. Enthusiastic gardeners often take this advice pretty hard. They love native orchids and want to see

*Orchids grown by
Lorne & Joan Heshka*
(Eugene Reimer)

Manitoba Native Orchids

them growing in their own gardens at home or at the cottage. But when one removes a plant from the wild, one also removes that plant's genetic information and that decreases biodiversity. Biodiversity is necessary for the survival of plant populations, and therein lies the problem for their continued survival.

The good news for gardeners is that it is now possible to grow and enjoy native orchids in one's garden without transplanting them from the wild. Several reputable greenhouses in Canada are now offering laboratory propagated native orchids for sale.

These plants have been grown from seed and do exceptionally well in a home garden because, unlike wild plants, they have not formed a symbiotic relationship with the fungi, trees and shrubs in their environment – which is destroyed when the native species are transplanted. The

nurseries ship them at the appropriate planting time and include planting instructions. All one has to do is sit back and wait for them to bloom. You will enjoy them all the more knowing that you are helping to preserve wild orchid populations. Several kinds are available including slipper orchids like Showy and Yellow Lady's-slippers. They are hardy and beautiful and spread over time by root propagation into lovely clumps.

A photograph on page 100 shows a lovely, lab-propagated plants grown by local orchid expert, Lorne Heshka, proudly exhibited at the Manitoba Orchid Society's Annual Show. Please see the Native Orchid Conservation Inc. website at <www.nativeorchid.org> for a list of reputable Canadian greenhouses that sell native orchids they have grown from seed.

Happy gardening!!

Tips for Planting Pots

Every plant container should have good drainage holes in the bottom. Fine screen, landscape cloth or coffee filters prevent soil from escaping through the drainage holes and keep insects from entering the pots. Trays beneath the pots will prevent damage to decks.

Adding slow release fertilizer when planting pots promotes good growth and blooms over about a three month period. In mid-July a second addition of slow release should maintain them for the remainder of the summer. Regular liquid fertilizer applications every two weeks will also help sustain both plants and bloom and prevent chlorosis.

Trial & Error(s)
by Dan Furlan

Dan Furlan, a dedicated novice, is always amazed at the beauty and magic that springs from the planting of a tiny seed. He continues to learn through trial and error every season, and can be found battling ants and squirrels in Silver Heights, Winnipeg. MB.

How do you become a gardening wizard? Are they born like Harry Potter, or do they spend years in damp greenhouses contemplating cuttings and mulch? I don't know, but a while back I was seized with the desire to create beautiful flowerbeds, works of art, the wonder of the neighbourhood. Well, that's how it started!

Enthusiasm precedes expertise. It certainly did in my case, as I had never grown anything except mould (unplanned!). With no knowledge of the gardeners' art, this was a decidedly low tech operation. Special hydroponic technology, expensive lights and record hydro bills intimidated me, so I opted for the use of sunny window ledges in the late days of winter. In fact, after planting, the seeds are under soil cover anyway, so all they need is warmth, but not direct sunlight. This can give your family time to adjust to your new project (if they ever do).

What to plant? I admit that, too frequently, the beauty of a flower seed package rather than more practical considerations has opened my wallet.

They all look good, so I have a collection of great seed packages, still full, as I didn't know some of the basics, such as: will that plant do well in the place I have in mind? Sun, shade or a combination? Is it short, medium, or tall? When does it bloom? All summer? May to June, or for two days in August? How far does it spread, possibly crowding out other favourites?

Most, but not all, seed companies have redeemed themselves in spades by sharing that basic information on the back of the package, so that the greenest rookie can make a good judgement. Is it one, for example, that can be easily started indoors and flourish with a minimum of care? I have had great luck with nasturtiums, ageratum and sunflowers of all kinds, and disasters with many others.

Take poppies and petunias for example. The seeds are almost invisible – little black specks one fifth the size of a chunk of pepper! These little beauties are difficult to plant unless you use tweezers and a magnifying glass. Others may have success with them, but my expertise and patience hasn't reached that level. Even then, when tamping them into the earth, you can't tell if they stayed in the soil, or are still sticking to your finger!

Nasturtiums and sunflowers on the other hand can have seeds the size of a kernel of corn, very easy to plant, and you know when you have too many in the same pot! They also have a tremendous germination rate, both in terms of speed and percentage of success.

As for containers, which ones are best suited for seed planting? I will admit to scrounging the garbage for empty plastic containers before I learned the joys of the little fibre pots available at most home and garden stores. Shop early for the fibre containers you will need. They go fast in the stores. These biodegradable, eco-friendly containers come in flats and in a variety of sizes and shapes to suit any need. Simply fill them with soil, plant the seeds and water, then place in a sunny spot in the house once the seeds sprout. If you take them outside, when evening temperatures are still cool, bring them in at night, but leave the flats out during the sunny spring days. When the outside temperature is warm enough, you merely plant the fibre pots directly into the soil without having to disrupt the sprout.

Before the final planting, dampen and break the bottom of the container so the roots can break out easily. It is wise to label all the flats or containers you are using to ensure you remember what is in each one. Masking tape and a marker pen works well, unless, as I did, you leave them out in the rain, so the words get washed off! Better yet, cover the writing with scotch tape to prevent hours of guessing – "I wonder what this one might be!" As you'll soon find, most sprouts look the same, unless the leaves are unique.

This will get you started on the mechanics of the process, so now let's return to what to plant.

Sunflowers, in particular, sprout so fast you can almost hear them cheering each other on! These first sprouts are what you have been looking for, ever since you seeded, and the sight of the first one brings untold joy to the rookie planter! Both sunflowers and nasturtiums grow quickly, which further adds to your pleasure and sense of accomplishment. "Look Ma, a sprout!" Sunflowers come in all sizes from towering giants over 2 to 2.5 m (6-8 ft), to the increasingly popular and decorative 45 to 90 cm (18-36 in) dwarfs, which can be the central focus of pots and containers, as well as flowerbeds. Check out the selection, the variety is remarkable.

Another favourite is the nasturtium with it's lovely variegated leaves, beautiful blooms and tendency to spread all over. Climbing vine varieties are also available, extending more than 2 m (6 ft) in length! Be warned, however, the sprouts grow quickly and have a tendency to become entwined with each other before you get to the transplanting stage. Pulling them apart can be harder than separating glued spaghetti!

I have enjoyed learning about this start-up phase of gardening so much that, each spring I now have not only a great supply for my own needs, but unique gifts for friends and family who think I have discovered some deep mystical secrets of the garden. When you give some one a sunflower that grows to over 2 m (+7 ft) high, they remember it!

I have only highlighted two of the easiest flowers to start with. Why don't you jump in and do your own trials and errors? 🍂

A Healthy Garden; Back To Basics or New Basics; What Does That Mean?
by Valerie Denesiuk

I recently spent two delightful days listening to various presenters speak on a variety of topics and make various recommendations at the 2010 Manitoba Horticulture Association. Curiously, many of the speakers almost seemed to either conflict, or at least disagree with other speakers. Eventually, I came to a realization that very few things in gardening are absolutely correct, or absolutely wrong. After all, they can grow grass on cement these days!

Much of what a grower needs to consider are: what are their expectations, what is their situation, and how much work are they prepared to put in, to achieve those expectations.

Currently, the interest in gardening – whether rural or urban – is increasing year by year. Motivations for gardening are everything from a desire for beautiful surroundings, a healthy outdoor activity, or a desire to grow what you eat. Today's gardeners want the assurance that they are eating a healthy product. The trend isn't necessarily about going back to the way that our grandparents gardened - because that wasn't necessarily the ideal. Gardeners today have access to a wealth of information, on plants, products, tools, and methods. From planting heritage or heirloom seeds, to using fibreglass containers with a specially developed lightweight soilless mix on a skyscraper balcony or roof; there is no shortage of options.

A Healthy Garden today can be planted in many places: rural, in your back yard, in a community garden, in planters or containers on a townhouse patio, or on a window sill in your apartment. Whether your gardening choice is floral, edible or potage, depends on what you desire or need. Consideration for the earth you plant in, the seeds or plants you use, how you provide nutrition for your plants, and how you care for your plants – all contribute to the health of both your garden and yourself.

Identifying and Managing Cutworms
by Dr. John Gavloski

John works in the Crops Knowledge Centre at Manitoba Agriculture, Food and Rural Initiatives in Carman, MB. where he conducts monitoring programs on some of the insects of greatest concern in field crops, and develops and delivers written material and presentations on insects in crops.

Cutworms are the larvae (caterpillars) of several species of night-flying moths in the family Noctuidae, and are a natural part of the prairie habitat. The larvae are called cutworms because some species cut young plants as they feed on stems at or below the soil surface. There are also species categorized as climbing cutworms that move up plants and feed on foliage, buds and shoots. Most species of cutworms feed on a wide range of plants. Cutworm larvae curl up into a tight C-shape when disturbed. The adults do not cause damage to plants.

Species of Cutworms
In Manitoba, seedlings of spring-planted crops may be damaged in late-May or June by sporadic high levels of some species of cutworms. Although there are lots of types of cutworms in Manitoba, there are some species that tend to be more abundant in gardens and fields. The redbacked cutworm (*Euxoa ochrogaster*), the darksided cutworm (*Euxoa messoria*) and dingy cutworm

(*Feltia jaculifera*) are often common species (Turnock et al. 1993, Ayre and Lamb 1990). The army cutworms (*Euxoa auxiliaris*) may also be abundant and a concern occasionally. Variegated cutworm (*Peridroma saucia*) may be a concern later in the summer. Knowing the predominant species of cutworm when populations are high can be helpful, because the different species can damage plants in different ways, and when and how long they are present may differ.

Redbacked cutworm larva (middle) and pupae

Larva of redbacked cutworm (left) and darksided cutworm (right)

Redbacked cutworms overwinter as eggs. Eggs hatch in April, and initially larvae are quite small and harder to find. Normally you can find larvae of redbacked cutworms anytime from about mid-May until the end of June. They are an early season problem. By the end of June they have usually pupated and problems for the current year are done. Redbacked cutworms may cut plants at or just above the surface and the tops of smaller plants may be entirely consumed.

Darksided cutworms overwinter as eggs and hatch during the first period of extended warm weather in the spring. As well as feeding on the leaves, older larvae may cut plants at ground level.

Dingy cutworms overwinter as partly-grown larvae. So early in the season they may be larger than some cutworm species that overwinter as eggs. Dingy cutworms are primarily leaf feeders, and rarely cut plants. The adult moths are active from mid-July until September and have been known to lay eggs on sunflower heads when they are in bloom (*see colour photo on page 97*).

Army cutworm (*Euxoa auxiliaris*) may move into Manitoba as it migrates from the Rocky mountains to lower elevations, but rarely are they at as damaging levels in Manitoba as they can be in Alberta and Saskatchewan.

Looking for Cutworms
During the day cutworms are usually below the soil or debris and come to the surface at night to feed. So during the day you may see damage left on plants, but no cutworms. Watch for plants cut off near the ground or plants that are noticeably wilting (when cutworms chew on the stems but do not sever the plant). You may also see droppings on the ground, which can indicate cutworms were

there. To verify cutworms are present, run your hand over the soil, rolling over soil clumps and other potential hiding places within a one foot square area of the damage. Digging around the immediate area of a damaged plant can confirm whether cutworms likely caused the damage.

The depth of cutworms in the soil during the day may depend on the age of larva and how moist the soil is. For example, in a study from Ontario on darksided cutworm, older larvae were observed just under the soil surface in wet weather. However, in dry weather they were found at a depth of 8 to 10 cm (3 to 4 inches) from the soil surface (Cheng, 1973). Most younger larvae rested in the soil during the day at a depth of 6-13 mm (¼ to ½ in.) near the base of the host plant.

Larvae normally have 6 stages of development (known as instars) before they become fully grown. Between each instar stage, the larvae 'moult' or shed their skin. During moulting the larvae are inactive and remain several centimeters below the soil surface. Some studies have found 20 to 50% of the cutworm population were in a pre-moult or recent post-moult stage and were not feeding. Laboratory studies have shown the moulting period during which the larvae are inactive comprised approximately 33 percent of the entire larvae life stage. Feeding cutworms can be identified by the presence of greenish mid-gut

contents visible through the semi-transparent underside. A moulting cutworm will not have food in its gut. Once the larvae complete their last instar stage, they burrow deeper into the soil and form earthen cells where they pupate.

Also pay attention to the stage of larvae and how many plants are being damaged or destroyed. If you are seeing a lot of damage and most larvae are still young, about 12 mm (½ inch) or less, that means you have quite a young population of larvae and they will be doing a lot more feeding. Many of our common species can be up to 38mm (1.5 inches) long.

Factors Regulating Cutworm Populations

Higher levels of cutworms may persist for a few years, followed by a few years of lower levels. Factors contributing to population increases for some of our common species are not well known, but may include hot, dry conditions in August, and low parasite populations.

Parasites may play a large role in keeping cutworm numbers low. A study in Saskatchewan found that larvae of the redbacked cutworm were parasitized by 4 species of bee flies, at least 4 species of tachinid flies, and several species of parasitic wasps (King and Atkinson, 1928).

Ground beetles can be important predators of cutworms; a study in Alberta found 7 species of ground beetles feeding on larvae and pupae of redbacked cutworms in the field (Frank, 1971).

Adult ground beetles are usually active at night and hide during the day under stones, loose bark, boards, or other debris. Because cutworms are also nocturnal, ground beetles can be effective in reducing their numbers.

Bacterial diseases of cutworms can be common under certain conditions, and several fungal diseases of cutworms thrive in cool damp weather (King and Atkinson, 1928). Birds that eat cutworms include crows, blue jays, catbirds, house wrens, robins, and meadowlarks.

Control Tips

Handpicking - If damage by cutworms is noticed on particular plants, digging in the soil around the plants may expose the cutworms. Another approach is to look after dark when the cutworms are out of the ground, in which a flashlight may be required.

Cutworm collars placed around plants prior to feeding by cutworms are another potential solution where practical. This involves wrapping the lower part of the stem with something to keep the cutworms from feeding on them, or placing cylinders made from empty cans (with bottoms removed) around each plant. The cutworm collars must be pushed down into the soil approximately one inch to be effective.

Cultivation - If it is evident that there is a high cutworm population in a field or garden prior to seeding in the spring, young cutworm larvae may be starved before seeding by allowing volunteer growth to reach three to five centimetres (1.2 to two inches), cultivating and then seeding 10 to 14 days later. The tricky part about making this practical is knowing beforehand that you have a high cutworm population early, well before crops are seeded.

Predators and Parasites - Numerous beneficial insects, including predatory ground beetles and parasitic wasps and flies prey upon cutworms and reduce the population. Some species of birds also prey upon cutworms. Take steps to preserve such beneficial organisms in and around gardens. Reducing unnecessary spraying for other pests and providing refuges may help to encourage beneficial organisms.

Insecticides - products registered for use on cutworms are available in most hardware stores. Because of their potential effect on non-target species, this should be used as a last resort.

If applying insecticides for cutworms, best results occur if insecticide applications for cutworms are made in the evening. Sometimes it is most economical to just treat infested patches and not entire fields or gardens.

Not all cutworms will be killed immediately after an insecticide is applied, and control will increase over a few days as more cutworms are exposed to or ingest the insecticide. Recall that moulting larvae will not be feeding; that can cause a significant delay in control of those individuals when insecticides are used as a control strategy. So if you still find some living cutworms after an insecticide application, don't necessarily conclude the insecticide is not working. Give it some time for moulting larvae to resume feeding.

Once cutworms start pupating their damage is done for the year. So if the damage is not too severe and larvae are large, it may be best to just wait for them to pupate and see if hand picking can provide good results (depending on the size of the garden). You could even try placing some of the cutworms that you find in a bird feeder (providing insecticides have not been used) to give the birds an extra treat. 🐦

All Photos by John Gavloski

See page 97 for colour photos

References

Ayre, G.L. and R.J. Lamb. 1990. Life histories, flight patterns, and relative abundance of nine cutworms (*Lepidoptera: Noctuidae*) in Manitoba. The Canadian Entomologist 122: 1059-1070.

Cheng, H.H. 1973. Observations on the bionomics of the dark-sided cutworm, *Euxoa messoria* (*Lepidoptera: Noctuidae*), in Ontario. The Canadian Entomologist 105: 311-322.

Frank, J.H. 1971. *Carabidae* (*Coleoptera*) as predators of the red-backed cutworm (*Lepidoptera: Noctuidae*) in Central Alberta. The Canadian Entomologist 103: 1039-1044.

King, K,M. and N.J. Atkinson. 1928. The biological control factors of the immature stages of *Euxoa ochrogaster* Gn. (*Lepidoptera, Phalaenidae*) in Saskatchewan. Annals of the Entomological Society of America 21: 167-188.

Turnock, W.J., B. Timlick and P. Palaniswamy. 1993. Species and abundance of cutworms (*Noctuidae*) and their parasitoids in conservation and conventional tillage fields. Agriculture, Ecosystems and Environment 45: 213-227.

Recommended Reading

The Lost Garden by Helen Humphreys – A work of fiction set during the 2nd World War in Britain when the government, as part of the war effort, appropriated estates for the growing of food for soldiers.

The Secret Life of Plants by Peter Tompkins – The world of plants and its relation to mankind as revealed by the latest scientific discoveries. *"Plenty of hard facts and astounding scientific and practical lore."*

Pruning Shrubs
by Brad Gurr

Brad Gurr is an I.S.A. Certified Arborist and Plant Health Care Specialist dedicated to the care and preservation of trees. For more information on this subject or any plant health care related questions please feel free to contact Brad online at gurrb@yahoo.com

Landscapes can help to transform houses into homes. Trees and shrubs not only contribute pleasant feelings to our surroundings, but they also add up to 15% to the value of your property.

It often takes several years for newly planted shrubs to establish and then, before you know it, they are on their way to becoming leggy overgrown monsters.

Most shrubs will appreciate even the smallest amount of pruning and reward you with rejuvenated foliage and more abundant buds.

Time to prune

The first key to correctly pruning your shrub is to know what you are growing. Proper identification is essential before pruning your shrub. Many shrubs flower on last year's growth (old wood) and if you are pruning yearly you may never get flowers. The classic example of this is the lilac, which is a spring blooming shrub. Shrubs like these should only be pruned immediately after they bloom to ensure a good set of flower buds for next year.

In contrast to the old wood flowerers, some shrubs only bloom on new growth. These shrubs should be pruned before the growing season begins.

As with so much of nature, there are shrubs that don't fall into either of these categories and flower from both last year's growth and new growth. These typically flower later in the growing season and can be pruned while dormant or right after blooming.

There are some shrubs that we grow

Pruning tools (Brad Gurr)

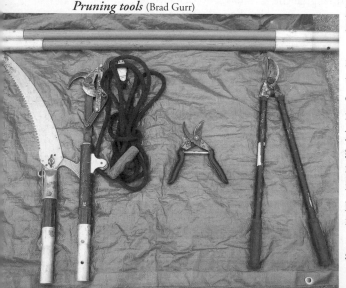

Pruning Chart		
Location of Flowers	**Best Time to Prune**	**Typical Plants**
Last year's growth	Right after flowering	Lilac, Forsythia, Saskatoon
New growth	Before growing season	Clematis, Spirea, Hydrangea
New and old	Right after flowering or while dormant	Potentilla, Rose, Mock Orange

strictly for foliage like red osier dogwood, elderberry, willows, and barberry. This group should generally be pruned in the winter season before growth begins. Moose 'prune' dogwoods in the winter and so should you.

Most conifers such as spruce, juniper and cedars can be pruned at anytime – however, pines are the exception. Pines are best pruned in early summer when the new growth is emerging. These long shoots, known as candles, can be cut or pinched off at the half-way point and the shrub will set new buds for future growth. Prune pines after the shoot has elongated and you will be left with a half shoot. Without buds on the end it will lose its needles and leave you with a dead stick.

Tools to prune

The old adage: "the right time to prune is when the saw is sharp," probably doesn't tell the whole story, but pruning with dull tools is always a disaster. The bests results come from professional-quality tools that are in good condition.

Most professionals use hand bypass pruners and pole pruners day in and day out. Bypass pruners work like scissors with two sharp blades that are opposite each other, passing each other to make a clean cut. Anvil pruners bring the sharp blade down onto a flat surface, damaging the bark, causing die back at the point of pruning. For cuts up to 1.25 cm (.5 in), a pair of sharp hand pruners works best. Bypass loppers are over sized hand pruners that will cut branches up to 5 cm (2 in) in diameter. Loppers are sized to fit in between hand pruners and pole pruners and often stay on the shelf while the latter two tools do all the work.

A bypass pole pruner will work on overhead branches between 1.25–2.5 cm (0.5–1.0 in). They also can be used for cutting low branches without bending over. For most homeowners three small 1.25 m (4 ft) screw-together poles will be enough for shrub pruning. They are easier to fit in the trunk of your car as well. Interchangeable saw heads can be attached for tall branches or removed and used as a hand saw to cut branches larger than one inch that won't fit into your pole pruner. Professional pole saw blades are readily available and will fit wooden hand saw handles as well. Good tools will literally last you a lifetime so take the time to ask questions and get professional grade.

Terminology for pruning

Before we continue, we should have a basic understanding of a few of the terms used to describe the anatomy of shrubs. (See image at bottom of page)

Buds are dormant plant parts. Inside each bud is a complete shoot or flower. Buds are described based on their position on the twig. Terminal buds are located at the end of a twig and lateral buds are located below the terminal bud on the sides of the twig. Buds can be arranged opposite each other on the twig or in a zigzag pattern alternating sides along the twig. The location of each bud or group of buds is called a node. The piece of twig between the buds is called the internode.

Techniques for pruning

As a general rule pruning cuts should take place just past the node, at a distance equal to the width of the twig. Cutting too close to the node will damage the bud and cause die-back. Never cut in the middle of the internode. Cutting in the middle of the internode will result in an unsightly stub that will die back and may be an entry point for disease or insects. Two

broad terms for pruning are 'heading back' and 'thinning out.'

Heading back is best described as when you indiscriminately reduce the size of a shrub to conform to a preset size or shape. For instance, you may want to prune your carragana hedge into a 1.3 by 1 m (4 by 3 ft) box. You would accomplish this by using a power shear to cut back the twigs in a uniform fashion. The caragana would quickly sprout a bushy broom on each tip and cover up the unsightly cuts that would result. The problem with heading back shrubs and hedges with this method is that eventually you end up with an umbrella of dense foliage at the tips of each leggy stem and little else below. Formal hedging often requires that you vary your technique by occasionally thinning out the dense canopy by cutting a series of windows in it to allow light and air to penetrate the inside of the plants.

Thinning is a much more sustainable method of pruning that involves selectively removing branches back to the appropriate unions with other branches. As you can imagine, this isn't done with a power shear. When thinning a hedge you need to determine your overall goal, for example, thinning by 25% or by opening up the hedge every third of a metre (foot) or so. You would then go through the hedge and cut out

(Brad Gurr)

lateral bud   *terminal bud*

node   *internode*   *node*

dead, diseased and crossing branches below the canopy by a foot or so every few feet. Next, remove healthy branches back to the appropriate unions in selected locations. This can be done after shearing and still maintain a formal look with a few small gaps. The hedge will respond by putting out new growth inside and below the existing canopy layer. Over time this method would allow you to reduce the overall size of the hedge without having it end up looking thin or over pruned.

Thinning is the method of choice when you want to maintain a shrub at a certain size and have a more natural form. When pruning shrubs in this style, take a tip from your carpenter: 'Measure twice – cut once.'

You may notice that a tape measure was not included in my list of tools. You need to step back, take a look at the shrub and measure with your eyes. Cut a bit and then step back and view your progress. Before removing larger branches, give them a shake and see how they relate to the rest of the plant. Then, remove larger branches in stages, checking the form of the plant as you go. Once you have made your choice, reach into the centre of the shrub and cut the branch just slightly above the node of an outward facing bud. This will allow new growth to move away from the centre of the shrub and avoid crowding. If you have a hole to fill, prune back to above a bud that faces the hole.

Make a few cuts and then step back and have a look. Eventually you will reach a point that looks good to you – then stop. If the shrub is viewed from multiple angles, be sure to look at it from all sides. You can make the cuts at an angle if you wish – a clean cut at any angle is best.

Rejuvenation pruning is an extreme form of heading back that can be valuable when dealing with shrubs in mature landscapes. Over time some shrubs will become too leggy and unmanageable. You see this often in older gardens. One radical method of saving old plants is to rejuvenate them. Again, lilacs are the classic example of this. Lilacs need to have the older branches removed to allow the new growth to flourish. You can do this by removing the older stems back to 6 inch stubs. Leave any new shoots to take over. Typically you would remove 1/3 of the older shoots per year. In three years you will have all new shoots and a much invigorated plant. You will lose some flowers in the first few years, but will be rewarded with a bounty in the years to come. 🐦

A note of caution:
Some plants are susceptible to diseases spread by pruning tools. Members of the rose family, such as cotoneaster and mountain ash, should be pruned with sterile tools to prevent the spread of fire blight. Black knot of cherry is another disease easily spread by unsterilized tools. The solution to this problem is dousing your tools with alcohol between cuts. Cut, sterilize, cut, sterilize and sterilize between plants.

Small Pear and Cherry/Plum Tree Cultivars in Northern Plains Landscapes

by Dr. Dale E. Herman

Dale is a professor of Horticulture and Forestry with the Department of Plant Sciences, North Dakota State University.

Interest by the public in small ornamental landscape trees has increased markedly over the past 25 years. Small 15 to 28 feet (five to nine meters) flowering trees tend to fit well in residential lots with limited space and one-story ranch-type homes. Smaller trees can also be grown satisfactorily under utility lines. In addition, large trees block much of the potential sunlight available to a residential lot which reduces the success of growing quality turf, gardens, and flowers due to excess shading and the probability of increased disease problems.

Flowering crabapples have been a very popular small tree choice for decades. As woody plant evaluations have proceeded at North Dakota State University (NDSU), we have noted a number of pear and cherry/plum cultivars that have (or may have) excellent potential for expanding the diversity of adaptable small trees for planting in Northern Plains landscapes. Some of the most exciting and promising cultivars are discussed below.

Pyrus - Pear

Ussurian Pear (*Pyrus ussuriensis*) is rated as the hardiest pear species. It is winter hardy in United States Department of Agriculture (USDA) Hardiness zone 3 and is native to northeastern Asia. This pear has been available for many years as seedlings for planting in shelterbelts and farmstead windbreaks. However, seedlings are quite variable in vigour, growth habit and other characteristics. Two superior cultivars that are clonally propagated have been introduced for landscape planting. These include:

Prairie Gem Flowering Pear - *Pyrus ussuriensis* 'MorDak'

A seedling selection of the Ussurian pear introduced at NDSU. The superior qualities of this cultivar are very distinct when grafted plants are grown near seedling Ussurian pear rootstock. Prairie Gem produces a more coarsely-twigged tree with very dense branching. It has a distinctly oval growth habit, becoming globose with age. Foliage is clean, bright emerald-green and semi-glossy. The thick, leathery-textured leaves are of excellent quality throughout the growing season, turning yellow in autumn. It has excellent fireblight resistance. White flowers blanket the tree in spring. Trees do not fruit unless a different pollinator pear is nearby. This is advantageous, since the 1 to 1¼ inch (2½ to 3.2 cm) rounded yellow fruits are not of culinary value. It is winter hardy in USDA hardiness zone 3. The dense, rounded growth habit of Prairie Gem results in an attractive, tailored small tree that grows to 25 feet (8 meters) and is suitable for shade as well as for residential use or as a park specimen. Available in nursery trade. Propagated by budding and/or grafting.

Mountain Frost Pear
- *Pyrus ussuriensis* 'Bailfrost'

A seedling selection of the Ussurian pear introduced by Bailey Nurseries, Inc., St. Paul, MN. This selection has good vigour and a narrower, more upright growth habit. Attractive white flowers cover the tree in spring, and its semi-glossy foliage is fairly leathery and dark green. The one-inch yellow pomes are not produced unless a different pollinator pear is nearby. Its mature width is approximately 5–6 feet (1.5–1.8 m) narrower than Prairie Gem and it is also winterhardy in USDA zone 3. Available in nursery trade.

Callery Pear
- *Pyrus calleryana*

Callery Pear is a dark green, lustrous leaved pear native to Korea and China. Leaves tend to be crimped or wavy along the margins. In the fall, brilliant yellow to red-purple fall colours develop. Numerous superior cultivars with variation in form have been introduced, including round to spreading and oval to distinctly upright pyramidal or conical. Many white flowers are produced and fruits are only ⅓ - ½ inch (.8–1.3 cm) wide and russet-dotted. Therefore, the pomes are of no ornamental value but also not messy. Callery pear, as represented by numerous superior landscape cultivars, has been a very popular ornamental small tree in much of the eastern half of the U.S. as well as the far western U.S. However, it is rated as USDA zone 5 in hardiness and therefore, lacks sufficient hardiness in the Northern Plains. NDSU has evaluated several cultivars and one cultivar is considerably hardier than all others. This cultivar merits widespread trial planting in USDA zones 3-4 to further determine its potential value for this region. A brief description follows:

Autumn Blaze Pear
- *Pyrus callerayana* 'Autumn Blaze'

Introduced by Dr. Westwood at Oregon State University, and reputed to be the hardiest Callery pear cultivar. It has been evaluated for seven years in NDSU trials with no winter injury to date, even at -30 to -35⁰ F (-34 to -37⁰ C) over a period of several winters. It is upright, rounded in growth habit, has glossy reddish-tinged young leaves maturing to dark green. Expected mature height is 25–30 feet (7.6–9.1 m) by

20–25 feet (6–7⅝ m) wide. It has strong lateral branch attachments. One authority rates it as susceptible to fireblight, which will need further evaluation in the Northern Plains. In NDSU trials, it produces brilliant red autumn colour in mid to late October. Available in nursery trade.

Korean Sun Pear
- Pyrus fauriei 'Westwood'

Pyrus fauriei is a smaller-statured pear species native to Korea. It has much smaller leaves than the pears discussed above. The cultivar 'Westwood' was received in 1998 and planted in NDSU trials. After 10 years, trees average 13+ feet (10+ m) tall by 8+ feet (2½+ m) wide. Expected height is 14–18 feet (4¼–5½ m), a very small tree. Flowers are white and the ½ inch (1¼ cm) fruits are not messy and russet-dotted, like those on Callery pear. Plant form is informally rounded and leaves are medium green and fine textured. The most exciting facets of this pear are winter hardiness in USDA zone 3 in a 10-year trial and its outstanding autumn coloration, namely, a fluorescent red with bright pink to orange hues, depending on the year. Available in nursery trade.

Prunus - Cherry/Plum

Princess Kay Plum
- Prunus nigra 'Princess Kay'

'Princess Kay' is a selected cultivar of Canada plum with showy, fragrant, double-white flowers in early May, which last for 7–10 days. The species has single flowers. It was introduced by the University of MN and is hardy in zones 2–3. It is essentially sterile, producing very few fruits. Trees produce very dark green, somewhat rough or rugose leaves, which turn to reddish shades in autumn. Trunk and branches are dark brown to black with large whitish lenticels. Trees grow oval to round in form reaching 15 feet (4½ m) tall by 8–10 feet (2½–3 m) wide. Good soil drainage is required. 'Princess Kay' is a choice, small ornamental flowering tree and is available in nursery trade.

Sargent Cherry
- Prunus sargentii

This cherry is native to northern Japan and Korea. Authorities rate this species as the most handsome of the larger tree cherries for northern states and its hardiness as USDA zones 4 to 5. Consequently, this species had not been evaluated in NDSU trials, until a named cultivar (discussed below) was received for trial in 2000. In the spring of 2008, we obtained plants of this species, plus the cultivars 'Columnaris' - Columnar Sargent Cherry and 'Rancho' - Rancho Sargent Cherry from Oregon nurseries for trial evaluation. Both 'Columnaris' and 'Rancho' were selected for narrower, more columnar growth habits than characteristic of the species. 'Rancho' is described as even narrower in form than 'Columnaris'. Since the above have not yet been fully evaluated, further comments will be restricted to a cultivar that has been tested at the NDSU Absaraka Horticulture Research Farm.

Pink Flair Sargent Cherry
- *Prunus sargentii* 'JFS-KW58'

Based upon seven years of evaluations, Pink Flair merits widespread evaluation in the Northern Plains. It has not suffered any winter injury to date at the Absaraka site in USDA hardiness zone 3. Single pink flower clusters ornament the trees in spring. No fruits have been observed to date but are described as 1/3 inch (.8 cm) long, ovoid, purple-black drupes ripening in July. Leaves are semi-glossy and dark green. Fall colour has varied from attractive red-purple to orange-red in NDSU trials. J. Frank Schmidt & Son Co. (nursery grower in Oregon) lists orange-red for autumn colour in its catalogue description. Expected height is 25 feet (7½ m) and spread, 15 feet (4½ m), with an upright, narrow vase-like form. Bark is polished purplish with tannish-cream lenticels, but colour may change somewhat as trees age. Could this be the first flowering tree cherry with pink flowers that proves to be hardy in zone 3–4? Available in nursery trade.

Emerald Charm Cherry
- *Prunus* x 'Morgenson' (2007,
collaborative NDSU introduction)

In the mid-1980's, Greg Morgenson, manager of Lincoln-Oakes Nurseries, Bismarck, ND, collected seed from a planting of Mongolian Cherry (*Prunus fruticosa*) in the Northern Plains. Some authors list the common name as European Dwarf Cherry or European Ground Cherry Bush. This species is native in central and eastern Europe to Siberia and typically grows as a multi-stemmed suckering, dense shrub 4–6 feet (1¼–1⅞ m) tall. Emerald Charm, a unique seedling selection, grows into an attractive small tree reaching 20–25 feet (6–7½ m) by 15–18 feet (4½–5½ m) wide. It grows upright, multi-branched, and vase-shaped in form with a uniformly spreading crown. It may be grown as a single or multi-stemmed specimen similar to Japanese tree lilac. A collaborative release by NDSU, Emerald Charm is a putative hybrid between *P. fruticosa* and an unknown cherry species. It has good vigour under clean cultivation, averaging 1¼ feet (⅓ m) of growth annually over a 16-year period. Growth is most rapid in earlier years. Emerald Charm produces masses of small, white flowers in spring, followed by dark green, very lustrous leaves, which are smaller than other cherry species. The thick-textured foliage holds up well during summer heat stress, becoming attractive yellow in autumn colour. Emerald Charm is apparently sterile, having produced no fruit after 16 years, even though planted in proximity to five other cherry species. It has been very hardy in zone 3, one to two zones colder than the hardiness of many cherry species and cultivars. Bark colour is a dark reddish-brown and unlike Amur Chokecherry (*P. maackii*), no winter bark splitting has been observed. Propagation by mid-August budding on *P. maackii* and *P. cerasus* 'Meteor' (Meteor Sour Cherry) seedling rootstocks was very successful and eliminates suckering. Budding on *P. avium* (Sweet or Mazzard Cherry), a somewhat less hardy rootstock, was not as successful. This small tree will offer an attractive landscape alternative with superior foliage to most crabapple and other smaller tree species. We are encouraging wholesale nursery firms to begin producing this new cultivar so it can be made available to the public for planting in the future.

Amur Chokecherry - *Prunus maackii*

This cherry species, native to Manchuria and Korea, is also listed under the more preferable common names of Amur Cherry and Manchurian Cherry. It has been planted as an ornamental small, rounded tree for many years in northern regions for its white flower racemes, variably exfoliating golden-orange to coppery-cinnamon coloured showy bark, and zone 3 hardiness. However, in more recent years, this species has lost some of its popularity due to a longevity problem. Trees often develop ill-defined bark splitting or frost cracks which cause tree decline. Small 1/4 inch (⅝ cm) red, matur-

ing to black, rounded fruits ripen in August. Two improved cultivars have been introduced by Jeffries Nurseries, Portage la Prairie, MB in recent years. 'Jefree' - Goldrush grows 25 feet (7½ m) tall by 20 feet (6 m) wide and is reputed to be resistant to trunk frost cracking, with flaky coppery-orange bark. 'Jefspur' - Goldspur is a new dwarf selection growing 15 feet (4½ m) tall by 10 feet (3 m) wide. It is well suited for confined urban landscapes, being more upright and compact, with tufty dark green foliage. The latter cultivars are commercially available in Canada and hopefully may become available in the future for planting in the northern United States.

Although flowering crabapples have been the most popular ornamental tree in the United States for over 40 years, apple scab, fireblight, cedar-apple rust and other diseases have definitely reduced the value of many crabapple cultivars. The time is right for nurserymen, landscape architects/designers, as well as consumers, to promote greater diversity in Northern Plains landscape plantings. The *Pyrus* and *Prunus* cultivars discussed in this article could expand the palette of small landscape tree choices. To top it off, you haven't even gone astray if you love the family *Rosaceae*, because they are 'first cousins' to the genus *Malus* - Crabapple. 🐾

(Ed Czernecki)

Daylilies – A Brief History
by Barb Laschkewitsch and Bryce Farnsworth

*Research Specialists
Department of Plant
Sciences-North Dakota
State University,
Fargo, ND, USA*

From *Hemerocallis* 'Apricot' (Yeld 1893) to *H.* 'Omaha Sunshine' (Kaskel-Baker 2005), the daylily beds at North Dakota State University have a variety sure to please just about anybody. Over 1500 cultivars of daylilies (genus *Hemerocallis*), both historic (pre-1970) and contemporary (post-1970), are on the campus of North Dakota State University in Fargo, North Dakota.

The daylily has a long and varied history. Written records indicate the daylily was cultivated and used in China as far back as 2697 B.C. for food, medicinal and ornamental purposes. Due to trade between China and Europe, the daylily found its way to Europe in the 1500's A.D. where herbalists of the time, Rembert Dodoens, Charles de l'Ecluse (Clusius) and Mathias de l'Obel (de Lobel or Lobelius) described and illustrated the plant. Originally given the names of *Asphodelus, Lilasphodelus, Liriosphodelus* and *Lilium nonbulbosum*, it was Linnaeus, in his first edition of **Species Plantarum** (1753), who gave the rugged plants the genus name of *Hemerocallis*. From the Greek *hemera* 'a day' and *kallos* 'beauty', the name literally means 'beauty for a day', in reference to the fact that each individual flower lasts only a day.

Despite having such an interesting background, it wasn't until the turn of the twentieth century that the daylily began its journey as a popular garden plant. Also, despite having been first introduced to and used in European gardens, it's the North Americans who have done the most with breeding the plant into the popular garden ornamental it has become today.

In his book, ***Hemerocallis*, The Daylily** (1989 Timber Press, Inc.) R. W. Munson, Jr. breaks the 'Breeding

Years', as he calls them, into three separate eras: The Early Years, 1900-1950; the Middle Years, 1950-1975; and the Present and Future Years, 1975-1995. He breaks them down this way, not because of any special event or landmarks, but because of the breeders who were instrumental in helping the daylily 'evolve' into what we see in gardens today.

**The Early Years
According to Munson:**
Although George Yeld of England developed *H*. 'Apricot', the first hybrid daylily of which there is a definite record, it is Dr. Arlow Burdette Stout (1876-1957) of the United States who is considered 'the father' of daylily breeding in North America. Described as a collector, grower, breeder and scientist, he is also the author of **Daylilies-The Wild Species and Garden Clones Both Old and New of the Genus Hemerocallis** (originally published in 1934 by Macmillan in New York), a book which is still considered to be the ultimate authority on daylily species. One goal of Dr. Stout's was to prolong the blooming season by working with late blooming species. His *H*. 'Autumn Prince', introduced in 1941, was a late blooming yellow-gold. The very first cultivar he introduced was *H*. 'Mikado' in 1929, followed by *H*. 'Wau-Bun' (1929), *H*. 'Bijou' (1932) and many others.

George Yeld of England and Amos Perry, also of England, were experimenting with daylilies but because of plant dissemination problems, their work did not have the impact in North America that Dr. Stout's did. However, one of George Yeld's introductions, *H*. 'J. S. Gayner' (1928) was heavily used by breeders in the United States during the late '40's and 50's. Other important breeders during this time mentioned by Munson in his book are Ralph Wheeler, Ophelia Taylor, Elizabeth (Miss Betty) Nesmith, Hooper P. Connell, Mary Lester and Carl S. Milliken.

**The Middle Years
According to Munson:**
The 25 years represented from 1950-1975 saw perhaps the most exciting advancements in breeding for the daylily. Over 15,000 cultivars were registered with the American Hemerocallis Society (AHS) and more than 450 people were breeding, naming and/or selling daylilies during this time.

Breeders of importance during this era included:
• Dr. Ezra Kraus, a professor of botany and breeder of daylilies and chrysanthemums.
• David F. Hall, a lawyer who was a breeder of *Iris* initially, and then daylilies. His breeding work introduced the colors pink and rose into the daylily.
• Elmer A. Claar, a Chicago businessman who is credited with bringing creped and ruffled yel-

lows as well as rich, broad-petaled red into the daylily pool.

(Fran Wershler)

- W. B. MacMillan of Abbeville, Louisiana was known for featuring cultivars with low scapes, evergreen foliage and broad, full, round, flat, and ruffled flowers. The form of flower he developed was referred to as 'the MacMillan' and was still used as a comparison form when Munson's book was written in 1989.
- Edna Spalding, also of Louisiana, was also known for her pink and purple selections.
- Husband and wife team, Frank and Peggy Childs of Jenkinsburg, Georgia also contributed greatly to the daylily world. Their main contribution probably came in the form of the clear pink color of several of his varieties.
- Virginia Peck was one of the early breeders of tetraploid daylilies. Her *H.* 'Dance Ballerina Dance' was the earliest tetraploid with extensive ruffling which has been a very important advance.
- James Marsh was one of the Chicago area hybridizers who became best known for his work with pinks and lavenders. He was an early convert to the tetraploids. Many of his introductions were in two series - The Chicago series and the Prairie series.
- Brother Charles Reckamp spent more than forty years hybridizing daylilies. He worked mostly with pastel colors and was one of the first to develop a gold edge on the petals.
- Steve C. Moldovan spent most of his life in the breeding of daylilies. He was one of the breeders in the Chicago area and he used southern varieties on northern ones in order to obtain clones which did well over a wider area.
- R. W. (Bill) Munson, Jr. was part of a family of Hemerocallis breeders. His mother, sister, niece and great niece, have all been active in the work. He is primarily noted for the 'watermark' - a chalky zone around the throat.
- Hugh Russell released more than 1200 varieties of daylily over his lifetime. He had the largest daylily nursery in the world at Spring, Texas.

(Additional information on the above hybridizers also came from the book **Daylilies - A Fifty Year Affair** written by Frances Gatlin and published by the American Hemerocallis Society in 1995.)

One of the more significant (and perhaps controversial) developments to emerge during this time was that of the tetraploid daylily. Increased genetic knowledge in the 1950's led some breeders to wonder what would happen if the diploid daylily could be converted to a tetraploid. With the use of colchicine (an alkaloid isolated from the Autumn Crocus (*Colchicum autumnale*)), breeders were able to double the normal chromosome number of the daylily. The process of getting the plants to double their chromosome numbers with colchicine was something not easily accomplished and initially, only a handful of breeders were up to the tedious, often difficult task. Even if a breeder did successfully double the number of chromosomes, the induced tetraploid lacked the high fertility of a diploid and seed production from a successful tetraploid was not easy. So, why would the breeders want to induce tetraploids if it was a tedious task

and the resulting plant might not be reproduced by seed? Tetraploid flowers are normally larger, colors are brighter and more intense, scapes are stronger and sturdier, and the plants have greater vegetative vigor.

Initially, three breeders persevered at the task of developing tetraploids: Hamilton Traub, Quinn Buck, and Robert Schreiner. As their successes grew and the techniques were more refined, breeders such as Orville Fay, Bob Griesbach, Virginia Peck and Toru Arisume began developing their own approaches and techniques. They were followed by James Marsh, Brother Charles Reckamp, Bill Munson, Ida Munson, Frank and Peggy Childs, Steve Moldovan, Willard Barrere, Edgar Brown, Lucille Warner and Nate Rudolph.

From 1960-1965, only 17 induced tetraploid daylilies were registered with the AHS. By 1968, 66 seedling tetraploids (cultivars from tetraploid parents) were registered, and by the time Munson's book was written in 1989, over 5,000 tetraploids had been registered.

The Present and Future Years
According to Munson:

Interest in daylily breeding and development continues to grow. World wide interest is increasing with breeding programs emerging

(Sandy Venton)

in Europe and Australia. Although Munson ends this era at 1995, we know that interest in the daylily is at an all time high with over 50,000 cultivars registered by the AHS.

Trends in Daylily Breeding

There seem to be many trends in daylily breeding all happening at the same time. Certainly traditional breeding of the 'bagel' type continues very strongly among most of the large breeders. At the same time there is new interest in the spider types which had fallen into disuse over the years.

Much of the early breeding was done in the north. Breeders gradually moved south because they could obtain bloom in a year or so from seed whereas we in the north can take as long as 3 years. Bloom in a year allows a breeding program to move forward with improvements much faster. There are now a lot more amateur and professional breeders in the north. The advantage for those of us living up here is obvious—if a plant is bred up here on The Prairies, it should be able to handle whatever Mother Nature throws at it.

Some breeders are going back to the past for germplasm. Some are using old varieties as well as the species with success.

Our AHS region is composed of Iowa, Manitoba, Minnesota, Nebraska, North Dakota, and South Dakota. We have hybridizers who are doing traditional breeding as well as the unconventional, using older varieties and species which were not used by the early breeders.

The Daylily Collection at NDSU

To view some of the historic daylilies mentioned in this article, plan a visit to the historic daylily beds at the Horticulture Demonstration and Research Plots at North Dakota State University in Fargo, ND, USA. They are open to the public throughout the growing season and guided tours are available on request. Besides the daylily beds, the area also has a bedding plant trial area, an iris collection and miscellaneous perennials on display. Please contact Bryce Farnsworth at 701-793-8812 or Barb Laschkewitsch at 701-231-8163 for more information. 🦌

Recommended Reading

To learn more about the daylily, the following books are recommended:

The Color Encyclopedia of Daylilies. Ted. L. Petit and John P. Peat. (2000 Timber Press, Inc.)

Daylilies - A Fifty Year Affair. Frances Gatlin (1995 American Hemerocallis Society)

Daylilies The Wild Species and Garden Clones, Both Old and New, of the Genus *Hemerocallis* by A. B. Stout (1986 Sagapress, Inc.)

The Gardener's Guide to Growing Daylilies. Diana Grenfell. (1998 Timber Press, Inc.)

***Hemerocallis* Day Lilies.** (translated from the German by Alexander Helm). Walter Erhardt. (1992 Timber Press, Inc.)

***Hemerocallis,* The Daylily** by R. W. Munson, Jr. (1989 Timber Press, Inc.)

The Weird And Clever World Of Carnivorous Plants
by Joyce Graham Fogwill

Pitcher plant - Sarracenia purpurea (Joyce Graham Fogwill)

Joyce is very interested in carnivorous plants and lends her time and talents to the Carnivorous Plant Collection at the Assiniboine Park Conservatory. She is passionate about science education for children. She was an instructor in the Chemical and Bioscience Technology Program at Red River College until her retirement.

The busy little bumblebee* moves from flower to flower in the acid boggy meadow, teeming with honey bees, bumblebees, flies, ants, mosquitoes and other insects. The wind wafts a subtle inviting aroma from a colourful red 'flower'. The bee wanders down the red-veined cavern covered with downward pointing hairs. The path downward soon becomes smooth and waxy and the bumblebee cannot reverse its way back to the entrance. It suddenly loses its footing on the waxy surface and falls into liquid at the bottom of the 'flower'. It cannot escape and it drowns. This is no flower, this is a trap and the bee is now food for this clever carnivore which 'eats' insects – *Sarracenia purpurea* – the North American Pitcher plant.

Carnivorous plants? Plants that feed on animals? Is this true? Yes, there are plants that feed on animals such as insects, other small invertebrates and even small lizards and mice. These unique plants have reversed nature's normal order of animals eating plants. These weird plants are found all over the world, including Manitoba.

The Assiniboine Park Conservatory has a large collection of Carnivorous plants on public display. The collection consists of representative species of carnivorous plants native to various parts of the world such as Borneo, Canada, Europe, Malaysia, South Africa and the United States.

These plants are photosynthetic but since little or no nutrients are available to them in their natural habitats, they have developed the ability to trap and digest animal matter (usually small insects) to supplement their nutritional requirements, principally nitrogen and potassium. This nutritional adaptation allows these carnivorous plants to thrive in soils where most other plants cannot.

Carnivorous plant habitats are varied and include rain forests, acid bogs, barrens, mountainous and non-mountainous areas, rocky (sometimes moss covered), wet and other inhospitable areas. Opinions vary, but these remarkable flowering plants belong in seven to nine plant families, 15 to 17 genera with up to 550 species or more and an increasing number of hybrids, subspecies, and varieties. Their distribution is worldwide, over different climatic zones in places such as Australia, Borneo, Canada, Europe, Southeast Asia, South Africa, Malaysia, United States, Venezuela's Tepuis (plateaus) and Mexico.

Carnivorous plant habitats in Manitoba include the Gull Lake Wetlands, located in the southeast corner of Lake Winnipeg, immediately north of the Brokenhead First Nation (Scanterbury bog). Species reported are *Sarracenia purpurea, Drosera rotundifolia, Pinguicula vulgaris* and *Utricularia vulgaris.*

Carnivorous plants which are native to temperate and colder regions like Manitoba undergo winter dormancy in their natural habitats. Most tropical species of carnivorous plants do not have a dormant period.

See the colour section for photographs of a few of the variety of ingenious trapping mechanisms and adaptations of these plants. They have developed clever disguises such as unusual and exotic shapes, pleasant aromas, showy colours with masking patterns and innovative plant structures to attract their prey. Their adaptations lure the unsuspecting prey to enter the traps from which they rarely can escape.

Dionaea muscipula - *Venus Fly Trap with open trap about to close on prey*
(Joyce Graham Fogwill)

Examples from the Assiniboine Park Conservatory collection at include:

Sarracenia – trumpet pitchers, *Nepenthes* – monkey cups, *Drosera* – sundews, *Dionaea* – Venus Fly Traps and *Pinguicula* – butterworts.

Sarracenia – The North American Pitcher plants grow from ground level to as much as one meter (3 feet) tall. Their habitats include swamps, bogs and sandy peaty wetlands.

Sarracenia purpurea – is indigenous to Canada and its habitat extends as far north as the southern part of the Northwest Territories. Their leaves are modified to form hollow traps, with a lid; the inner part with nectar secreting glands. The large lid acts as a colourful veined landing platform, insects are directed downward and fall to the bottom of the trap. The plant's digestive aids may include enzymes, wetting agents, insect narcotics and bacterial action.

Nepenthes are tropical pitcher plants (sometimes called Monkey cups) and usually grow as climbing or scrambling vines with elaborate, attractive pitchers. They are found in southeast Asia, Borneo and Sumatra, south China, Indonesia, Malaysia, Seychelles, Australia, New Caledonia, India and Sri Lanka. They prefer sunny ridges, slopes and stunted forests with bright diffuse light. Pitchers (cups) form at the end of each leaf connected by a leaf petiole. Tendrils coil around branches so the vine gets support to reach the forest canopy. Their prey include insects and even small lizards and frogs.

Dionaea – Venus Fly Traps are native to the Carolinas in the eastern United States. They are found in grassy plains in damp, sandy, acidic peat and boggy soils which are fringed or dotted with pine trees which have periodic fires. The trap leaves are 5–10 centimetres (2–4 inches) long and have two V-shaped, spiny, slightly fleshy hinged pads, each with three small trigger hairs. When the triggers are touched in quick succession by the insect, the trap snaps shut and the outer 'fangs' form a cage preventing escape. Digestive juices exude from special cells in the Venus Fly Trap to digest the insect. Traps with prey will remain closed from 7 to 14 days before opening to expose the dry remains of the prey.

Sarracenia leucophylla - *The white-topped pitcher plant* (Joyce Graham Fogwill)

Drosera – Sundews. Their habitats include a wide range of climatic zones in many parts of the world such as Europe, North America, Africa, Asia and Australia. Their habitats are varied and include snow covered mountains, warm dry plains, swamps and jungles. They may be erect, climbing, scrambling, fanleafed, rosette or pygmy – both tuberous or non-tuberous. They have modified leaves each with club-shaped hairs with a sugary sticky secretion at the tips of the hairs. The trapped insect causes the hairs to bend around the prey, which is digested and released when the nutrients are absorbed.

Pinguicula – Butterworts: These plants are native to North and South America and may be found in peat bogs, beside slow flowing streams and on rocks where water seeps. They form flat rosettes with greenish yellow leaves. The leaves have sessile glands which produce clear sweet smelling mucilage that causes the leaves to gleam in the sunlight and attract their prey.

There are other Carnivorous plants which are not currently in the Collection at the Assiniboine Park Conservatory. These include:

Heliamphora – Sun pitchers, Sun Cups. These are found primarily on the "Tepuis", table top sandstone plateaus of Venezuela, Guyana, and Brazil at elevations ranging from 1000 to 3000 metres (3200–9800 feet). The pitchers are tubular shaped, green to red, with reduced lids called -'nectar spoons'. They range from 4–40 cm (1.6 to 20 in) tall, depending on the habitat.

Cephalotus follicularis – The Albany Pitcher Plant is native to southwest Australia. The leaf is shaped like a small pouch. Their habitat is among 60 cm (24 in) tall grasses in sandy peaty soil.

Darlingtonia californica –The Cobra Lily. Their habitat is around bogs, streams, and springs in sphagnum moss and rock cracks in both high and low altitudes in western Oregon.

Aldrovanda – The Waterwheel Plant. This is a floating aquatic plant with a snap trap. They are worldwide and are found in various areas such as Australia, Europe and Asia.

Utricularia –Bladderworts occur in fresh water and wet soil. They are distributed worldwide

Drosophyllum – The Portuguese sundew is found in the coastal areas of Portugal, Spain and Morocco. Byblis is found in North Australia and New Guinea.

Conclusion: These wondrous carnivorous plants, occupying such harsh environments, have developed unique adaptations which ingeniously reverse nature's normal process of animals eating plants. 🦌

See page 91 for colour photos.

References:
Cheers, Gordon. **A guide to Carnivorous Plants of the World**. 1992. Harper Collins Publishers
Temple, Paul. **Carnivorous Plants.**1993. Cassel Educational Limited for The Royal Horticultural Society
*Story source: Graham Fogwill, J., 2009: **Bubs -The Bumblebee and her most unfortunate fortunate adventure**. Author- House.

Gardening on the Eve of Climate Change
by Carla Keast

Carla is a freelance writer and landscape design consultant. She has a Master of Landscape Architecture and a Bachelor of Science degree and has been published in the Manitoba Gardener, The Cottager, and the Winnipeg Free Press.

In the face of significant weather change as a result of global warming, how do we protect our gardens to keep them healthy? And just as important, can our gardens help heal our planet?

Exactly what changes to expect is one of the big uncertainties of climate change, which makes preparing for it somewhat difficult. There are a lot of ideas out there. Most are variations on three things: manage the plants; manage the water; and manage the carbon.

Managing plants means matching the growing conditions of the garden with the growing preferences of the plants, growing several varieties of plants rather than several of the same variety, growing plants that will withstand a variety of conditions, and adding some native plants to the garden.

There's talk of a longer growing season, which makes many of us hardiness zone 3 gardeners dream of being upgraded to zone 4 or 5. Unfortunately, our usual winter low temperatures are expected to remain, which means that our hardiness zone will probably not change.

What is likely though, is weather extremes: longer drought periods, longer rainy seasons, earlier than usual frost, later than usual frost – we prairie gardeners and our plants have developed a fairly decent resilience to surprise frosts. We protect the vulnerable plants, and the rest hunker down and 'tough it out' through the frosty nights. But that long wet rainy event that was supposed to be summer in 2009? And my goodness, it's late April (2010) and we haven't had a drop of rain.

As gardeners we know where the wet and dry spots are in our gardens. In the past, with reasonable weather and willing plants (and perhaps a bit of extra watering) we may have been able to grow plants that weren't that well suited to our gardens. During weather extremes, though, these are going to be the problem areas – low areas are going to become waterlogged sponges during wet spells and dry spots are going to become appalling collections of dust during drought. Knowing the wettest and driest places in our garden, and planting moisture lovers and drought lovers in those areas, will certainly help keep our plants alive.

I lost all of my Silver Princess Shasta Daisy (*Leucanthemum super-*

bum 'Silver Princess') and Moonshine Yarrow (*Achillea* 'Moonshine') in 2009. I had put them together in a low spot in a border, not because they love moisture, but because this was a location where they would deliver the most 'visual bang' from the deck and the kitchen window. In hindsight, the daisy probably had just the right moisture during more normal years. The site was probably much too moist for the yarrow, but it persevered, because that's what yarrow do. A summer of extreme moisture, however, was simply too much for the yarrow. I'll be replacing them, and relocating them to places that suit their growing preferences more precisely.

Another idea is to diversify. If you've lost plants, rather than simply replacing them, add some new ones to the mix. Not only am I going to move the yarrow to a drier location, I'm going to plant Silver Yarrow (*A. clavennae*) along side the 'Moonbeam'. The 'Silver Princess' can go to the edge of the low spot and I'll combine it with 'Becky' or 'Snow Lady' (*Lilium superbum* ' Becky', *L. superbum* 'Snow Lady'). With a few varieties of the right plants in the right places, some are bound to survive the next round of extreme weather.

Choosing plants that will withstand a wide variety of growing conditions contributes to a healthy garden. Daylily, Iris, Peony, Caragana, Honeysuckle, and Dogwood come to mind. While we probably don't want to restrict our gardens to these selec-tions, part of the reason they are so common is that they are so resilient.

In addition to weather extremes, there are also predictions that the prairies will experience more drought than we are used to. Adding some drought tolerant plants will help carry our garden through dry years. Including some native plants is always a good idea, as they've developed a variety of ways to survive harsh prairie conditions, and many of them are more likely to be drought tolerant.

With our growing understanding of the importance of water conservation, many of us have already started changing the way we manage our water. Many gardeners have implemented the use of soaker hoses and carefully managed lawn waterings. The focus of water management with an eye on climate change is not only to water more selectively, but to make better use of the water that arrives on site through rainfall or snowmelt. The old fashioned rain barrel is new again.

Many of us use mulch as a weed suppressant. But mulch is also a great way of collecting water. A layer of mulch in a bed or border will shatter raindrops into small fragments that can percolate down into the soil, rather than running off and carrying away the soil with it. Mulch has the added bonus of protecting the soil from the sun, which slows down evaporation significantly. A mulched bed needs considerably less watering than one with exposed soil.

Taking it a step further is the idea of creating areas within the garden to collect and hold rainwater and snowmelt, rather than draining it to the street. These areas are called downspout gardens and bog gardens. They can be dressed up with moisture loving plants to become a feature garden, or they can simply be a shallow ditch lined with landscape fabric and filled with stones. They are essentially a tiny retention pond that collects runoff and allows it to slowly percolate into the surrounding soil.

Managing plants and water is not big news to most gardeners. But what about managing carbon?

Global warming is all about the carbon cycle, something that most of us memorized half-heartedly in school thinking that it had very little to do with us personally, however, times change.

In very simple terms, carbon is the building block of organic life. Carbon doesn't break down. It serves its purpose and then gets passed along to its next job. The cycle part describes the way it circulates through our biosphere. Starting in the air, a plant uses it to grow a leaf; a bug eats the leaf and uses it to grow wings; a bird eats the bug and uses it to grow muscle; the bird dies and the carbon either gets released into the soil or into the air. A plant will take it back from the air and the cycle starts again. Some feel there's too much carbon in the air right now – carbon dioxide and other

greenhouse gases may be contributing to global warming.

What can we as gardeners do to reduce the amount of carbon dioxide in the atmosphere? Plants are very efficient at removing pollutants and trees in particular play an important role. Adding a tree or two to our garden can be your contribution to improving the environment in the community. Trees are also very effective at helping us to reduce our energy costs by providing shade for our homes in the summer and wind protection in the winter. In addition to the savings on energy costs, relying less on air conditioners and furnaces means that fewer air pollutants are released into the atmosphere.

Another valuable carbon management tool is composting. Not only is composting a healthy means of returning organic matter to the soil, but it's also a means of reducing our carbon footprint. Good composting practices move carbon back into the soil, where plants can make use of it. However, poor composting practise releases carbon into the air in the form of methane. This can be avoided by keeping the compost heap moist (but not too moist) and turned regularly. But to really manage the carbon in our garden, we need to compost all the organic material – all the fruit and vegetable wastes, leaves, grass clippings and small branches – rather than sending it to the landfill, where its decomposition produces methane.

Obviously, our gas powered garden tools are a significant source of carbon emissions. How do we part with them? Try topdressing the lawn with one of the new slow growing seed mixes. It won't eliminate the need for mowing but is supposed to reduce it considerably. Consider replacing low traffic areas of the lawn with some low maintenance ground covers. As for the leaves that collect in our bog gardens? A leaf rake removes most. The wind also helps out. I sometimes pluck a few others out by hand, and the rest, I simply ignore.

Keeping our gardens healthy in the face of climate change will require changes in how we garden. Some, we'll be able to control; others, maybe not. But as prairie gardeners, it seems to me that we have a head start — we've already learned how to be resilient and patient. 🐌

Rosemates
by Claire Bérubé

Claire is the Perennial Expert at Jardins St-Léon Gardens in St. Boniface, MB. She answers clients' questions and consults for the garden centre, as well as managing the Perennials, Shrubs, Roses and Herb departments.

Felix Leclerc – Canadian Artist series of roses
(Jim Kohut)

Ask any serious rose grower what they plant next to their rose bushes and you'll invariably get a dumbstruck look and reply "a rose of course!"

Some of us enjoy roses as a feature of our landscape, not as a mass planting, but rather as individual plants that are part of an ensemble.

Growing roses isn't just about roses, it's about incorporating them into the overall landscape. Although most serious rose gardeners think of roses as needing to be planted together in a particular, set aside bed with all their persnickety requirements, not every homeowner has the option or luxury of tearing up his front boulevard to accommodate twenty or more rose cultivars. Instead, most gardeners are looking to add just one or no more than a few rose bushes to their landscape.

This is where certain considerations or problems arise. Tea roses need room to breathe. Floribundas and grandifloras grow tall and wide. Explorers series climb or take over a three foot space and the older Parkland Series variety roses have a tendency to grow tall and flop over.

Some plants complement roses better than others. Some make us sigh in ecstasy while others make us close our eyes in shock. Some rosarians go strictly for fragrance, while others are more concerned with characteristics such as form, shape, climber, cover, rampant, hedge, and so on. Like my mother used to say: "Tastes are not to be discussed."

I'm partial to 'Lorraine Sunshine' false sunflowers (*Heliopsis helianthoides*) as a show-caser beside my 'Meidiland Red' rose, as the variegated leaves of the *Heliopsis* makes the dark green of the rose stand out. The rose is a dwarf variety and serves to 'anchor' the mostly cream leaves of the false sunflower to the bed's ground. Additionally, the false sunflower sacrifices itself by attracting the aphids that would otherwise attack my rose.

Irises, in particular the variegated leaved ones, tend to give length and structure to a ground cover rose. Popping up here and there, they bloom before the roses. *Iris pallida* (Sweet Iris or Dalmatian Iris) is a favourite as its sweet fragrance wafts up to my front porch a week before the rose does.

"What about grasses?" you ask. While miniature annual grasses such as Fibre Optic grass and the perennial blue fescue work well, I wouldn't recommend invasive grasses such as ribbon grass (*Phalaris arundinacea L* var. *variegata*). If you want your hybrid tea rose or any other plant in your flower bed to survive, stay away from this root and ground-eating devourer. An even worse plant is the dreaded bishop's gout weed or snow on the mountain (*Aegopodium podagraria* 'Variegata'). Now there's a plant to give any gardener nightmares—unless you have sold your home and are mad at your neighbour, I don't recommend you even plant a single rootlet!

Perennial geraniums tend to be good companions, blooming most of the early to mid-summer, supporting the shiny brightness of rose leaves with their muted, dark-green split and dentated leaves. The Dwarf Crane's-bill geranium (*Geranium cinereum*) varieties are short, tidy clumps of grey-green foliage that look like little puffs next to your plants. I use them as edgers. 'Ballerina' is a variety with a pale pink tone, 'Purple Pillow' has a dark, magenta flower, perfect to accent those pale pink and yellow shaded roses.

Be careful with shrubs. Don't plant them too close. Stay away from known suckering shrubs such as lilacs and Russian almond. Purple-leaved dwarfs such as 'Guincho Purple' elder (*Sambucus niger*) or a dark-leaved ninebark (*Physocarpus* 'Diabolo') look awesome next to a rugosa rose with dark or light pink flowers. Look for a leaf colour that will highlight not only the rose's bloom but also its leaves. For example take the 'Hansa' rose. Its rugosa leaves are crinkly and rough. Pair it with a smooth-leaved hosta that tolerates sun like 'Sum and Substance' or 'Sun Power' that loves all day sun and you have a winning, eye-popping combination.

If you have roses in shade, try placing a lime-leaved Coral Bell (*Heuchera*) or Foam Flower (*Tiarella*) as a ground cover under it. It will make your rose stand out; give it room to breathe and it might just reduce a little of the mildew factor.

Pair yellow roses with its complementary colour of blue or contrasting purple, such as delphiniums or salvias. Pink roses with silver foliage such as 'Silver Mound' or 'Valerie Finnis' wormwoods (*Artemisia specs.*), pair nicely with Lamb's ears (*Stachys lantana*) -although it might creep too much for you or the new giant-leaved salvia with its strikingly, bright blue flowers. Red roses go with almost anything: add yellow and you cry "Hot!", add silver and you say "Aah!", white and your eyes adjust easily.

Roses that have an upright habit are best suited for mixed borders and beds. As well, hybrid teas benefit from lower plants and medium height ones close by – but not next to them, providing buffers to strong summer winds and mulch retainers in winter. In summer they also provide a little bit of shade to the rose's root structure. Dwarf phloxes work well too, as long as you place them 30 cm (12 in.) away.

Plan your rosemates carefully and you'll surely enjoy a healthier and more appealing landscape. 🦋

Tips for Planting Pots

If one has an aversion to watering pots and containers, it's good to try using a selection of succulents and cactus in the pots. They are currently enjoying popularity because they require infrequent watering, will stand dry, bright, sunny locations and come is a great variety of shapes and sizes. Many succulents make good winter houseplants when the garden season is finished.

Phalaenopsis orchid
(Elena Gaillard)

Orchids - Not Just for Eccentric Millionaires
by Yvonne Dean

Yvonne Dean was the editor of The 2003 Prairie Garden.
She is a horticulturist and graphic designer currently living in Maple Ridge, BC.

Just thinking about orchids conjures up visions of exotic tropical islands, plant hunters and conservatories filled with lush greenery and blooms in spectacular shapes and colours, lovingly tended by an eccentric millionaire. Orchids have a reputation of being demanding plants whose mysterious ways are known only to a few dedicated fanatics, those who possess green hands instead of just a green thumb.

In truth, orchids are not all that difficult to grow, although they are often pricey and a millionaire's wallet would definitely help. As long as

their basic requirements of temperature, light, water and nutrients are met, they generally thrive and reward the patient gardener with long-lasting blooms. If you can grow an African violet, you can grow a *Phalaenopsis* orchid. Their ideal environments are quite similar.

Many orchids have similar needs. They are generally comfortable at the same room temperature we are with a slightly cooler temperature at night. There are three temperature ranges suited to growing orchids: 'cool' with nights between 10°–13° C (50°–55° F), 'intermediate' with nights between 13°–15.6° C (55°–60° F), and 'warm' with nights between 15.6°–18° C (60°–65° F). They require adequate light; generally not direct sun, but bright light throughout the day. Insufficient light is the most frequent cause of failure to bloom. With excessive light, the leaves will become yellowish; insufficient light, and they will turn a dark lush green.

A porous growing medium such as bark chips, perlite and peat moss, rather than soil, ensures proper drainage and most closely mimics their natural habitat. Most orchids like to be watered and then allowed to become almost dry before the next watering. A tray of moist pebbles placed underneath the pot will provide the necessary humidity. A 'weakly bi-weekly' fertilization schedule works best for most orchids. If the orchid is not in bloom, apply 30–10–10 fertilizer, mixed at one quarter to one half the recommended strength. For plants that are in bloom, a weak solution of 10–20–20 is all they require but feed only healthy plants and don't be in a hurry to repot. Every one to two years is generally adequate. Some orchids love to send out roots looking for things to cling to so this isn't necessarily an indication that they are rootbound.

Orchids are not generally bothered by insects. However, there are some pests to lookout for: mealy bug, scale insects and Phalaenopsis mites – these can devastate an orchid collection. Mealy bug and scale are often brought in with plants obtained from 'friends'. These 2 pests are very hard to eradicate and are known to infect your orchids with dangerous viral diseases. Phalaenopsis mites may be controlled by: spraying with miticides; higher humidity; and daily misting. They are microscopically small, but leave sunken yellowish areas on the leaves. Sow bugs and snails can also damage the roots of orchids.

Orchids will, however, sometimes, develop something white and fuzzy in the growing medium. This is 'snow mould' and the best solution is to dispose of the old growing medium. Make sure the roots and pot are clean before transferring the plant to new medium. The most common cause of snow mould is overwatering.

Overwatering can also cause black rot and root rot. If any part of the orchid looks black and mushy or brown (brown indicates root rot), particularly when combined with the appearance of wilted leaves, chances are it has one of these diseases. Remove the diseased area by cutting it away with a sterilized knife. Repot in fresh sterilized media and make sure to sterilize the pot as well, to prevent the transfer of the fungus. Keep the water out of your monopodial plant (for instance *Phalaenopsis* type growth).

One thing orchids don't like is tobacco smoke. Tobacco residue on your hands can give orchids a disease called tobacco mosaic. If you didn't have a reason to quit smoking before, you have one now!

There are three varieties that are relatively easy to grow: *Phalaenopsis, Cattleya* and the *Dendrobium*. Many cities have orchid societies that put on displays for the public to give you an idea of what each looks like. Speaking with orchid growers will also give you an idea as to the different needs of each.

The *Phalaenopsis* or moth orchid, with its long arching stems, is a familiar sight and probably one of the most popular houseplant orchids. It is certainly one of the easiest to grow. These orchids prefer bright light, (summer 500–1,000 foot candles, winter 1,500–2,000 foot candles), but avoid placing them in direct sun. If there is too little light, the leaves will become quite dark. Moth orchids require several nights below 17° C (63° F) to trigger blooms. After they have finished blooming, cut the flower stem back to just above a node on the stem. This will induce new growth after about a month, followed by blooms two to three months later.

Probably the most exotic and beautiful of all is the corsage, or *Cattleya*, orchid. Many of these varieties have a desirable fragrance. These orchids prefer bright light (2,000–3,000 foot candles) – a south window with sheers is perfect. These orchids can also stand higher temperatures (18° –27° C / 64–81° F) if there is increased airflow around the plant. If the plant is upright with no need for staking, the light is adequate. Insufficient light results in a dark green,

limp plant. Allow mature *Cattleyas* to dry out between waterings. As with most orchids, place the pot on a tray of moist pebbles to increase humidity. They will not tolerate overwatering.

The *Dendrobium* orchid is grown for its long arching sprays of blooms and is one of the largest groups within the orchid family. They require bright light and can tolerate higher temperatures up to 30° C (86° F) if the air circulation and humidity are increased. Again, they need to be placed on a tray of moistened pebbles. Cut back on watering in the fall after any new growth matures to produce new blooms. If all the leaves fall off your *Dendrobium* (belonging to the deciduous species), don't panic. They tend to do this. If the cane is still firm, relax. This is where the next flower spikes will appear.

There are many, many more types of orchids. These are just some of the more familiar and easiest to grow. As many as 25,000 species exist, found on every continent except Antarctica, and there are about 105,000 man-made hybrids. They range from absolutely breath-taking blooms to downright homely – flowers that only a dedicated orchid collector could love. If you have the chance to visit an orchid farm or orchid show, you'll be hooked on these spectacular plants. 🌢

Gardeners Beware:
Invasive Species to Avoid Planting!
by *Sandi Faber Routley and Cheryl Hemming*

---

*Sandi is an Invasive Species Technician and Cheryl is the
Coordinator of The Invasive Species Council of Manitoba.*

Spring brings with it the excitement and anticipation of gardening, and many of us can't wait to go to the nursery and pick out the most attractive, unique plants for our yards. While pondering which flowers to purchase, we rarely consider the affect these beautiful species would have on the surrounding environment if they were to escape. Perhaps we believe that by planting them in our yard, where they are contained and controlled, there is little chance they will be able to spread to natural areas. In addition, we generally trust the source of our plants, thinking it must be 'safe' to grow in Manitoba if it is being sold by a local nursery. In both cases, we may be sorely mistaken.

Every year gardeners bring home non-native plants and introduce them into the environment, and every year there are risks for some of these species to spread into natural areas and cause problems. The impact on the environment and economy caused by a few foreign species is, to say the least, 'not so pretty'. But how are you to know which plants are okay and which are not? Where can you get the facts you need in order to be properly prepared to identify plants that are dangerous? This is where we can help. The Invasive Species Council of Manitoba is a non-profit organization providing a collaborative approach to the prevention, early detection, management and potential eradication of invasive species in Manitoba. Our vision is to work together with our stakeholders and the public to maintain a healthy, bio-diverse landscape in Manitoba. By providing you with information and resources on invasive species, you will have the tools to assist in achieving this goal.

What Are Invasive Species?

Invasive species are plants, animals or other organisms that are growing out of their country or region of origin and are outcompeting or even replacing native organisms. Since they come from ecosystems in other parts of the world, 'unwanted invaders' escape their natural enemies. This means they are missing the natural checks and balances that would naturally contain them in their home environments. They have a distinct advantage over our native species whose populations are controlled by local predators, competitors, or disease.

Are You Involved with Dangerous Annuals?

From garden plants to escape artists, some alien species have found their way into our natural environment and wreaked havoc on native vegetation and agriculture land. In the past there have been a few annuals which have 'gotten away' and currently we are faced with the challenge of innovatively controlling and monitoring their spread. Kochia *(Kochia scoparia)*, scentless chamomile *(Matricaria perforata)*, and Himalayan balsam *(Impatiens glandulifera)* are examples of annuals which have invaded natural areas in Manitoba. If you have any of these species in your yard it is important to remove them, and this is why….

The **Himalayan Balsam** is a tall annual plant, originally from the western Himalayas, which is thought to have been introduced by foreign ships or from ornamental escapes. This species is found in gardens throughout Manitoba, and according to the City of Winnipeg Weed Inspector these impatiens are becoming a concern as they are found increasingly around the city. Himalayan balsam ejects seeds into rivers and streams which spread far and fast to new locations. It is highly competitive, difficult to remove, and is known to regularly suffocate native vegetation and take over entire areas.

Kochia is a summer annual broadleaf weed, also known as summer cypress and burning bush, which is on the increase in parts of Manitoba, particularly in the southwest region of the province.[1] This exotic was introduced to Canada from Asia and central Europe as an ornamental planting by European immigrants. A provincial weed survey conducted in 1997 ranked kochia as the 14th most abundant weed in southwest Manitoba, an increase from the 26th position in the 1986 survey.[1] It is considered a noxious weed in Manitoba, and preventing kochia seed set and spread are important aspects of the Noxious Weeds Act.[1] Kochia has the ability to spread rapidly and quickly establishes itself in natural areas, especially at a time of drought. It is a difficult weed to manage and has dominated areas of south western Manitoba.

The **Scentless Chamomile** is of European origin and can be an annual, biennial or short-lived perennial. During the last few decades its range has expanded rapidly. This plant has a dense, fibrous root system which traps soil and moisture, enabling the weed to survive for some time after being uprooted. The plant reproduces rapidly, able to produce over half a million seeds in any given year. Scentless Chamomile has become a serious weed of agricultural crops in Manitoba, leading to considerable yield reductions. It also forms dense monocultures, displacing native species.

Gardeners Beware!

Invasive species have become a major threat to the world's ecosystems, and Manitoba's lands and waters are no exception. We have ecosystems, agriculture lands, and recreational sites whose value and health depend on maintaining native species populations. While some invaders, such as purple loosestrife, leafy spurge and common carp are well established and widespread in the province, others are just starting to establish or find their way into natural areas. At this point, it is still possible to eradicate or even prevent their spread altogether.

Salt cedar (*Tamarix ramosissima, T. parviflora*) commonly known as 'Pink Cascade' and Tamarisk, has escaped from the garden into the wild in almost all the United States including North Dakota. Salt cedar is not yet on the Manitoba Noxious Weeds List and as a result it can be found at nurseries and garden centres throughout the province. It has, however, been identified as an invasive alien species by the Canadian Food Inspection Agency, named as one of The Nature Conservancy's 'dirty dozen' weeds, and listed as one of the World Conservation Union's 100 'worst invaders.'[2] It can grow to be a shrub or small tree, and was introduced to the western United States as an ornamental in the 1800's from its native habitat in Northern Europe and Asia. This invasive alien species is very aggressive and requires large amounts of water to survive. It concentrates salt in the soil which prevents native trees and shrubs from growing in the same area; reduces water tables with the vast amounts of water it consumes; and clogs waterways with its roots. Salt cedar has adapted to tolerate a wide variety of environmental conditions and is most often found along streams, waterways, drainage areas, moist pastures, flood plains and anywhere where there is wet soil for long periods of time.

Blueweed (*Echium vulgare*) is a biennial, occasionally annual or short-lived perennial which has not strongly established itself in Manitoba. Native to Europe, blueweed grows throughout Ontario in coarse sandy or gravelly soil in pastures, waste places and roadsides. The seeds from a blueweed plant can contaminate clover and other crop seeds as well as invade rangelands and pastures. Although most seeds fall to the ground near the plant, they have a rough coat which is able to stick to clothing, animal fur and feathers and be carried to new areas.

Prevention is the best protection against both these weeds, so promptly remove any of these plants from your property and report infestations.

How Can You Help?

It's easy! A common misconception is that there is nothing you can do. By taking an active role in prevention, early detention and rapid response, you are directly contributing to protecting habitats from invasive species. There are many things you can do right now, to reduce your chances of spreading invasive species!

Stop the spread at the source by not purchasing known invasive plants; removing any in your yard; and report sightings to the Invasive Species Council of Manitoba. To avoid introducing unwanted invaders there is the option of planting native plant species. If you do prefer to use non-native plants in your garden just be careful to choose 'friendly' alternatives that are labelled as non-invasive.

Ask your nursery or garden centre to identify unlabelled plants and avoid newly released exotic species as they may not yet be determined safe for release in our environment. Avoid purchasing wildflower mixes as they often contain non-native plants including Oxeye Daisy (*Chrysanthemum leucanthemum* syn. *Leucanthemum vulgare*), Dame's rocket (*Hesperis matronalis L.*), and Common Toadflax (*Linaria vulgaris*). If you find an invasive weed in your yard remove it promptly and then dispose of the plant properly by drying it in the sun for seven to ten days and then burning or double bagging the waste.

Landscapers and gardeners can now select from a wide variety of alternative perennial and annual plants (for both terrestrial and water gardens) which pose no threat to the environment. Native plants such as Meadow blazingstar (*Liatris ligulistylis*), Giant hyssop (*Agastache foeniculum*), Purple coneflower (*Echinacea angustifolia*) and Blue flag (*Iris versicolor*) provide excellent alternatives. A great source of information for growing native species can be found in the book "Naturescape Manitoba". Some non-native plants such as Spiked speedwell (*Veronica spicata*) and Garden sage (*Salvia* spp.*) also provide safe alternatives to Purple loosestrife.

Familiarize yourself with invasive species by joining the *Invasive Species Council of Manitoba Newsletter*, picking up a copy of *Invasive Species in Manitoba: River, Lake and Wetland Invaders Pocket Field Guide* or checking out the website <www.invasivespeciesmanitoba.com>. The council also produces an annual calendar with information and pictures of invasive species to watch out for. 🦫

See page 99 for colour photos.

Sources:
[1] Province of Manitoba, Manitoba Agriculture, Food and Rural Initatives. Website: *www.gov.mb.ca/agriculture/crops/weeds*
[2] The Nature Conservancy of Canada. Website: *www.natureconservancy.ca*

ISCM's "What Not to Plant" List for Gardeners

Due to the invasive characteristics of some ornamental plants (including plants for water gardens), the ISCM has compiled the following list of 16 species to avoid when planting:

Himalayan Balsam (*Impatiens glandulifera*) - Other common names: Himalayan Orchid, Indian Balsam, Policeman's Helmet, Poor Man's Orchid

Oxeye Daisy (*Leucanthemum vulgare*)

Scentless Chamomile (*Matricaria perforata*)

Common Baby's Breath (*Gypsophila paniculata*)

Common Tansy (*Tanacetum vulgare*)

Purple Loosestrife (*Lythrum salicaria, L. virgatum*) - Cultivars: Lythrum 'Morden Pink', 'Morden Gleam'

Dame's Rocket (*Hesperis matronalis*)

Creeping Bellflower (*Campanula rapunculoides*)

Salt Cedar (*Tamarix* spp.) - and cultivar Tamarisk, 'Pink Cascade'

Toadflax, **Dalmation** (*Linaria dalmatica*) or **Yellow** (*L. vulgaris*) - Other common name: Butter-and-eggs

Leafy Spurge (*Euphorbia esula*)

Wildflower Mixes

Yellow Flag Iris (*Iris pseudacorus*)

Flowering Rush (*Butomus umbellatus*)

Water Hyacinth (*Eichhornia crassipes*)

European Frog-Bit (*Hydrocharis morsus-ranae*)

The Water Garden that Almost Wasn't
by Tena Kilmury

*Tena Kilmury is an author, photographer, gardener,
with the Brandon Garden Club in Brandon, MB
and a director with the Manitoba Horticultural Association.*

When my husband and I bought 5 acres of land on the outskirts of Brandon in the early 1970s, it was just grain land with not a twig in sight. We built a house, garage, workshop and greenhouse, and planted shelterbelts to the north and west and a lane of Northwest poplars to the east. Next came a sweeping flower and shrub border in the frontyard, and then another in the backyard.

I yearned for a rock garden. When I was much younger I had lived on a farm in the Interlake and there was no problem finding rocks there. It was a different story here, as there were no stones on or near our acreage. My husband wasn't sure he wanted to haul rocks, as he'd spent many back-breaking hours in his youth clearing farmland of stones and hauling them away. But, being good-natured, he let me have my way, and today I have six rock gardens. Many of those rocks were hauled home in the half-ton, and the rest hitched a ride in the trunks of various vehicles over the years. My whole family now shares my rock 'fetish' and can't resist picking up a pretty piece of coloured granite and bringing it here to add to my collection.

One of the first rock gardens we built was in the backyard. We thought this particular rock garden would be the perfect backdrop for a water garden, as the water could be pumped up and over it, forming a waterfall. So we got to work and dug a hole about 2 metres long by 1.2 metres wide, and .6 metres deep (4 ft x 6 ft by 2 ft depth), pouring in cement for the bottom and walls. We landscaped the edges with low growing junipers and ground hugging plants, and added goldfish and water lilies. My husband fashioned a three-tiered waterfall out of disks from an old farm implement. This arrangement worked very well for many years, but last year I decided I would like to have a larger pond so I could have more water plants and larger fish. Maybe Koi?

A couple of years before I had made another rock garden in the backyard, as I just could not pass by beautiful rocks without hauling them home, and then, of course, I have to use them somehow. Our

The finished water garden
(Tena Kilmury)

above ground pool had served its purpose and had been removed, leaving a bare expanse of open lawn. I dug up an area and blended it in with the rest of the landscape by building another rock garden.

A few years previous to this, my husband had passed away, so for this endeavour I was on my own. To dig a pond by hand, especially of the size I envisioned, was out of the question. I laid out the garden hose in the size and shape I wanted, pegged the area and called in my good neighbour to dig the hole with his tractor and small backhoe. Off I went to the greenhouse to do some transplanting, leaving my neighbour to dig the hole.

When I returned home, my neighbour had already left and I surveyed the results. I was dumbfounded. He had dug it exactly to my specifications...but....it was MUCH larger than what I had seen in my mind's eye...like maybe a smaller version of the Grand Canyon? I stood and looked at this chasm and my heart sank to my boots. So many thoughts went through my mind. "How can I afford a liner big enough for this?" "Now I'll need a larger pump to circulate the water. What will that cost?" were just some of the thoughts amongst the competing clamour in my head.

Well, maybe I could just fill it in a bit around the edges and make the hole smaller. After a few shovelfuls of dirt I abandoned that idea. It was an insurmountable task for someone well past 65.

My kids are all married and have yards of their own to work on, so I didn't want to call on them for help. Even though it was my son who had suggested that it would be nice if I had a larger pond, the size of my present predicament was my own fault. Feeling like an idiot but knowing it was the sensible thing to do, I asked my good, patient neighbour to come back and fill in the hole. I would make do with the old pond.

When I phoned my neighbour to tell him my sad tale, he was absolutely silent for a few seconds. After all, he'd just dug that hole no more than two hours previously. I have no idea what thoughts went through his mind, but I could almost hear him saying to himself, "Now, isn't that just like a woman?" But, being the helpful neighbour he is, he came right away and filled in the hole, driving his tractor back and forth to tamp down the soil.

A few days later the whole family came for one of our frequent family barbeques, and my son asked, "Mom, what happened to your new pond?" I related my story and was told, "Why didn't you call me? I would have done that for you." I told him I'd thought it was just too big a job for him, on top of his own yard work, and with a new baby to care for and enjoy. Besides, it was all filled in again now and I would plant grass over the area again, and the old pond would just have to do.

Nothing more was said, but a few days later my son dropped by, and stood looking out the window at the ugly scar in the back lawn. He said, "Mom, why don't you let me dig the pond for you. It won't be as big as you'd first planned, but it will be bigger than the old pond. At least the digging will be easier now, since the dirt hasn't had time to settle from the first time." We shared a good chuckle over that episode.

A week later my son, with the help of my two teenaged grandsons, dug the pond again. The dirt was used to fill in the old pond so I could plant it up as an extension of the original rock garden.

We lined the bottom of the new hole with lengths of old carpet and I bought a liner from Bob's Greenhouse Plastics in Altona, Manitoba. I phoned them and told them the size of my pond, and they made the liner to specification. It is made from a supple enough material to follow the contours of the pond. The above-ground edges of the liner were camouflaged with flat rocks.

As it turned out, the old pump was large enough to circulate the water and my son made a filter out of an old plastic garbage can, lava rock, furnace filter material and quilt batting. This item is hidden out of sight behind the rock garden and shrubs. This set-up works wonderfully well, and keeps the water crystal clear all summer.

I have added lots of water plants, and even dug up a cattail (*Typha latifolia*) plant from a nearby slough, and it produced one spike in late summer. I was presented with a Mother's Day gift of two large Koi that grew to be 20–25 cm (8–10 in) long by summer's end and produced more than 30 babies. All of the fish were caught in the fall and transferred to fish tanks at my son's house for the winter.

I stored the water plants in my shed which is heated by a small electric heater to maintain a temperature just above freezing. The plants came back the following spring, but time will tell just how successful this project has been.

I can hardly wait to see what the pond will be like this year. And, no, there are no plans for a larger one..... at least, I don't think so! 🦐

A Brief History of the
Saskatchewan Rose Society

by Arnold F. Pittao

Arnold Pittao lives in Lloydminster, Alberta and is a certified Master Gardener. He has served on the Board of both National-Roses-Canada and the Canadian Rose Society. He is deeply involved with the Saskatchewan Rose Society.

As far as this writer is aware, Saskatchewan is the only province to have one Rose Society representing the interests of rosarians in the province. Certainly it is the only prairie province to do so . Considering that the province contains 220,000 square miles, that is a huge area to cover and the geographic distances remain the primary difficulty for the Society.

The inaugural meeting was held in February, 1998. The plans were laid, the name chosen, and the founding directors appointed: President Brian Porter, Vice-President Diann Putland, Secretary/Treasurer Doug Bradford and Directors Heather Adie (south), Amanda Ryce (north), Newsletter editor – Diann Putland.

From the beginning it was agreed that the strength of the newsletter would be what would hold the Society together, given the geographic separation.

Work proceeded on being registered and incorporated including devising a set of bylaws. The official incorporation took place later in the same year. The first rose show and annual general meeting was held in Rosetown, SK in July, 1999. What an appropriate name for a town in which to hold the first show! There were 12 exhibitors from around the province and the best rose of the show was 'First Love' entered by Florence McLean of North Battleford.

The challenge of staging a rose show embracing an entire province is significant. The first hurdle to cross is choosing the date for the show. For some areas, a show near the beginning of July will ensure that many of the once-blooming shrubs will be in-season, yet the same roses will bloom two to three weeks later in another area. However, for those who grow tender roses (of course with winter protection), the beginning of July is normally too early to have an abundance of blooms or sprays. By moving the show around the province, each area can choose a date most suitable to their geographic location.

A major hurdle is to attract exhibitors. The distance from one side of the province to the other is approximately 800 kilometres (500 miles) and a similar distance north to south represents the most populated region. That could mean that an exhibitor may need to travel almost 1600 kilometres (1,000 miles) to exhibit in a provincial show! Talk about dedication and effort! Anyone who has had to transport roses even a short distance knows of the problems that could and do occur. Think of the lead-time alone for selecting blooms, the hot weather that can prevail, the lack of 'smooth' highways, the time commitment, and the list goes on!

Composing the Show Schedule is also a challenge. Due to the climate of Saskatchewan, there are far more rosarians growing hardy roses than tender ones, yet, there still are classes for tender roses. So, with a bit of experimenting, we have devised a Schedule that meets our needs – the greatest number of sections are in the Hardy Shrub class which is divided by colour and then by specimen spray or specimen bloom form. There are also Novice, Miniature, Floral Art, and Flower Arranging classes; currently 14 of them in all with 128 sections.

Staging the show is kept simple. Traditional folding-tables are normally employed but this varies depending on the venue. White plastic covers the tables unless the tables themselves are white or near white in colour. Bristol board 2.5 cm (1 in) strips divide the sections; small signs indicate the sections; niches are used where required.

In procedure, things happen in much the same manner as any rose (or horticultural) bench show. Staging, judging, clerking, recording and tabulating are all normal duties.

However, consider the exhibitors – never have we had any roses shipped to a show. The odd time an exhibitor may send his/her entries along with another person. In general though, the dedicated few (we have had a maximum of 21 exhibitors) make the effort, travel the long distances, pay for their own travel and accommodation, and stage as good a rose show as you would find in any other province or state! The greatest number of entries we have had so far was in 2008 with 231 entries from 21 exhibitors.

Other than the personal satisfaction of winning, the rewards are few. Thirteen rosettes are awarded to various classes or sections, supplied by the Saskatchewan Rose Society. Five Aggregate awards are given to most points in: Large Flowered Rose Classes, Miniature Rose Classes, Novice Exhibitor Class, Floral Design Classes, and Flower Arranging Class. These are provided by local vendors or individuals. There is no prize money awarded. The Show/ AGM has been held at Rosetown, Regina, Churchbridge, Saskatoon, North Battleford, and Fort Qu'Appelle. There was only one year where it had to be cancelled due to drought conditions.

The summer of 2008 saw the Society initiate and host an Interprovincial Rose Show with Alberta. Held in Rosetown, SK. Twenty one exhibitors made the trek from as far away as Pincher Creek, AB to attend the show and, perhaps equally important, to enjoy fun and fellowship around the theme of roses. Alberta is reciprocating in 2010 and all rosarians will head for the Stampede City, Calgary with the same enthusiasm.

So why do people go to all this work and expense? The answer is simple – for the love of roses. It is not the financial reward that they seek, or else they would not come the distance. It is not the sense of 'duty' to attend – distances are far too great. It is for the love of the rose that brings people from every area of the province together once a year. Not only for the love of the flower, but also for the friendships that develop – despite the geographic separation.

The Society currently has about 60 members, scattered all across the province. The Board consists of a president, vice-president, secretary/ treasurer and four directors, one from each 'corner' of the province. Educational classes are held around the province and the quarterly newsletter *The Rose Rambler* continues to provide timely material to hold the Society informed. Members from as far away as Ontario and California join primarily to receive the newsletter. All back issues may be purchased in CDRom form. The book *Growing Roses in Saskatchewan* by Brian Porter and Arnold Pittao provides a wealth of prairie-based rose information. Copies may be ordered for $18 Cdn including postage from the Saskatchewan Rose Society, PO Box 2733, Lloydminster, SK S9V 0Z1.

The Society, which will celebrates its fourteenth anniversary in 2011, continues to meet the needs of rosarians across our province. 🍃

My Garden

My garden has no room for strife
Nor petty cares and woes.
It lightens my heart when a dewdrop
I find in the heart of a rose.
And the soft sweet trill of a songbird,
The perfume that wafts on the air
Gladdens my soul.
My life is enriched
By the beauty awaiting me there.

J. McKinnon

Boreal Gardens, Churchill, MB

by Diane and Bill Erickson

Diane and Bill live and garden in Zone 0 north of 58⁰ latitude in Churchill, MB. They own and run an experimental Arctic research project comprised of greenhouses and gardens growing various types of produce.

Both of us were employed by Pan American World Airways, Aero space Division at the Churchill Research Range until October, 1970 when CRR downsized from over 200 employees to 70. We had only recently married and were faced with a choice: move elsewhere or stay and find another way of making a living. We decided to stay and to accept the challenge of growing and marketing produce: tomatoes in a greenhouse situation, and to grow other crops on the land. Bill also operated a scheduled boat service to Prince of Wales Fort on the west side of the Churchill River in the summer months, and because we could not get Marine Insurance, we formed Boreal Projects as a Limited company.

We owned a home in Churchill, but faced expropriation because of redevelopment of the town at that time, thus a move was imminent. Bill began the construction of a house and greenhouse 1.6 kilometres east of Churchill on a quartzite ridge in 1974. The importance of the greenhouse was such that after the above-ground basement was poured, and the subfloor was put down on the first floor, the supports for the greenhouse half-arches were installed and covered with fibreglass glazing - all before the rest of the house was constructed.

The first produce under cover was grown under 'truck frames': metal frames for the backs of trucks which were usually covered with canvas. They were put up on timbers and covered with polyfilm. Raised beds were set up within the perimeter of the timbers and filled with local dirt (sandy soil and local peat moss). These were used to grow 'tender' crops such as: cucumbers, zucchini, beans, peppers and bush tomatoes. This was very successful.

At the suggestion of a friend of ours, Dr. Joseph Campbell, Plant Sciences Department at the University of Manitoba, we visited a Research Greenhouse in Truro, Nova Scotia when we were on our honeymoon in 1969. At the time, this project was the most successful of its kind in Canada. The method used was the Finnish peat basin and involved growing tomatoes in a bed of peat, with each bed having a liner of poly that went up its side to about 2.5 cm (1 in) to form a 'basin'. The peat was mixed with appropriate fertilizers and the plants were watered with 20-20-20, a water-soluble fertilizer. The tomatoes were trained up a string with all the suckers pruned out. This worked very well but the peat (which could retain up to 20 times its weight in water and still retain air spaces for the roots) had to be replaced every three to four years because it began to break down. It turned out that the cost of replacing the peat was the same as the cost of transportation - which was prohibitive since the return for the sale of the tomatoes was no where near the cost of the peat, fertilizer, water, heating, etc.

Currently a method called "Nutrient Film Technique" is used. (We first observed this method in New Zealand in 1979 at a research greenhouse in Palmerston North.) The plants grow in a stream of water to which the required nutrients are added. The nutrient solution is recycled hourly/half-hourly/every twenty minutes depending on the time of day, all controlled by a timer. This is NOT hydroponics, but rather a variant. In hydroponics the roots of the plant are in a medium such as peat, sawdust, sand, rock wool bags, etc. as in the Finnish Peat Basin method.

Dr. Campbell had started a Research Greenhouse in Thompson, MB with satellite sites at some northern reserves using 'Walk-in Tunnels - WIT', a term used in England for poly-covered hoop- shaped structures that were tall enough for one to stand upright as opposed to the cold frames that are smaller (eg. the truck frames). Two WITs were sited at Boreal Gardens but two different problems were encountered: the winter wind wrecked one structure almost immediately, and the other did not stand up to a curious polar bear who 'leaned' on it and ripped the poly. These structures worked well as protection for the plants. Cucumbers, tomatoes, green beans, peppers grew very well, but the vulnerability to the weather and wild life was a problem. This led to the next structure being designed and built by my husband and a summer student sent by Dr. Campbell to look for a local source of peat which, although available, was not abundant in any one location. As well it was too time and labour intensive to extract.

The structure was a 2x4 poly-covered framework. If one 4-foot wide panel was damaged, it could be easily replaced as compared to replacing the cover on the entire hoop-shaped structure. This worked well until an extremely cold winter when the poly literally pulled itself apart as it contracted—back to the drawing board! The structure was sound, but the covering had to be changed to a fibreglass covering as was used on the greenhouse arches.

Eventually SUPERTUNNEL (ST) was constructed and covered with fibreglass. At present 1100 square meters are under cover, and now a project to replace all the fibreglass with twin-wall lexan is underway. ST is essentially a big walk-in cold frame that can be operated from late April to late October depending on the year. Growing has started as early as March 31 and as late in the season as November 4. The new covering will increase the length of the growing season. As we have discovered, the problem is not so much keeping in the solar-heated warmth as trying to ventilate the 30+ C temperatures—a nice problem to have.

The tomatoes are started under lights at the end of February and then moved to the greenhouse, and into the 'sewer pipes' which are the 'beds' for the Nutrient Film Technique. The tomatoes are grown from May to October in the greenhouse which is heated with electricity in late April and early May and then not until late September.

Seedlings for bedding plants are also started under lights, then moved 'upstairs' to a north window (which in March receives enough light to continue growth) until they can be moved to the greenhouse or down to ST for transplanting into boxes for sale as bedding plants. These include petunias, marigolds, pansies, violas, strawflowers, calendula, lobelia, etc. Some years we also sell perennials such as Siberian Irises, shasta daisies, chives and rhubarb, all raised from plants in ST. Both the greenhouse and ST are heated using passive solar heat,

except for the spring period in the greenhouse. In the ST the raised beds all have bricks as a base, bricks in the aisles and a mass of dirt and rocks that serve as a heat sink. This is efficient and economical. Water for the greenhouse is collected from the spring run-off of melting snow behind the house and stored in an unheated structure but is circulated into the basement and returned to the water storage. ST is watered with run-off to start with, then the holding tank is refilled from a pond and a pump is used to water the plants in the beds.

There is a Boreal Gardens rule that holds for the sale of produce: we only sell what Diane and Bill cannot eat! Unfortunately, Bill can eat ALL the strawberries (day-neutral varieties grown as annuals) and raspberries (primal cane varieties). That was the case with rhubarb until the outdoor plants were moved under cover, and now rhubarb pies are sold to Gypsy's Bakery — as many as 130 pies a season.

These plants are very heavy feeders but fortunately we have a local source of very rich organic materials, particularly seaweed. We wait until late September to harvest the seaweed after the summer storms have moved it up the beach where it starts to break down. Along with 'lake bottom' (all the dust, dead insects, bird droppings that accumulate on the shallow lake bottoms), local sandy soil and the seaweed, we can have very rich soil. We also have a composter in ST into which go all the weeds (mainly chickweed) that add to the sandy soil. Seaweed is not as quite as rich as manure - kilogram for kilogram - but it sure smells like it!

As well as produce (tomatoes, cucumbers, zucchini) and bedding plants, Boreal Gardens markets the wild berries as jams and jellies. I have been picking and making jams and jellies most of my life in Churchill but only started to market them about 20 years ago. Most of the berries can be picked here at Boreal Gardens (36 acres of rock and muskeg) with additions from elsewhere (gooseberries, red currants, cloudberries). Bill is the champion blueberry-bilberry picker

and when my sister Terry comes home for a visit, she is invited into the berry patch as well. Four different sizes of jars are used to hold ten different products from the juice of the berries and the whole berries. Most of the product is sold to local vendors.

We offer tours of Boreal Gardens in the months of July and August or other times by appointment. Tours on Sunday in July and August are free for individuals, but groups are asked to make appointments and a fee is charged. Our phone number is 204-675—8866, our FAX number is 204-675-2660 and our mailing address is P.O. Box 6, Churchill, MB ROB OEO. 🐾

Diane's Crowberry Jam recipe

2 ½ lbs crowberries   ½ cup water
1 tablespoon lemon juice   1 package pectin (dry)

Combine the berries, water, lemon juice and pectin in kettle; mix well and bring to a boil. ADD 3 ½ pounds sugar (cup measure is too inexact) and bring to a full rolling boil; boil for one minute, stirring constantly. Remove from the stove and bottle. It is not necessary to can the jam - the berries are very high in Vitamin C. The yield should be about 8 to 10 cups (2 plus litres).

Crowberry or heathberry or curlew berry or Gray Goose berry: *Empetrum nigrum L.* is found all around the Arctic Ocean - circumpolar and as far south as all of Canada and parts of Central Russia. The berries are usually ready in early August; they are very juicy but insipid when eaten raw. However, heat seems to do something to them and the jam is very fragrant and G O O D !!! This was a favourite snack when we were kids on a walk or picnic: if you were thirsty, the berries moisture and slight medicinal flavour was satisfying.

The Rewards of Native Plants

by Lucille Verrier

Larger monarch caterpillar seeming to 'check' on recently hatched caterpiller
(Darlene McPherson)

Lucille is an artist, poet, author and gardener in Winnipeg, MB. She's happiest when immersed in nature or creating something beautiful. <www.illuminatingearth.com>

Gardening with plants indigenous to one's region is another simple step we can all take to reduce our environmental footprint and contribute to the well-being of us all. Whether you decide to incorporate only a few native species into your landscape, or to have entire sections of property dedicated to many varieties, you will make a significant difference. You'll also gain a special appreciation for our native flora as you learn how it interacts with our wildlife and realize the importance of its existence. There's no better way to reconnect with nature than when it's at your doorstep – including an urban one!

My own experience is a perfect example. Due to a persistent drainage problem we had in our sunken backyard, my husband and I were prompted to find a long-term solution. Forget the sump pump we used every spring melt or after a hard rain to prevent the basement from flooding. Instead, we decided we needed to replace the top layer of clay soil and invasive ground ivy with a thicker layer of good soil mix for our landscaping project. After some research, we agreed that using local plant species from the prairie region would be ideal for our goal to have a low maintenance, nature-friendly backyard. They've evolved with our climate over millennia, and consequently are very well adapted to survive the most challenging conditions and thrive with minimal care. This translates into being very good for both the eco-conscious home owner and the environment, since there's little need for fertilizers and pesticides. Once established, their root structure also reduces the need for watering, even during long periods of drought. Seeing as most species are perennials, this makes them cost efficient as they generally grow back faithfully each spring, unaffected by late frosts. Furthermore, they easily self-seed which replaces plants that are more short-lived. Their seedlings are also a great way to introduce neighbours, friends and family to these native gems. Initially, the spring and summer of 2003 were labour-intensive and costly since we transformed the entire backyard from the soil up. It was a very ambitious goal, but one that has greatly paid off in the years that have followed – including permanently solving our drainage problem.

Amid this urban environment of mostly lawns and concrete covering the ground, our average-sized backyard unexpectedly became an oasis of prairie. Over forty species of native plants cater to the diverse needs of wildlife and provide our own spirits with the calming and rejuvenating qualities of nature. There are flowers, grasses, ground-covers, vines, fruiting shrubs and young fruiting trees. Because of the concentration and variety of plants present, our yard attracts more species of birds, butterflies, dragonflies, bees, damselflies, beetles, small mammals and other small-scale wildlife than I ever saw growing up in the country! We've even witnessed the 'birth' of forty two beautiful Monarch butterflies *(Danaus plexippus)* in one summer as they each emerged from their dangling jewel-like pupas throughout the yard.

We felt privileged to experience such wonders, seldom seen by most people. Being a naturalist at heart, I began to document everything in gardener's journals as soon as our backyard received its first plants. Especially interesting has been the number of winged visitors that have used our garden over the years. I identify new species to our habitat annually and my list has become quite impressive, considering this is an urban yard. Following this article is a list of the winged species I've identified since spring 2003.

Despite its location and size, resident and migrating wildlife keep finding our prairie habitat and use the plants it offers for food, shelter, nesting materials and nurseries. Our shrubs and young trees provide protection and food in the form of nectar, berries and leaves. The numerous flowering species provide nectar for many, including butterflies, bees, moths and hummingbirds. Once their blooms turn into seed heads, many varieties of birds feed on these seeds. This source of nutrition is especially important during fall and spring migration. Our grasses such as Switchgrass *(Panicum virgatum)* also attract seed feeders. We've even seen small Eastern Cottontail rabbits *(Sylvilagus floridanus)* stand upright on our stone path to reach the nodding seed heads. A number of our plants are also hosts for beautiful varieties of butterflies whose caterpillars feed on the leaves. Our garden provides multi-layers of cover for wildlife including count-less insect species which feed birds as well as dragonflies, spiders and many predatory insects. Each plant species is beautiful and promotes the diversity of our backyard habitat. Interestingly, because this ecosystem is attractive to so much fauna, nature has rewarded us in unexpected ways. The most obvious of these surprises has been the introduction of additional native plant species. I suspect their seeds were defecated by visiting birds and germinated where they fell. We've acquired Early Blue Violet *(Viola adunca),* Northern Bog Violet *(Viola nephrophylla),* Harebell

White-throated Sparrow
(Zonotrichia albicollis)
(Cephas)

(Campanula rotundifolia) and Kalm's Lobelia *(Lobelia kalmii).* Diminutive and so pretty, these flowers are a delight to discover in our garden.

If that wasn't enough to convince someone to grow native plants, consider that you're helping wildlife and the environment while nurturing your spirit. You're also contributing to the preservation of many indigenous plant species that have become rare in their natural habitats. If most urban and suburban residents grew native plants on their properties, these artificial environments would become less of an obstacle for the wildlife that depends on local species for their survival. Subsequently, everyone would play a key role in maintaining the delicate balance of our environment, for which we're all responsible. Knowing we've made a difference with our own property gives us a special sense of fulfilment and joy.

There are many good publications on the market and sites on the internet that give readers 'how to' suggestions and useful information to get started. I recently discovered *Wild About Gardening* by the Canadian Wildlife Federation. It has a wonderful *Backyard Habitat Certification* which acknowledges the efforts of gardeners who welcome wildlife to their gardens. For more information, you can go to their website at: *www. wildaboutgardening.org.* We are currently in the process of getting our own backyard certified. ❧

Birds

- American Robin *(Turdus migratorius)*
- Hermit Thrush *(Catharus guttatus)*
- Swainson's Thrush *(Catharus ustulatus)*
- Palm Warbler *(Dendroica palmarum)*
- 'Myrtle' Yellow-Rumped Warbler *(Dendroica coronata)*
- Magnolia Warbler *(Dendroica magnolia)*
- Yellow Warbler *(Dendroica petechia)*
- Common Yellowthroat Warbler *(Geothlypis trichas)*
- House Wren *(Troglodytes aedon)*
- Blue Jay *(Cyanocitta cristata)*
- Mourning Dove *(Zenaida macroura)*
- Fox Sparrow *(Passerella iliaca)*
- Song Sparrow *(Melospiza melodia)*
- Chipping Sparrow *(Spizella passerina)*
- White-throated Sparrow *(Zonotrichia albicollis)*
- Harris's Sparrow *(Zonotrichia querula)*
- Lincoln's Sparrow *(Melospiza lincolnii)*
- English Sparrow *(Passer domesticus)*
- Hairy Woodpecker *(Picoides villosus)*
- 'Slate-Coloured' Dark-Eyed Junco *(Junco hyemalis)*
- House Finch *(Carpodacus mexicanus)*
- American Goldfinch *(Carduelis tristis)*
- Common Grackle 'Bronzed form' *(Quiscalus quiscula)*
- European Starling *(Sturnus vulgaris)*
- American Crow *(Corvus brachyrhynchos)*
- Ruby-throated Hummingbird *(Archilochus colubris)*
- Black-capped Chickadee *(Poecile atricapillus)*
- Great Crested Flycatcher *(Myiarchus crinitus)*
- Least Flycatcher *(Empidonax minimus)*.

Butterflies And Moths

- Monarch *(Danaus plexippus)*
- Black Swallowtail *(Papilio polyxenes asterius)*
- Orange Sulphur *(Colias eurytheme)*
- Mourning Cloak *(Nymphalis antiopa)*
- Pearl Crescent *(Phyciodes tharos)*
- Red Admiral *(Vanessa atalanta)*
- White Admiral *(Limenitis arthemis)*
- Painted Lady *(Vanessa cardui)*
- American Lady *(Vanessa virginiensis)*
- Variegated Fritillary *(Euptoieta claudia)*
- Milbert's Tortoiseshell *(Nymphalis milberti)*
- Question Mark *(Polygonia interrogationis)*
- Cabbage White *(Pieris rapae)*
- Peck's Skipper *(Polites peckius)*
- European Skipper *(Thymelicus lineola)*
- Viceroy *(Limenitis archippus)*
- Spring Azure *(Celastrina ladon)*
- Pale Beauty *(Campaea perlata)*.

Dragonflies And Damselflies

- Common Green Darner *(Anax junius)*
- Variable Darner *(Aeshna interrupta)*
- Ruby Meadowhawk *(Sympetrum rubicundulum)*
- White-Faced Meadowhawk *(Sympetrum obtrusum)*
- Northern Bluet *(Enallagma cyathigerum)*
- Familiar Bluet *(Enallagma civile)*
- Common Spreadwing *(Lestes disjunctus)*.

50 Years Ago –
My Garden Companions
are my Timing Guides

by Mary Mclaughlin

*This article was
originally printed in
The 1961 Prairie Garden*

Baltimore Oriole
(David Brezinski)

My garden is my sanctuary where I find peace and contentment, received for free both in body, mind and spirit, values in abundance untold.

My garden is also a place to experiment, to enjoy, and a thing to share.

I have three 'Don't' rules that I insist on being carried out: I Don't do any fussing — Don't allow any cussing — and Don't take any bossing.

I keep a bird calendar as well as a garden one. While the seasons vary from year to year, I find the timing of the bird arrivals is seldom wrong. Since I love both birds and flowers, gardening gives me a wonderful opportunity to join in the harmony and study nature at work.

Someone said: "Plant flowers for your heart." Even if your heart isn't so good plant flowers anyway and it will feel better for it. So I seed pansies on Feb. 14, Valentine's Day. And from March 20-25, Asters, Carnations. Castor-oil Plant, Celosia, Dahlias (annual). Gloriosa Daisy. Gaillardias, Hollyhock Lobelia, Petunias, Pinks, Salvia and Sweet William.

April 1-10: When the crows and cranes arrive I plant Calliopsis, Chrysanthemums (annual), Morning Glory, Phlox Drummondii Satin Flower, Portulaca and Stocks.

April 10-15: When the meadow larks greet me with their heart-lifting song I plant African Daisy, Alyssum, Butterfly flower, Love-in-a-mist Marigolds African and French, Nicotina and Swan River Daisy. During the same time when my friend "Flicka", the woodpecker is sounding off the old dead tree stump — where the year before a family of little Flickers were housed — I know it's time to start my outdoor planting. At this time, I plant Bachelor's buttons. Candytuft and Sweet Peas.

May 10-15: It's the week of the Red-Winged Blackbird Symphony. There must be hundreds of them that gather in a favourite maple tree just to the back of the house. They seem to have a leader, then all join in. Oh, what a melody! How often I wish that I could have it recorded and play it when the thermometer dips down to 25-30 below.

During Symphony Week I seed the last of the annuals —Bells of Ireland, Calendula, Clarkiá, Cosmos, Larkspur, Lavetera, Lupins, Mignonette, Nasturtiums, Night scented Stocks, California Poppies, Salpiglosis, Strawflowers, Sunflower, Sweet Sultan and Zinnias. When the Zinnias and Nasturtiums are up and there is risk of frost, I take the hoe and cover them up with soil in the evening and repeat the next evening. In the morning, I just gently push the soil off the plants with my fingers and they are not harmed in any way.

June 1-5: "Brownie" the Mocking Bird has arrived and is standing in the highest poplar tree telling all the world that he is happy to be back. Time to set out the bedding plants that are most hardy African Daisy, Asters, Carnations, pinks, Gaillardias, Snapdragons, Phlox, Stocks, Sweet William and the Verbenas.

June 10-15: "Peter" the Oriole arrives and declares that "Peter Peter Will do" but the only thing he seems to want to do is sing and look for grubs but that is good enough for me. That means time to finish setting out all the rest of the bedding plants and hope for the best. I like to set the plants out late in the day and sometimes I work as long as I can see if I can get away with it. The Moose Jaw creek runs right by the garden. I usually go down and wash my hands before leaving the garden. One time I ended up by getting my face showered as well. "The Boss", that is the beaver, showed his disapproval of my working overtime by suddenly slapping the water with his tail with a great splash that sent moonlit ripples far and wide. It was a rather shocking experience but amusing too.

July 15-20: The Humming birds arrived, two ruby throated gentlemen and their iridescent green gowned ladies. I'm glad the window boxes and beds are well filled with their favourite blossoms. They practically disappear in the petunias. There's lobelia, delphinium, soapwort Verbenas and who can resist Scabiosa? We usually enjoy watching them go after the nectar. It makes planting flowers worthwhile. 🐿

Award for Excellence
The International Peace Garden and CEO, Doug Hevenor, 2010 Winner of The Prairie Garden Award for Excellence
by Linda Pearn

Dr. Dale Herman and Doug Hevenor (Sandy Venton)

The Prairie Garden Award for Excellence for 2010 was presented to The International Peace Garden (IPG) and its CEO, Doug Hevenor, at a luncheon at Larter's at St. Andrews, Manitoba on September 3, 2010. This is the 11th year this Award has been given for Excellence in Horticulture on the Northern Great Plains.

The International Peace Garden, a 2,339 acre (947 hectares) Botanical Garden which lies along the borders of Manitoba and North Dakota, opened in 1932 and is devoted to World Peace. A simple boundary marker – a cairn built of stones gathered from both sides – is flanked by two flag poles bearing the flags of the two nations. A narrow terraced channel of water flows through the center, the 49th parallel, of the Formal Garden. Among the many attractions are a Sunken Garden, Floral Clock, Floral Canadian & American Flags, 9/11 Memorial, Bell Tower and Peace Tower. The Peace Garden annually hosts numerous camps for music, band, vocal and other educational groups.

Doug Hevenor hopes to make the Peace Garden a destination for tourists, bus trips and visitors from both sides of the U.S./Canadian border.

Doug Hevenor, the current CEO, joined IPG in 2005. He obtained his Horticultural training at the Niagara Parks Commission School of Horticulture in Ontario. Doug has lived and gardened in most of the Plant Hardiness Zones in Canada and United States. He has been influential in progress and new development at the IPG. Under his leadership, the Sunken Garden has been re-developed. Recently, 600 trees, 7,000 shrubs, 75,000 perennials and 20,000 bulbs have been planted in one of the largest landscape designed areas in the center of North America. As well, he has helped to bring about the decision to erect a fence to exclude white-tailed deer from some of the plantings. Doug is passionate about Horticulture and this passion is transferred to his activities at The International Peace Garden. The nominator, Dr. Dale Herman, states "He is an outstanding CEO, an efficient manager, a lobbyist, an engineer, a public relations expert, a horticulturist par-excellence and more, all wrapped in one leader." The Peace Garden operates with a Board of Directors composed of interested people from both Canada and the United States of America.

The Prairie Garden Award for Excellence is awarded annually to an individual or group making a significant contribution to the advancement and/or promotion of horticulture on the Northern Great Plains. Areas of involvement may include community activity, plant introduction or breeding, preservation of horticultural sites, teaching, research, extension or photography.

The Prairie Garden Committee is a volunteer group which publishes an annual gardening book focusing on horticulture in the prairies. The Prairie Garden, Western Canada's only gardening annual, was first published in 1937. 🦫

More information about the award and previous winners can be seen at:
www.theprairiegarden.ca/award.html

International Peace Gardens U.S./Canada boundary marker

The Prairie Garden
Award for Excellence

has been presented annually since 2000 by The Prairie Garden in order to recognize horticultural achievements.

Eligibility

The Prairie Garden Award for Excellence shall be awarded to an individual or group making a significant contribution to the advancement and/or promotion of horticulture on the Northern Great Plains. Areas of involvement may include community activity, plant introduction or breeding, preservation of horticultural sites, teaching, research, extension and photography.

The Award

The award shall be cash in the amount of one thousand dollars ($1000.00) and a suitably inscribed plaque.

Nomination Process

Letters of nomination should include in-depth details with appropriate documentation of the candidate's achievements in horticulture. This will be the only source of information used to compare to other nominations.
All nominations must be received by May 31, 2011.

Nominations should be submitted to:
The Prairie Garden Awards Board
P.O. Box 517
Winnipeg, Manitoba   R3C 2J3

Announcement & Presentation

The recipient will be announced by September 1, 2011 with a presentation ceremony to follow as soon as practical thereafter. The winner will be featured in The 2012 Prairie Garden.

*"**The Prairie Garden**" is an annual horticultural publication published by a group of volunteers for the furtherance of prairie horticulture.*

Themes for The Prairie Garden Back Issues

We have back issues in varying quantities. Please use the form on the next page to order any of the following to complete your reference library.

2010 – Annuals & Biennials
2009 – Deciduous Shrubs *
2008 – Roses
2007 – The Edible Landscape
2006 – Myth, Magic & Meditation
2005 – Lilies
2004 – Pleasing Prairie Places *
2003 – Themes & Extremes
2002 – Landscape Design
2001 – Container Gardening
2000 – Herbs
1999 – Perennials *
1998 – Trees for The Prairies
1997 – Propagation
1996 – New Themes in Prairie Landscape
1995 – Accessible Gardening
1994 – Xeriscaping – Gardening in Dry Conditions *
1993 – ~~Garden Herbs~~ *Sold Out*
1992 – Garden Oddities
1991 – Sustainable Landscaping
1990 – ~~Bulbs and Perennials~~ *Sold Out*
1989 – ~~50 Years of Prairie Garden~~ * *Sold Out*
1988 – Gardening Indoors
1987 – Perennials on The Prairies
1986 – New Ideas
1985 – Large Area Gardening *
1984 – ~~Small Gardens~~ *Sold Out*
1983 – Better Living Through Gardening
1982 – New Concepts, Gardening in Winter
1981 – Native Heritage
1980 – Mostly Trees and Shrubs *
1979 – ~~Mostly Annuals~~ *Sold Out*
1978 – ~~Gardening Hints~~ *Sold Out*
1977 – Flower Arranging *

* Issue contains an index of that year & previous 4 year's contents

The Prairie Garden
PO Box 517, Winnipeg, Manitoba R3C 2J3
Phone: (204) 489-3466; Fax: (204) 489-1644
Email: editor@theprairiegarden.ca / www.theprairiegarden.ca

❑   The 2011 Prairie Garden $12.00
Special quantity prices to horticulture societies and garden clubs:
10 – 49 copies $7.75; 50 – 149 copies $7.25
150 or more copies $6.75
Volume discounts to commercial outlets on request.

❑ Please add my name to the STANDING ORDER LIST in order that I
may receive a copy of *The Prairie Garden* every year starting with the
2012 issue. I will send my remittance upon receipt of each issue.
Standing Orders are charged at a discount rate.
(Do not check this box if your name is already on the Standing Order List)

BACK ISSUES (while quantities last) 2010:Annuals and Biennials – $6.00
Previous issues (listed on the previous page) prior to 2010
will be sold at $4.50 each while stock remains

POSTAGE AND HANDLING CHARGES APPLY ON ALL ORDERS
1 book – $2.95; 2-4 books – $10.25; 5-10 books – $17.25
11 books or more – Canada Post Weight Charges to apply
Postage will be charged at cost on all orders received from outside Canada.
All prices in Canadian dollars.
These prices supercede all previous price lists and are subject to change without notice.

✂ --- ✂

Name			
Address			
City	Prov/State		P.C./Zip
Qty	Year / Issue	Price Ea	Price
		Subtotal	
Please enclose cheque payable to:		Postage & Handling	
"The Prairie Garden"		**TOTAL**	